VOCA EDGE

수능·기초

E-field Academy

BLUE

더디퍼런스

VOCA EDGE

STORYTELLING VOCABULARY

- **지은이**   E-field Academy (정오은)

  (도움을 주신분: Chuck Chucklin, Jane Cohen, 오정수, 최사라, 배수현, 김형숙)

- **펴낸곳**   더디퍼런스
- **펴낸이**   조상현

- **등록번호**   제 2015-000237호
- **주소**   서울특별시 마포구 마포대로 127, 304호
- **TEL**   02-725-9988
- **FAX**   02-6974-1237
- **URL**   www.thedifference.co.kr

ISBN   979-11-86217-24-5 (53740)

VOCA
EDGE

BLUE

더 디퍼런스

Introduction

Every student knows acquiring English vocabulary is a basic necessity for learning the English language. However, not many are aware that simply memorizing vocabulary words is not enough. In order to master a language, students need to spend more time learning how to use these words and what they really mean. Yet, students still spend countless hours memorizing rather than learning.

Even worse is the fact that most vocabulary books are extremely difficult and boring. Fortunately, there is a way for everyone to change their perspective on learning vocabulary. Now you can develop your vocabulary in an enjoyable way. The VOCA EDGE series will help you simultaneously enlarge your vocabulary and improve your English.

This series uses an integrated approach to learning English. Listening, reading, writing and comprehension are all covered in this series.

One of the key features of this series is that it revolves around the daily lives of several characters and the challenges they face in growing up. By reading each episode, students will learn the natural and functional use of English vocabulary.

Each level of this series comes with one textbook and one audio component. Each book is organized into 12 chapters, each of which consists of 2-4 related units. Each book also deals with a variety of unique and interesting topics, and the series is graded to an appropriate length and depth to suit the needs of students with varying levels of English proficiency.

After studying each unit, students will be challenged to review the words and expressions they learned through a series of related questions and activities. Students can listen to the entire script in MP3 format. We invite you to let this series help you take the next step in your journey towards becoming a more proficient speaker of English. We are confident that the VOCA EDGE series can help you make a dramatic improvement in your English ability.

Structure

- ## Reading Passages

  The Reading passages cover a wide variety of topics ranging from teen life to social issues. Each sentence in the reading passages contains target vocabulary students have to learn. Each of the characters has their own personality and the real life topics will help students understand the context more easily. In addition, it will motivate students to learn vocabulary used in the passages with confidence.

- ## Words

  Students are encouraged to read the definitions. They are also encouraged to read the sentences and derivations of the target vocabulary that students need to learn.

- ## Check Again!

  These sections provide students with a chance to practice words and idiomatic expressions learned in each unit using a variety of approaches.

- ## Voca Plus

  The Voca Plus section is added at the end of each chapter. This section provides students with basic information about how some English words are composed including their derivations. In addition, culture tips related to each chapter are included.

Contents

Bomi
A middle school third grade student. An inquisitive teenage girl.

Hoony
Bomi's younger brother

Seri
Bomi's younger sister

Sara
Bomi's best friend

Mom
Bomi, Hoony, and Seri's
mother

Dad
Bomi, Hoony, and Seri's
father

VOCA EDGE

BLUE

watched family videos. What is puberty? Visit my blog Girls and boys use different facilities

Hoony attends a science camp. There will be a talent show. We went on a safari tour. I pre

ally, I got accepted. We're in the same boat. I go to a growth clinic. Mud cookies are

garage. Hoony went on a trip to the War Memorial. Sara composed music for Brownie

cide campaign. The recent food scandal is horrible. Dad is interested in art investment.

me intelligence systems. Cloning can be good and bad. Plants can grow without sunli

drifted ashore! I watched family videos. What is puberty? Visit my blog Girls and boys use a

eam project. Hoony attends a science camp. There will be a talent show. We went

Relationships count most. Finally, I got accepted. We're in the same boat. I go to a growt

essons. My dad's car is in the garage. Hoony went on a trip to the War Memorial. Sara com

chool is doing an anti-suicide campaign. The recent food scandal is horrible. Dad is intere

Mom is impressed by home intelligence systems. Cloning can be good and bad. Plants car

drills. Two whales drifted ashore! I watched family videos. What is puberty? Visit my blog Gi

club. We have a team project. Hoony attends a science camp. There will be a talent

championship. Relationships count most. Finally, I got accepted. We're in the same boa

aking taekwondo lessons. My dad's car is in the garage. Hoony went on a trip to the W

unning for president. Our school is doing an anti-suicide campaign. The recent food sco

egular customer of ABC Mart. Mom is impressed by home intelligence systems. Cloning c

Astronauts need to know special drills. Two whales drifted ashore! I watched family videos.

oday. I want to join the drama club. We have a team project. Hoony attends a science

attend the wonder dog championship. Relationships count most. Finally, I got accepted. V

pancakes. Hoony is taking taekwondo lessons. My dad's car is in the garage. Hoony wen

the send button. Kite will attend the wonder dog championship. Relationships count mos

e! We made homemade pancakes. Hoony is taking taekwondo lessons. My dad's car is

at an interesting festival! Sara's brother is running for president. Our school is doing an an

has skin trouble. Mom has become a regular customer of ABC Mart. Mom is impressed b

Why do floods and droughts alternate? Astronauts need to know special drills. Two whale

ent facilities. We love you, Kite We moved today. I want to join the drama club. We have

safari tour. I pressed the send button. Kite will attend the wonder dog championshir

ic. Mud cookies are terrible! We made homemade pancakes. Hoony is taking taekwond

ed music for Brownie. What an interesting festival! Sara's brother is running for president. Ou

in art investment. Seri has skin trouble. Mom has become a regular customer of ABC Mar

w without sunlight. Why do floods and droughts alternate? Astronauts need to know speci

d boys use different facilities. We love you, Kite We moved today. I want to join the dram

v. We went on a safari tour. I pressed the send button. Kite will attend the wonder do

o to a growth clinic. Mud cookies are terrible! We made homemade pancakes. Hoony

Chapter 1. Teen Life

Memorial. Sara composed music for Brownie. What an interesting festival! Sara's brothe

Unit 1. I watched family videos.

l is horrible. Dad is interested in art investment. Seri has skin trouble. Mom has become

Unit 2. What is puberty?

e good and bad. Plants can grow without sunlight. Why do floods and droughts alterna

Unit 3. Visit my blog.

t is puberty? Visit my blog Girls and boys use different facilities. We love you, Kite We move

p. There will be a talent show. We went on a safari tour. I pressed the send button. Kite w

e in the same boat. I go to a growth clinic. Mud cookies are terrible! We made homemac

a trip to the War Memorial. Sara composed music for Brownie. What an interesting festive

Chapter 1
Teen Life

Unit 1. I watched family videos.

celebrate one's first **birthday**

exchange engagement **rings**

Episode

Dear Mom,

I found some videos of special family occasions. ● One was on my first birthday. ● Many people came to celebrate it. ● There was a special ceremony. ● A man announced that I had to do something. ● There were many symbols on the table. ● I had to choose one of them. ● It was a big challenge for me then. ● My uncle guessed that I would choose a golf ball. ● He may have wanted me to win glory as a champion. ● Mom predicted I would choose a pencil. ● That means I will be very intelligent. ● But my choice was a 10,000 won bill. ● Dad smiled and said, "She will become wealthy. ● She will possess a lot of money."

The other video was at my aunt and uncle's engagement party. ● It was at a lovely banquet hall. ● They were exchanging something. ● They were two beautiful engagement rings! ● The rings symbolize everlasting love. ● They looked like a very happy couple. ● Everyone raised their glasses and toasted them.

엄마에게,

나는 특별한 가족 행사를 담은 비디오들을 찾아냈어요. 하나는 나의 첫돌 때였어요. 많은 사람들이 와서 축하해 주었어요. 특별한 의식이 있었어요. 한 남자가 내가 무언가를 해야 한다고 발표했어요. 탁자 위에 여러 상징물이 있었어요. 나는 그 중 하나를 골라야 했어요. 그때 그것이 내겐 큰 도전이었죠. 삼촌은 내가 골프공을 고를 것이라고 추측했지요. 그분은 내가 챔피온의 영광을 얻기를 원했나 봐요. 엄마는 내가 연필을 고를 거라고 예언했어요. 그것은 내가 아주 똑똑할 거라는 뜻이에요. 하지만 나의 선택은 만 원짜리 지폐였어요. 아빠는 미소를 지으며 "얘는 부자가 될 겁니다. 많은 돈을 소유하게 될 거예요."라고 말했어요.

다른 비디오는 숙모와 삼촌의 약혼식 파티 때였어요. 그것은 아름다운 연회장에서 있었어요. 그들은 무언가를 교환하고 있었어요. 그것은 두 개의 아름다운 약혼 반지였어요! 반지는 영원한 사랑을 상징해요. 그들은 아주 행복한 한 쌍처럼 보였어요. 모두 잔을 들어 그들을 위해 건배했어요.

occasion
[əkéiʒən]

n. 행사, 경사

I found some videos of special family occasions.
나는 특별한 가족 행사를 담은 비디오들을 찾아냈어요.

• occasional a. 가끔의, 때때로의   • occasionally ad. 가끔

birthday
[bə́:rθdèi]

n. 생일

One was on my first birthday.
하나는 나의 첫돌 때였어요.

celebrate
[séləbrèit]

v. 축하하다

Many people came to celebrate it.
많은 사람들이 와서 축하해 주었어요.

• celebration n. 축하

ceremony
[sérəmòuni]

n. 의식

There was a special ceremony.
특별한 의식이 있었어요.

announce
[ənáuns]

v. 발표하다

A man announced that I had to do something.
한 남자가 내가 무언가를 해야 한다고 발표했어요.

• announcement n. 발표

symbol
[símbəl]

n. 상징물, 상징

There were many symbols on the table.
탁자 위에 여러 상징물이 있었어요.

• symbolize v. 상징하다   • symbolic a. 상징적인

choose
[tʃuːz]

v. 선택하다

I had to choose one of them.
나는 그 중 하나를 골라야 했어요.

• choice n. 선택   • choose - chose - chosen

challenge
[tʃǽlindʒ]

n. 도전
v. 도전하다

It was a big challenge for me then.
그때 그것이 내겐 큰 도전이었죠.

guess
[ges]

v. 추측하다
n. 추측

My uncle guessed that I would choose a golf ball.
삼촌은 내가 골프공을 고를 것이라고 추측했지요.

glory
[glɔ́:ri]

n. 영광

He may have wanted me to win glory as a champion.
그분도 내가 챔피언의 영광을 얻기를 원했나 봐요.

• glorious a. 영광스러운 • win glory 영광을 얻다

predict
[pridíkt]

v. 예언하다

Mom predicted I would choose a pencil.
엄마는 내가 연필을 고를 거라고 예언했어요.

• prediction n. 예언

intelligent
[intélidʒənt]

a. 지적인, 똑똑한

That means I will be very intelligent.
그것은 내가 아주 똑똑할 거라는 뜻이에요.

• intelligence n. 지성, 지능

bill
[bil]

n. 지폐

But my choice was a 10,000 won bill.
하지만 나의 선택은 만 원짜리 지폐였어요.

wealthy
[wélθi]

a. 부유한

Dad smiled and said, "She will become wealthy.
She will possess a lot of money."
아빠는 미소를 지으며 "얘는 부자가 될 겁니다. 많은 돈을 소유하게 될 거예요"라고
말했어요.

• wealth n. 부, 재산

possess
[pəzés]

v. 소유하다

Dad smiled and said, "She will become wealthy. She will possess a lot of money."

아빠는 미소를 지으며 "얘는 부자가 될 겁니다. 많은 돈을 소유하게 될 거예요"라고 말했어요.

• possession n. 소유, 소유물

engagement
[engéidʒmənt]

n. 약혼

The other video was at my aunt and uncle's engagement party.

다른 비디오는 숙모와 삼촌의 약혼식 파티 때였어요.

• engage v. 약혼시키다

banquet hall
[bǽŋkwit hɔːl]

n. 연회장

It was at a lovely banquet hall.

그것은 아름다운 연회장에서 있었어요.

exchange
[ikstʃéindʒ]

v. 교환하다 n. 교환

They were exchanging something.

그들은 무언가를 교환하고 있었어요.

ring
[riŋ]

n. 반지

They were two beautiful engagement rings!

그것은 두 개의 아름다운 약혼 반지였어요.

everlasting
[èvərlǽstiŋ]

a. 영원한

The rings symbolize everlasting love.

반지는 영원한 사랑을 상징해요.

couple
[kʌ́pəl]

n. 남녀 한 쌍

They looked like a very happy couple.

그들은 아주 행복한 한 쌍처럼 보였어요.

toast
[toust]

v. 건배하다 n. 건배

Everyone raised their glasses and toasted them.

모두 잔을 들어 그들을 위해 건배했어요.

Check Again!

A Translate each word into Korean.

1. occasion ....
2. celebrate ....
3. symbol ....
4. predict ....
5. glory ....
6. banquet hall ....
7. exchange ....
8. everlasting ....
9. possess ....
10. toast ....

B Translate each word into English.

1. 의식 ....
2. 약혼 ....
3. 선택하다 ....
4. 지적인 ....
5. 부유한 ....

C Fill in the blank with the appropriate word. Refer to the Korean.

1. Her b _____ is on April Fool's Day.

   그녀의 생일은 만우절 날이에요.

2. He a _____ the new Miss Peaches of the village.

   그는 그 마을의 새로운 복숭아 아가씨를 발표했습니다.

3. They secretly met after school to e _____ comic books.

   그들은 만화책을 교환하기 위하여 방과 후 비밀리에 만났다.

4. Every week, the six members begin a new c _____ .

   매주마다 여섯 맴버들은 새로운 도전을 시작합니다.

5. He won g _____ as an Olympic champion at only 20.

   그는 겨우 20살에 올림픽 챔피온의 영광을 얻었다.

Chapter 1
Teen Life

Unit 2. What is puberty?

a **period** of growing up

have a great **fashion sense**

be **concerned** **about** something

Episode

Dear Diary,

We watched a video **program** at school today. ● It was about **puberty**. ● Puberty is a **period** of growing up. ● During puberty there are **physical** changes to our bodies. ● We also grow up **mentally**. ● And we feel new **emotions**.

The program was very **helpful** to me. ● I am **experiencing** many of those changes right now. ● It **reminded** me of Mr. Lee. ● He is our new **single** English teacher. ● He has a great **fashion** sense. ● He is very **humorous**, too. ● Sara **refers** to him as a **witty** man. ● Lately, I am very **conscious** of him. ● My heart **beats** faster when I see him. ● Teachers' Day is **coming up** soon and I want to give him a special present. ● But I'm **concerned** about what he will think. ● Will he be **pleased**? ● Or will he think it is **awkward**? ● I hope he **treats** me differently. ● I hope he **notices** me more. ● If he doesn't, I will feel so **rejected**. ● What if my friends **tease** me?

다이어리에게,

우리는 오늘 학교에서 비디오 프로그램을 보았어. 사춘기에 관한 거였어. 사춘기는 성장하는 시기래. 사춘기 동안에는 우리 몸에 신체적인 변화가 일어나. 우리는 정신적으로도 성장하게 돼. 그리고 새로운 감정을 느끼게 돼.

그 프로그램은 나에게 아주 도움이 되었어. 지금 당장 나는 그런 변화를 많이 경험하고 있어. 그 방송은 이 선생님을 생각나게 했어. 그분은 우리의 새로운 총각 영어 선생님이야. 그분은 패션 감각이 뛰어나. 아주 익살스럽기도 하지. 사라는 그분을 재치 있는 분이라고 말하지. 요즘 나는 그분을 몹시 의식하게 돼. 그분을 보면 내 심장 박동이 빨라져. 스승의 날이 곧 다가오는데 나는 그분에게 특별한 선물을 드리고 싶어. 하지만 나는 그분이 어떻게 생각할지가 걱정돼. 그분이 마음에 들어 할까? 아니면 그것이 어색하다고 생각할까? 나는 그분이 나를 다르게 대해 주었으면 해. 내게 더 관심을 보여 주었으면 해. 그렇지 않으면, 나는 정말 퇴짜 맞은 기분이 들 거야. 내 친구들이 놀리면 어떻게 하지?

program
[próugræm]
n. 프로그램, 방송

We watched a video program at school today.
우리는 오늘 학교에서 비디오 프로그램을 보았어.

puberty
[pjú:bərti]
n. 사춘기

It was about puberty.
사춘기에 관한 거였어.

period
[píəriəd]
n. 시기, 기간

Puberty is a period of growing up.
사춘기는 성장하는 시기야.

physical
[fízikəl]
a. 신체의

During puberty there are physical changes to our bodies.
사춘기 동안에는 우리 몸에 신체적인 변화가 일어나.

• physically ad. 신체적으로

mentally
[méntəli]
ad. 정신적으로

We also grow up mentally.
우리는 정신적으로도 성장하게 돼.

• mental a. 정신의

emotion
[imóuʃən]
n. 감정

And we feel new emotions.
그리고 우리는 새로운 감정을 느끼게 돼.

• emotional a. 감정의   • emotionally ad. 감정적으로

helpful
[hélpfəl]
a. 유익한

The program was very helpful to me.
그 프로그램은 나에게 아주 도움이 되었어.

experience
[ikspíəriəns]
v. 경험하다   n. 경험

I am experiencing many of those changes right now.
지금 당장 나는 그런 변화를 많이 경험하고 있어.

remind
[rimáind]

v. 생각나게 하다

It reminded me of Mr. Lee.
그것은 이 선생님을 생각나게 했어.

- remind A of B A에게 B를 생각나게 하다
- reminder 생각나게 하는 사람(것)

single
[síŋgl]

a. 독신의

He is our new single English teacher.
그분은 우리의 새로운 총각 영어 선생님이야.

fashion
[fǽʃən]

n. 패션, 유행

He has a great fashion sense.
그분은 패션 감각이 뛰어나.

- fashionable a. 유행하는 • fashion sense n. 패션 감각

humorous
[hjúːmərəs]

n. 익살스러운,
유머스러운

He is very humorous, too.
그분은 아주 익살스럽기도 해.

- humor n. 유머, 익살

refer
[rifə́ːr]

v. 언급하다

Sara refers to him as a witty man.
사라는 그분을 재치 있는 분이라고 말하지.

- reference n. 언급, 참조 • refer to A as B A를 B라고 언급하다

witty
[wíti]

a. 재치 있는

Sara refers to him as a witty man.
사라는 그분을 재치 있는 분이라고 말하지.

- wit n. 기지, 재치

conscious
[kánʃəs]

a. 의식하고 있는

Lately, I am very conscious of him.
요즘 나는 그분을 몹시 의식하게 돼.

- be conscious of ~을 의식하다

beat
[biːt]

v. 심장이 뛰다
n. 박자, 비트

My heart beats faster when I see him.
그분을 보면 내 심장 박동이 빨라져.

come up
[kʌm ʌp]
v. 다가오다

Teachers' Day is coming up soon and I want to give him a special present.
스승의 날이 곧 다가오는데 나는 그분에게 특별한 선물을 드리고 싶어.

concerned
[kənsə́:rnd]
a. 걱정하는

But I am concerned about what he will think.
하지만 나는 그분이 어떻게 생각할지가 걱정돼.
- concern v. 걱정시키다 n. 걱정, 염려
- be concerned about ~에 대해 걱정하다

pleased
[pli:zd]
a. 마음에 드는,
즐거워 하는

Will he be pleased?
그분이 마음에 들어 할까?
- please v. 즐겁게 하다 • pleasure n. 즐거움

awkward
[ɔ́:kwərd]
a. 어색한

Or will he think it is awkward?
아니면 그분은 그것이 어색하다고 생각할까?

treat
[tri:t]
v. 대우하다

I hope he treats me differently.
나는 그분이 나를 다르게 대해 주었으면 해.
- treatment n. 대우, 처리

notice
[nóutis]
v. 주의하다, 주목하다
n. 주의, 주목, 통지

I hope he notices me more.
나는 그분이 내게 더 관심을 보여 주었으면 해.
- noticeable a. 주목할 만한

rejected
[ridʒéktid]
a. 퇴짜 맞은

If he doesn't, I will feel so rejected.
그가 그러지 않으면, 나는 정말 퇴짜 맞은 기분이 들 거야.
- reject v. 거절하다, 사절하다

tease
[ti:z]
v. 놀리다

What if my friends tease me?
내 친구들이 놀리면 어떻게 하지?

Check Again!

A Translate each word into Korean.

1. program ....

2. puberty ....

3. physical ....

4. mentally ....

5. experience ....

6. humorous ....

7. conscious ....

8. awkward ....

9. notice ....

10. rejected ....

B Translate each word into English.

1. 감정 ....

2. 유익한 ....

3. 독신의 ....

4. 심장이 뛰다 ....

5. 걱정하는 ....

C Fill in the blank with the appropriate word. Refer to the Korean.

1. They r to him as a child.

   그들은 그를 아이라고 불러요.

2. Her hair r me of a poodle.

   그녀의 머리는 푸들을 생각나게 해요.

3. He has a strange f sense.

   그는 패션 감각이 **독특**해요.

4. We were p with our presents.

   우리는 선물이 마음에 들었어요.

5. He t everyone like a friend.

   그는 모든 사람을 친구처럼 대해요.

Chapter 1
Teen Life

Unit 3. Visit my blog.

put some pictures **on** one's blog

a boy **in his Superman costume**

need some special **hair treatment**

hold one's breath

Episode

Dear Diary,

I'm going to put some new pictures up on my blog. ● Here are my siblings, Seri and Hoony.

Seri's lips are glittering. ● She loves to wear lip gloss. ● She acts like such a princess. ● But she has a bad temper. ● I remember the last argument we had. ● Our rooms looked like battlefields!

Look at Hoony in his Superman costume. ● He believes it gives him superpowers! ● He thinks even a timid child can look brave in this costume. ● He looks like an ordinary preschooler. ● But look at his graduation picture. ● He looks so serious. ● It's a pretty big contrast. ● I want to select some pictures of Mom and Dad, too. ● But Dad looks so bald in most of them. ● He really needs some special hair treatment. ● Here's Mom in a striped swimming suit. ● The long stripes make her look thinner. ● And Mom is holding her breath. ● She obviously wanted to look as thin as possible. ● She looks very uncomfortable.

다이어리에게,
나는 내 블로그에 새 사진을 올릴 거야. 여기는 내 형제 자매 세리와 후니야.

세리의 입술은 반짝거려. 그녀는 립글로스 바르기를 좋아해. 그녀는 진짜 공주처럼 행동한다니까. 하지만 화를 잘 내. 우리가 마지막으로 말다툼한 것이 기억나. 우리 방들이 전쟁터 같아 보였어!

수퍼맨 복장을 입은 후니를 봐. 그 애는 그것으로 초능력을 얻는다고 믿어! 소심한 아이도 이 옷을 입으면 용감하게 보인다고 생각하지. 그는 평범한 유치원생처럼 보여. 하지만 졸업식 사진을 봐. 아주 진지해 보이거든. 꽤 큰 차이가 나네. 나는 엄마와 아빠의 사진도 몇 장 고르고 싶어. 하지만 아빠는 대부분의 사진에서 머리가 많이 벗겨진 모습이야. 아빠는 정말 머리에 특별 관리 좀 받아야 해. 여기에 엄마는 줄무늬 수영복을 입고 있어. 긴 줄무늬가 그녀를 더 날씬하게 보이게 해. 그리고 엄마는 숨을 참고 있어. 엄마는 분명히 가능한 한 날씬하게 보이고 싶었을 거야. 엄마는 아주 불편해 보여.

blog
[blɔ́g]

n. 블로그

I'm going to put some new pictures up on my blog.
나는 내 블로그에 새 사진을 올릴 거야.

• blog=Web+log: 자신의 관심사에 따라 자유롭게 글을 올릴 수 있는 웹사이트

sibling
[síbliŋ]

n. 형제, 자매

Here are my siblings, Seri and Hoony.
여기 나의 형제 자매 세리와 후니야.

glitter
[glítər]

v. 반짝이다, 빛나다

Seri's lips are glittering.
세리의 입술은 반짝거려.

• glittering a. 반짝이는, 빛나는

lip gloss
[lip glɔːs]

n. 립글로스

She loves to wear lip gloss.
그녀는 립글로스 바르기를 좋아해.

princess
[prínsis]

n. 공주

She acts like such a princess.
그녀는 진짜 공주처럼 행동한다니까.

• prince n. 왕자

temper
[témpər]

n. 기질, 성질

But she has a bad temper.
하지만 그녀는 화를 잘 내.

argument
[ɑ́ːrgjumənt]

n. 말다툼

I remember the last argument we had.
우리가 마지막으로 말다툼한 것이 기억나.

• argue v. 말다툼하다

battlefield
[bǽtlfiːld]

n. 전쟁터

Our rooms looked like battlefields!
우리 방들이 전쟁터 같아 보였어!

• battle n. 전투

costume
[kάstʃuːm]
n. 복장

Look at Hoony in his Superman costume.
수퍼맨 복장을 입은 후니를 봐.

superpower
[súːpərpàuər]
n. 초능력

He believes it gives him superpowers!
그 애는 그것으로 초능력을 얻는다고 믿어!

timid
[tímid]
a. 소심한

He thinks even a timid child can look brave in this costume.
그는 소심한 아이도 이 옷을 입으면 용감하게 보인다고 생각해.

brave
[breiv]
a. 용감한

He thinks even a timid child can look brave in this costume.
그는 소심한 아이도 이 옷을 입으면 용감하게 보인다고 생각해.

ordinary
[ɔ́ːrdənèri]
a. 평범한

He looks like an ordinary preschooler.
그는 평범한 유치원생처럼 보여.

graduation
[græ̀dʒuéiʃən]
n. 졸업식

But look at his graduation picture.
하지만 그의 졸업식 사진을 봐.

• graduate v. 졸업하다 n. 졸업생

serious
[síəriəs]
a. 진지한

He looks so serious.
그는 아주 진지해 보이거든.

contrast
[kάntræst]
n. 대조, 현저한 차이

It's a pretty big contrast.
꽤 큰 차이가 나네.

select
[silékt]
v. 선택하다

I want to select some pictures of Mom and Dad, too.
나는 엄마와 아빠의 사진도 몇 장 고르고 싶어.

• selection n. 선택

bald
[bɔːld]
a. 대머리의

But Dad looks so bald in most of them.
하지만 아빠는 대부분의 사진에서 머리가 많이 벗겨진 모습이야.

treatment
[tríːtmənt]
n. 취급, 치료

He really needs some special hair treatment.
아빠는 정말 머리에 특별 관리 좀 받아야 해.

• treat v. 치료하다

striped
[straipt]
a. 줄무늬의

Here's Mom in a striped swimming suit.
여기에 엄마는 줄무늬 수영복을 입고 있어.

• stripe n. 줄무늬

thinner
[θínər]
a. 더 가는
　(thin의 비교급)

The long stripes make her look thinner.
긴 줄무늬가 그녀를 더 날씬하게 보이게 해.

• thin a. 가는, 날씬한   • thin - thinner - thinnest

breath
[breθ]
n. 숨

And Mom is holding her breath.
그리고 엄마는 숨을 참고 있어.

• breathe v. 숨을 쉬다   • hold one's breath v. 숨을 참다

obviously
[ábviəsli]
ad. 명백히, 분명히

She obviously wanted to look as thin as possible.
엄마는 분명히 가능한 한 날씬하게 보이고 싶었을 거야.

• obvious a. 명백한, 분명한

uncomfortable
[ʌnkʌ́mfərtəbl]
a. 불편한

She looks very uncomfortable.
그녀는 아주 불편해 보여.

• comfortable a. 편안한

Check Again!

A Translate each word into Korean.

1. sibling ....   2. glitter ....

3. battlefield ....   4. ordinary ....

5. graduation ....   6. contrast ....

7. treatment ....   8. striped ....

9. obviously ....   10. uncomfortable ....

B Translate each word into English.

1. 공주 ....

2. 말다툼 ....

3. 복장 ....

4. 진지한 ....

5. 대머리의 ....

C Fill in the blank with the appropriate word. Refer to the Korean.

1. He is showing his bad t   today.

그는 오늘 성질을 부리고 있어요.

2. This hero has amazing s   .

이 영웅은 놀라운 초능력을 가졌어요.

3. You can s   a Korean or English menu.

한글 또는 영문 메뉴를 선택할 수 있어요.

4. This diet hasn't made me t   .

이 다이어트가 나를 날씬하게 만들어 주지 않았어요.

5. How long can you hold your b   underwater?

물밑에서 얼마 동안 숨을 참을 수 있어요?

✚ 명사 만들기 1

동사에 –tion 혹은 –sion 등을 붙여서 명사로 만들 수 있다.

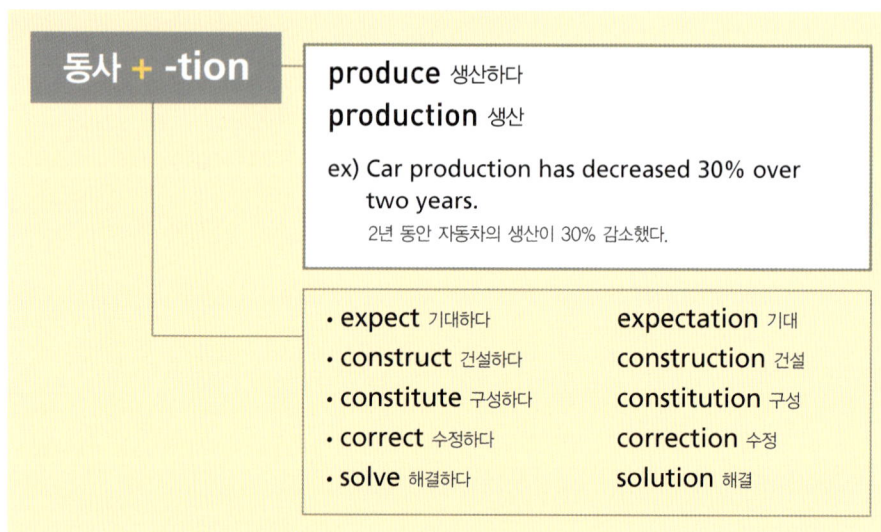

동사 + -tion

produce 생산하다
production 생산

ex) Car production has decreased 30% over two years.
2년 동안 자동차의 생산이 30% 감소했다.

- **expect** 기대하다   **expectation** 기대
- **construct** 건설하다   **construction** 건설
- **constitute** 구성하다   **constitution** 구성
- **correct** 수정하다   **correction** 수정
- **solve** 해결하다   **solution** 해결

동사 + -sion

fuse 융합하다
fusion 융합, 통합

ex) This food is a fusion of Korean and Italian cuisine.
이 음식은 한국과 이태리 조리법이 융합되어 있다.

- **admit** 입학을 허락하다   **admission** 입학
- **decide** 결정하다   **decision** 결정
- **divide** 나누다   **division** 분할, 분배
- **invade** 침입하다   **invasion** 침입
- **express** 표현하다   **expression** 표현

Daily Activities

- take a shower 샤워하다
- get dressed 옷을 입다
- have a meal 식사하다
- read a newspaper 신문을 읽다
- take a nap 낮잠 자다
- do exercise 운동하다
- take a stroll 산책하다

Types of Cloth 옷감의 종류

+ natural fiber 천연섬유
+ synthetic fiber 인조섬유
+ silk 실크
+ cotton 면
+ wool 양모
+ leather 가죽
+ polyester 폴리에스테르

VOCA EDGE

BLUE

Chapter 2. My home and Neighborhood

Unit 4. Girls and boys use different facilities.

Unit 5. We love you, Kite.

Unit 6. We moved today.

Chapter 2
My home and Neighborhood

Unit 4. Girls and boys use different facilities.

like **violent** computer games

like going to **a shopping mall**

have better access to the subway

Episode

Dear Diary,

I was thinking about our neighborhood **facilities**. ● They should **satisfy** most people. ● Boys and girls go to different places for **entertainment**. ● We have different **tastes**.

Our neighborhood has **Internet cafes** for boys. ● The **rates** are cheap there. ● Some even have air **purifiers**. ● Others are very **spacious**. ● You can play the most **up-to-date** games there. ● And the computers there have **wider screens**. ● I don't like **violent** computer games. ● But boys say they are **educational**, too. ● They say they are learning **self-defense** skills!

Our neighborhood also has a **shopping mall** for girls. ● **Unlike** boys, girls like going there. ● We can **hang out** there for hours. ● It has a huge **multi-theater**, too. ● Dad **mentioned** that we might move to another neighborhood. ● He **frequently** goes to the sports center there. ● It has **similar** facilities to this one. ● But it also has better **access** to the subway. ● It sounds **perfect**, but I'll still **miss** this neighborhood.

....

다이어리에게,

나는 우리 동네 시설들에 대해 생각해 봤어. 그것들은 대부분의 사람들을 만족시켜야 해. 남자 애들과 여자 애들은 오락을 즐기는 곳이 틸러. 우리는 취향이 다르거든.

우리 동네는 남자 애들을 위한 인터넷 카페가 있지. 그곳은 요금이 싸. 어떤 곳들은 심지어 공기 청정기도 있어. 또 어떤 곳들은 아주 넓어. 거기서 가장 최신의 게임들을 즐길 수 있지. 그리고 컴퓨터들은 화면도 더 넓어. 나는 폭력적인 컴퓨터 게임을 안 좋아해. 하지만 남자 애들은 그것도 교육적이라고 해. 호신술을 배운다고 하네!

우리 동네에는 여자 애들을 위한 쇼핑몰도 있어. 남자 애들과는 다르게 여자 애들은 거기에 가는 것을 좋아하지. 우리는 몇 시간씩 그곳을 돌아다닐 수 있어. 그곳에는 큰 복합 영화상영관도 있어. 아빠는 우리가 다른 동네로 이사 갈 수도 있다고 하셨어. 아빠는 그 동네 스포츠 센터에 자주 가시거든. 거긴 이곳과 비슷한 시설을 갖추고 있어. 하지만 거기서는 지하철을 더 쉽게 이용할 수 있지. 아주 완벽한 것 같지만 나는 그래도 이 동네가 그리울 거야.

facilities
[fəsílətiz]

n. 설비, 시설

I was thinking about our neighborhood facilities.
나는 우리 동네 시설들에 대해 생각해 봤어.

satisfy
[sǽtisfài]

v. 만족시키다

They should satisfy most people.
그것들은 대부분의 사람들을 만족시켜야 해.

• satisfaction n. 만족

entertainment
[èntərtéinmənt]

n. 오락

Boys and girls go to different places for entertainment.
남자 애들과 여자 애들은 오락을 즐기는 곳이 달라.

• entertain v. 즐겁게 하다

taste
[teist]

n. 취향, 기호

We have different tastes.
우리는 취향이 다르거든.

Internet cafe
[íntərnèt kæféi]

n. 인터넷 카페

Our neighborhood has Internet cafes for boys.
우리 동네는 남자 애들을 위한 인터넷 카페가 있지.

rate
[reit]

n. 요금, 비율, 속도

The rates are cheap there.
그곳은 요금이 싸.

purifier
[pjúərəfàiər]

n. 청정기, 정화기

Some even have air purifiers.
어떤 곳들은 심지어 공기 청정기가 있어.

• pure a. 순수한   • air purifier n. 공기 청정기

spacious
[spéiʃəs]

a. 넓은, 훤히 트인

Others are very spacious.
또 어떤 곳들은 아주 넓어.

• space n. 공간

up-to-date
[ʌp tə deit]

a. 갱신한, 최신의
(=newest)

You can play the most up-to-date games there.
거기서 가장 최신의 게임들을 즐길 수 있지.

• update v. 새롭게 하다, 최신화하다

---

wider
[wáidər]

a. 더 넓은
(wide의 비교급)

And the computers there have wider screens.
그리고 그곳 컴퓨터들은 화면도 더 넓어.

• wide a. 넓은 • wide-wider-widest

---

screen
[skri:n]

n. 화면, 스크린

And the computers there have wider screens.
그리고 그곳 컴퓨터들은 화면도 더 넓어.

---

violent
[váiələnt]

a. 폭력적인

I don't like violent computer games.
나는 폭력적인 컴퓨터 게임을 안 좋아해.

• violence n. 폭력 • non-violent 비폭력적인

---

educational
[èdʒukéiʃənl]

a. 교육적인

But boys say they are educational, too.
하지만 남자 애들은 그것도 교육적이라고 해.

• education n. 교육

---

self-defense
[sélf-diféns]

n. 자기방어, 호신

They say they are learning self-defense skills!
그들은 호신술을 배운다고 하네!

• defend v. 방어하다 • self-defense skill 호신술

---

shopping mall
[ʃápiŋ mɔ:l]

n. 쇼핑몰, 상가

Our neighborhood also has a shopping mall for girls.
우리 동네에는 여자 애들을 위한 쇼핑몰도 있어.

---

unlike
[ʌnláik]

prep. ~와는 달리

Unlike boys, girls like going there.
남자 애들과는 다르게 여자 애들은 거기에 가는 것을 좋아해.

hang out
[hæŋ aut]
v. 시간을 보내다, 슬슬 거닐다

We can hang out there for hours.
우리는 몇 시간씩 그곳을 돌아다닐 수 있어.

multi-theater
[mʌ̀lti-θí(:)ətər]
n. 복합 영화상영관

It has a huge multi-theater, too.
그곳에는 큰 복합 영화상영관도 있어.

mention
[ménʃən]
v. 언급하다
n. 언급

Dad mentioned that we might move to another neighborhood.
아빠는 우리가 다른 동네로 이사 갈 수도 있다고 하셨어.

frequently
[frí:kwəntli]
ad. 자주

He frequently goes to the sports center there.
아빠는 그 동네 스포츠 센터에 자주 가셔.

• frequency n. 빈도   • frequent a. 빈번한

similar
[símələr]
a. 비슷한

It has similar facilities to this one.
거긴 이곳과 비슷한 시설을 갖추고 있어.

• similarity n. 유사성

access
[ǽkses]
n. 접근, 이용
v. ~에 접근하다

But it also has better access to the subway.
하지만 거기서는 지하철을 더 쉽게 이용할 수 있지.

• have access to ~에 접근할 수 있다

perfect
[pɔ́:rfikt]
a. 완벽한

It sounds perfect, but I'll still miss this neighborhood. 아주 완벽한 것 같지만 나는 그래도 이 동네가 그리울 거야.

• imperfect a. 불완전한

miss
[mis]
v. 그리워하다, 놓치다

It sounds perfect, but I'll still miss this neighborhood. 아주 완벽한 것 같지만 나는 그래도 이 동네가 그리울 거야.

• missing a. 실종된

Check Again!

A Translate each word into Korean.

1. facilities ....   2. entertainment ....

3. purifier ....   4. spacious ....

5. unlike ....   6. educational ....

7. self-defense ....   8. multi-theater ....

9. frequently ....   10. access ....

B Translate each word into English.

1. 만족시키다 ....

2. 그리워하다 ....

3. 요금 ....

4. 폭력적인 ....

5. 비슷한 ....

C Fill in the blank with the appropriate word. Refer to the Korean.

1. He has a strange t   in clothes.

   그는 옷에 대한 취향이 특이해요.

2. This store sells the most u   fashion footwear.

   이 상점은 가장 최신 유행하는 신발들을 판매한다.

3. Some boys were h   out behind the building.

   남자애들 몇 명이 건물 뒤에서 서성대고 있었어요.

4. Those two are p   for each other.

   그 둘은 서로에게 딱 어울려요.

5. How big is your computer s   ?

   네 컴퓨터 화면은 얼마나 크니?

Chapter 2
My home and Neighborhood

Unit 5. We love you, Kite.

deserve a reward

a **homeless** dog on the street

have to **persuade** someone

pat someone **on the head**

Episode

Dear Kite,

What a handsome dog you are, Kite! • Bring the remote control over to me. • Here is a reward for you. • You deserve it! • You look so full of pride. • You sit there so well-behaved. • I'll never forget the day I found you. • I found you underground. • You were a homeless dog on the street. • And you weren't a typical dog. • You seemed scared of people. • I decided to bring you home, but Mom didn't like my decision. • I really had to persuade her. • Every day she complained about you. • You left dog hair everywhere. • You barked at everyone. • And you weren't toilet-trained. • But just look what happened to you. • You have improved so much. • You even learned some tricks! • Now you are the center of attention. • You are our treasure. • Even Mom patted you on the head this morning! • We even like it when you lick our cheeks. • We love you, Kite.

카이트에게,

너는 정말 멋진 개야, 카이트. 내게 리모콘 좀 가져오렴. 자, 이것은 너에게 주는 상이야. 너는 그것을 받을 만해! 너는 아주 자긍심이 넘쳐 보여. 너는 그 자리에 아주 얌전하게 앉아 있구나. 나는 너를 발견한 날을 절대로 잊지 못할 거야. 나는 너를 지하도에서 발견했어. 너는 거리에 버려진 주인 없는 개였어. 그리고 너는 보통 개들과 같지 않았어. 너는 사람들을 두려워하는 것 같았어. 너를 집으로 데려오기로 결정했지만 엄마는 내 결정을 못마땅하게 여기셨어. 나는 엄마를 아주 열심히 설득해야 했어. 매일 엄마는 너에 대해 불평하셨어. 너는 사방에 개털을 남기고 다녔지. 너는 누구에게나 짖어댔어. 그리고 너는 용변을 가릴 줄 몰랐어. 하지만 너에게 무슨 일이 일어난 건지 한번 봐. 너는 아주 많이 나아졌어. 너는 몇 가지 재주까지 익혔잖아! 너는 이제 관심의 주요 대상이야. 너는 우리의 보물이야. 엄마까지 오늘 아침에 너의 머리를 쓰다듬어 주었잖아. 우리는 네가 우리 뺨을 핥을 때도 좋아. 우리는 너를 사랑해, 카이트.

remote control
[rimóut kəntróul]

n. 리모콘

Bring the remote control over to me.
내게 리모콘을 갖다 줘.

reward
[riwɔ́ːrd]

n. 보상, 상, 보수

Here is a reward for you.
이것은 너에게 주는 상이야.

deserve
[dizə́ːrv]

v. ~을 받을 만하다

You deserve it!
너는 그것을 받을 만해!

pride
[praid]

n. 자존심, 자긍심

You look so full of pride.
너는 아주 자긍심이 넘쳐 보여.

• proud a. 자존심이 있는

well-behaved
[wél-bihéivd]

a. 행실이 단정한

You sit there so well-behaved.
너는 그 자리에 아주 얌전하게 앉아 있구나.

• behave v. 행동하다

forget
[fərgét]

v. 잊다

I'll never forget the day I found you.
나는 너를 발견한 날을 절대로 잊지 못할 거야.

underground
[ʌ́ndərgràund]

ad. 지하에서
a. 지하의

I found you underground.
나는 너를 지하도에서 발견했어.

homeless
[hóumlis]

a. 집 없는,
　　기르는 사람이 없는

You were a homeless dog on the street.
너는 거리에 버려진 주인 없는 개였어.

typical
[típikəl]
a. 전형적인

And you weren't a typical dog.
그리고 너는 보통 개들과 같지 않았어.

scared
[skɛərd]
a. 두려워하는

You seemed scared of people.
너는 사람들을 두려워하는 것 같았어.

- scare v. ~를 겁나게 하다   • scared of ~를 두려워하는
- scary a. 무서운, 두려운

decide
[disáid]
v. 결정하다

I decided to bring you home but Mom didn't like my decision.
나는 너를 집으로 데려오기로 결정했지만 엄마는 내 결정을 못마땅하게 여기셨어.

- decision n. 결정   • decisive a. 결정적인, 단호한
- decide+ to V ~하기로 결심하다

persuade
[pəːrswéid]
v. 설득하다

I really had to persuade her.
나는 그녀를 아주 열심히 설득해야 했어.

- persuasion n. 설득

complain
[kəmpléin]
v. 불평하다

Every day she complained about you.
매일 그녀는 너에 대해 불평을 했어.

- complaint n. 불평, 불만

everywhere
[évrihwὲər]
ad. 사방에

You left dog hair everywhere.
너는 사방에 개털을 남기고 다녔지.

bark
[baːrk]
v. 짖다

You barked at everyone.
너는 누구에게나 짖어댔어.

- bark at ~를 보고 짖다

toilet-trained
[tɔ́ilit-tréind]
a. 용변을 가릴 줄 아는

And you weren't toilet-trained.
그리고 너는 용변을 가릴 줄 몰랐어.

- toilet n. 변기, 변소

happen
[hǽpən]
v. 발생하다, 일어나다

But just look what happened to you.
하지만 너에게 무슨 일이 일어난 건지 한번 봐.

• happen to ~에게 일어나다
• happening n. (우연히 일어난) 일, 사건

improve
[imprúːv]
v. 나아지다, 개선되다

You have improved so much.
너는 아주 많이 나아졌어.

• improvement n. 향상

trick
[trik]
n. 재주, 묘기

You even learned some tricks!
너는 몇 가지 재주까지 익혔잖아!

center
[séntər]
n. 초점, 중심

Now you are the center of attention.
너는 이제 관심의 주요 대상이야.

attention
[əténʃən]
n. 주의, 주목

Now you are the center of attention.
너는 이제 관심의 주요 대상이야.

treasure
[tréʒər]
n. 보물

You are our treasure.
너는 우리의 보물이야.

pat
[pæt]
v. 쓰다듬다

Even Mom patted you on the head this morning!
엄마까지 오늘 아침에 너의 머리를 쓰다듬어 주었잖아!

lick
[lik]
v. 핥다

We even like it when you lick our cheeks.
우리는 네가 우리 뺨을 핥을 때도 좋아.

Check Again!

A Translate each word into Korean.

1. deserve ....   2. well-behaved ....

3. typical ....   4. scared ....

5. underground ....   6. persuade ....

7. everywhere ....   8. toilet-trained ....

9. improve ....   10. treasure ....

B Translate each word into English.

1. 발생하다 ....

2. 리모콘 ....

3. 자존심 ....

4. 잊다 ....

5. 짓다 ....

C Fill in the blank with the appropriate word. Refer to the Korean.

1. She is always c_____ about something.

   그녀는 늘 무언가에 대해 불평해요.

2. The r_____ was a trip to Tokyo Disneyland.

   상은 동경 디즈니랜드로의 여행이었어요.

3. Many h_____ people sleep at the station.

   많은 노숙자들이 역에서 자요.

4. Where did you d_____ to go?

   어디로 가기로 결정했어요?

5. The man showed us a neat card t_____.

   그 남자는 우리에게 멋진 카드 묘기를 보여 줬어요.

Chapter 2
My home and Neighborhood
Unit 6. We moved today.

detach a poster **from** the wall

disconnect the water

plug in

Episode

Dear Diary,

We **packed** all our things from our old house today. ● I **detached** my Volcanoes poster from the wall. ● The wall looked so **empty** without it. ● There was so much **trash**. ● When I turned on the **faucet**, I noticed the water was already **disconnected**. ● This **area** where we lived for so long began to seem strange to me, now. ● I **remained still** for a few minutes. ● Dad drove the car out of the **parking lot**. ● It seemed like the car was **separating** us farther from our old house. ● Soon, it was just a **dot**. ● The weather **forecast** said it would rain. ● It was **pouring** rain in my heart, too. ● Soon the truck arrived at our new apartment and began **unloading**. ● We had a **permit** to use the elevator. ● Some of our boxes had 'Fragile' written on them. ● So they needed to be treated with **care**. ● Hoony **certainly** has a short **memory**. ● He is **behaving** like we've always lived here. ● By evening, everything was **plugged in**. ● I have a **worry**, though. ● I wonder if I can **locate** our new house after school tomorrow.

다이어리에게,

우리는 오늘 옛날 집에서 짐을 모두 쌌어. 나는 벽에서 나의 볼케이노 포스터를 떼어냈어. 그것이 없으니까 벽이 텅 빈 것 같았어. 쓰레기기 엄청 많았어. 수도 꼭지를 틀어 보고, 나는 물이 이미 끊겨진 것은 알았어. 우리가 아주 오랫동안 살았던 이곳이 이제는 내게 낯설게 느껴지기 시작했어. 나는 몇 분 동안 가만히 있었어. 아빠가 주차장에서 차를 몰고 나갔어. 차는 우리를 옛 집으로부터 더욱 멀어지게 하는 것만 같았어. 그것은 곧 점 하나가 되었지. 일기예보에서 비가 올 것이라고 했어. 내 마음에도 비가 퍼부었어. 곧 트럭이 우리 새 아파트에 도착해서 짐을 내려놓기 시작했어. 우리는 엘리베이터 이용 허가를 받았어. 어떤 상자에는 '깨지기 쉬운'이라고 적혀 있었어. 그래서 그것들을 조심해서 다루어야 했어. 후니는 확실히 기억이 짧다니까. 그는 우리가 늘 이곳에서 살았던 것처럼 행동해. 저녁 무렵엔 모든 것이 플러그 가 꽂혔어. 하지만 내게 한 가지 걱정이 있어. 내일 방과 후에 내가 우리 새 집을 잘 찾을 수 있을지 의문이야.

pack
[pæk]
v. 짐을 싸다

We packed all our things from our old house today.
우리는 오늘 옛날 집에서 짐을 모두 쌌어.

• unpack 짐을 풀다

detach
[ditǽtʃ]
v. 떼어내다

I detached my Volcanoes poster from the wall.
나는 벽에서 나의 볼케이노 포스터를 떼어냈어

• detachment n. 분리 • detached a. 분리된

empty
[émpti]
a. 빈, 아무것도 없는

The wall looked so empty without it.
그것이 없으니까 벽이 텅 빈 것 같았어.

• emptiness n. 텅 빔, 공허함

trash
[træʃ]
n. 쓰레기

There was so much trash.
쓰레기가 엄청 많았어.

faucet
[fɔ́:sit]
n. 수도 꼭지

When I turned on the faucet, I noticed the water was already disconnected.
수도 꼭지를 틀자, 나는 물이 이미 끊겼음을 알았어.

disconnect
[dìskənékt]
v. 연결을 끊다

When I turned on the faucet, I noticed the water was already disconnected.
수도 꼭지를 틀어 보고, 나는 물이 이미 끊겨진 것을 알았어.

• disconnection n. 단절, 분리

area
[ɛ́əriə]
n. 구역, 지역

This area where we lived for so long began to seem strange to me, now.
우리가 아주 오랫동안 살았던 이곳이 이제는 내게 낯설게 느껴졌어.

remain
[riméin]
v. ~인 채로 남아 있다

I remained still for a few minutes.
나는 몇 분 동안 가만히 있었어.

still
[stil]

a. 움직이지 않는
ad. 여전히

I remained still for a few minutes.
나는 몇 분 동안 가만히 있었어.

parking lot
[páːrkiŋ lɑt]

n. 주차장

Dad drove the car out of the parking lot.
아빠는 주차장에서 차를 몰고 나갔어.

• park v. 주차하다   • lot n. 토지의 한 구획

separate
[sépərèit]

v. 분리시키다

It seemed like the car was separating us farther from our old house.
차는 우리를 옛 집으로부터 더욱 멀어지게 하는 것만 같았어.

• separation n. 분리
• separate A from B A를 B로 부터 분리시키다

dot
[dɑt]

n. 점

Soon, it was just a dot.
그것은 곧 점 하나가 되었지.

forecast
[fɔ́ːrkæst]

n. 예보
v. 예보하다

The weather forecast said it would rain.
일기예보에서 비가 올 것이라고 했어.

pour
[pɔːr]

v. 퍼붓다

It was pouring rain in my heart, too.
내 마음에도 비가 퍼부었어.

unload
[ʌnlóud]

v. 짐을 내려놓다

Soon, the truck arrived at our new apartment and began unloading.
곧 트럭이 우리 새 아파트에 도착해서 짐을 내려놓기 시작했어.

• load v. 짐을 싣다

permit
[pəːrmít]

n. 허가(증)
v. 허락하다

We had a permit to use the elevator.
우리는 엘리베이터 이용 허가를 받았어.

• permission 허락, 허가

fragile
[frǽdʒəl]

a. 깨지기 쉬운

Some of our boxes had 'Fragile' written on them.
어떤 상자에는 '깨지기 쉬운' 이라고 적혀 있었어.

• fragility n. 부서지기 쉬움, 여림

care
[kɛər]

n. 주의, 조심
v. 주의하다

So, they needed to be treated with care.
그래서 그것들을 조심해서 다루어야 했어.

• with care 조심스럽게 • careful a. 주의하는, 조심하는

certainly
[sə́ːrtənli]

ad. 확실히, 틀림없이

Hoony certainly has a short memory.
후니는 확실히 기억이 짧다니까.

• certain a. 확실한

memory
[méməri]

n. 기억

Hoony certainly has a short memory.
후니는 확실히 기억이 짧다니까.

• memorize v. 기억하다, 암기하다
• have a short memory 기억이 오래가지 않다

behave
[bihéiv]

v. 행동하다

He is behaving like we've always lived here.
그는 우리가 늘 이곳에서 살았던 것처럼 행동해.

• behavior n. 행동

plug in
[plʌg in]

v. 플러그를 꽂다

By evening, everything was plugged in.
저녁 무렵엔 모든 것이 플러그가 꽂혔어.

worry
[wə́ːri]

n. 걱정
v. 걱정을 하다

I have a worry, though.
하지만 내게 한 가지 걱정이 있어.

• worried a. 걱정을 하는

locate
[loukéit]

v. 위치를 알아내다

I wonder if I can locate our new house after school tomorrow.
내일 방과 후에 내가 우리 새 집을 잘 찾을 수 있을지 의문이야.

• location n. 위치

Check Again!

A Translate each word into Korean.

1. detach ....
2. faucet ....
3. disconnect ....
4. remain ....
5. forecast ....
6. permit ....
7. fragile ....
8. care ....
9. worry ....
10. locate ....

B Translate each word into English.

1. 짐을 싸다 ....
2. 쓰레기 ....
3. 주차장 ....
4. 퍼붓다 ....
5. 짐을 내려놓다 ....

C Fill in the blank with the appropriate word. Refer to the Korean.

1. The school seems e_____ without you.

   당신이 없으니까 학교가 텅 빈 것 같아요.

2. She b_____ like she didn't care.

   그녀는 관심 없는 척 행동했어요.

3. You forgot to p_____ in the DVD player.

   당신은 DVD 플레이어의 플러그를 꽂는 것을 잊었어요.

4. A line s_____ the boys from the girls.

   선이 남자애들과 여자애들을 갈라놓았어요.

5. He c_____ has a big stomach.

   그는 확실히 위가 커요.

✚ 명사 만들기 2

동사에 -ment 혹은 형용사에 -ness 등을 붙여서 명사로 만들 수 있다.

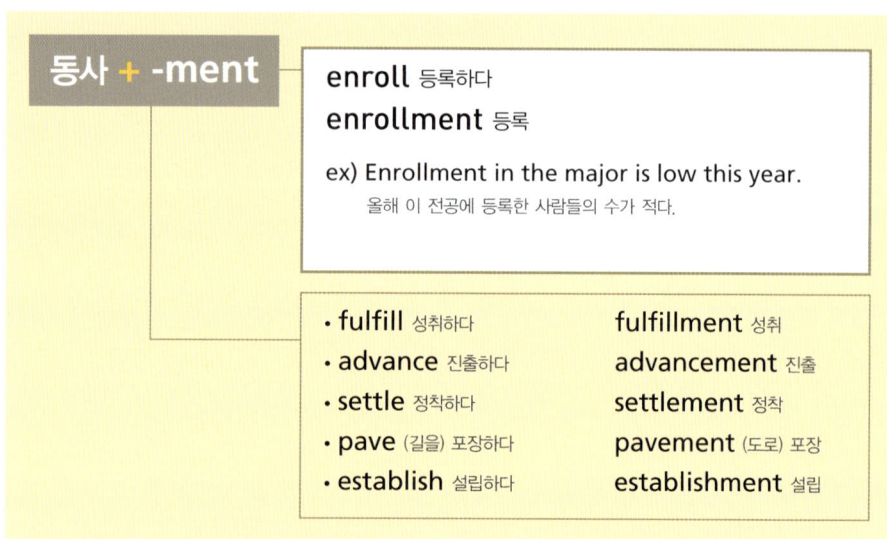

동사 + -ment

enroll 등록하다
enrollment 등록

ex) Enrollment in the major is low this year.
올해 이 전공에 등록한 사람들의 수가 적다.

- **fulfill** 성취하다   **fulfillment** 성취
- **advance** 진출하다   **advancement** 진출
- **settle** 정착하다   **settlement** 정착
- **pave** (길을) 포장하다   **pavement** (도로) 포장
- **establish** 설립하다   **establishment** 설립

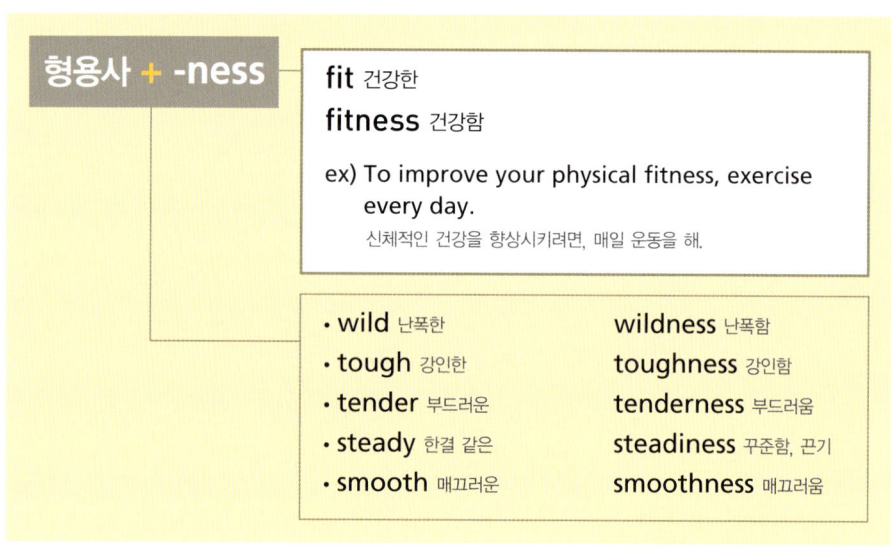

형용사 + -ness

fit 건강한
fitness 건강함

ex) To improve your physical fitness, exercise every day.
신체적인 건강을 향상시키려면, 매일 운동을 해.

- **wild** 난폭한   **wildness** 난폭함
- **tough** 강인한   **toughness** 강인함
- **tender** 부드러운   **tenderness** 부드러움
- **steady** 한결 같은   **steadiness** 꾸준함, 끈기
- **smooth** 매끄러운   **smoothness** 매끄러움

Philosophies

- materialism 물질주의 - materialist 물질주의자
- capitalism 자본주의 - capitalist 자본가, 자본주의자
- Communism 공산주의 - Communist 공산주의자
- Confucianism 유교주의 - Confucianist 유교주의자
- socialism 사회주의 - socialist 사회주의자

Religious Places & People 종교적 장소와 성직자

+ temple 사원
+ cathedral 성당
+ church 교회
+ mosque 이슬람 사원
+ monk 수도승
+ priest 성직자, 사제
+ minister(= pastor) 목사

VOCA EDGE

BLUE

Chapter 3. Learning

Chapter 3
Learning

Unit 7. I want to join the drama club.

see **an ad**

fill out an application

prepare a short **performance**

Episode

Sara: I was just at the administration office. ● I saw an ad there.

Bomi: Was it about the drama club?

Sara: Yeah, they are choosing new members. ● It informs you about how to join. ● If you want, you can fill out an application in the office. ● Then submit it to the woman there.

Bomi: Were there any other requirements?

Sara: Yes, there are a few steps you have to take. ● First, you must take an aptitude test. ● They want you to prove that you can be a good actor. ● The test is to prepare a short performance. ● It must be recorded and then submitted.

Bomi: And is the second step an interview?

Sara: Yes. You will be given some lines to memorize. ● Then you have to perform in front of your peers. ● You might have to play a greedy man like Scrooge. ● One of my friends was asked to play a professor. ● The other one was asked to play a queen from the Chosun Dynasty.

Bomi: Oh, what if I forget my lines?

Sara: You won't. Be confident!

Bomi: Thanks. I really want to perform this semester. ● I'd better rush over to the administration office.

....

사라: 방금 행정실에 들렸는데 거기서 광고를 하나 봤어.
보미: 연극반에 관한 거였니?
사라: 응, 신입 회원을 뽑고 있어. 어떻게 가입할 수 있는지 거기에 나와 있어. 원하면, 사무실에서 신청서를 작성해. 그리고 기기에 있는 여자분에게 제출하면 돼.
보미: 또 다른 요구사항이 있니?
사라: 응, 몇 가지 단계가 있어. 우선, 적성검사를 받아야 해. 그들은 네가 좋은 배우가 될 수 있다는 것을 입증해 주길 바래. 시험은 짧은 연기를 준비하는 거야. 그것을 녹화해서 제출해야 돼.
보미: 두 번째 단계는 면접이니?
사라: 응. 너에게 대사 몇 마디를 외우라고 줄 거야. 그런 다음, 동료들 앞에서 연기를 해야 돼. 스크루지처럼 욕심 많은 남자 연기를 해야 할 수도 있어. 내 친구 한 명에게는 교수 연기를 하라고 했어. 또 다른 아이에게는 조선시대의 왕후를 연기하라고 했어.
보미: 아, 내가 대사를 잊어버리면 어떡하지?
사라: 그러지 않을 거야. 자신감을 가져!
보미: 고마워, 나는 정말로 이번 학기에 공연을 하고 싶어. 서둘러서 행정실로 가 봐야겠어.

administration
[ædmìnəstréiʃən]
n. 행정

I was just at the administration office.
나는 방금 행정실에 들렸어.

• administer v. 관리하다, 운영하다

ad
[æd]
n. 광고
(=advertisement)

I saw an ad there.
나는 거기서 광고를 하나 봤어.

• advertise v. 광고하다

drama
[drɑ́:mə]
n. 연극

Was it about the drama club?
연극반에 관한 거였니?

• dramatic a. 극적인

member
[mémbər]
n. 회원

Yeah, they are choosing new members.
응, 신입 회원들을 뽑고 있어.

• membership n. 회원임, 회원 자격

inform
[infɔ́:rm]
v. 알려주다

It informs you about how to join.
어떻게 가입할 수 있는지 거기에 나와 있어.

• information n. 정보

application
[æ̀plikéiʃən]
n. 신청서, 지원서

If you want, you can fill out an application in the office.
원하면, 사무실에서 신청서를 작성해.

• apply v. 신청하다, 지원하다 • applicant n. 신청자

submit
[səbmít]
v. 제출하다

Then submit it to the woman there.
그리고 거기에 있는 여자분에게 제출하면 돼.

requirement
[rikwáiərmənt]
n. 필요, 요구

Were there any other requirements?
또 다른 요구 사항이 있니?

• require v. 필요로 하다 • required a. 의무적인

step
[step]
n. 단계

Yes, there are a few steps you have to take.
응, 몇 가지 단계가 있어.

- take a step 조치를 취하다

aptitude
[æptitùːd]
n. 적성

First, you must take an aptitude test.
우선, 적성검사를 받아야 해.

prove
[pruːv]
v. 증명하다

They want you to prove that you can be a good actor.
그들은 네가 좋은 배우가 될 수 있다는 것을 입증해 주길 바래.

- proof n. 증거

performance
[pərfɔ́ːrməns]
n. 연기, 공연

The test is to prepare a short performance.
시험은 짧은 연기를 준비하는 거야.

- perform v. 연기하다, 공연하다

record
[rikɔ́ːrd]
v. 녹음(녹화)하다
n. 녹음(녹화)

It must be recorded and then submitted.
그것을 녹화해서 제출해야 돼.

- recorder 녹음기

interview
[íntərvjùː]
n. 면접
v. 면접하다

And is the second step an interview?
그리고 두 번째 단계는 면접이니?

- interviewer n 면접관 • interviewee n 면접받는 사람

line
[lain]
n. 대사

You will be given some lines to memorize.
너에게 대사 몇 마디를 외우라고 줄 거야.

peer
[piər]

n. 동년배, 또래

Then you have to perform in front of your peers.
그런 다음 너는 동료들 앞에서 연기를 해야 돼.

greedy
[grí:di]

a. 탐욕스러운

You might have to play a greedy man like Scrooge.
너는 스크루지처럼 욕심 많은 남자 연기를 해야 할 수도 있어.

• greed   n. 탐욕

professor
[prəfésər]

n. 교수

One of my friends was asked to play a professor.
내 친구 한 명에겐 교수 연기를 하라고 했어.

dynasty
[dáinəsti]

n. 왕조

The other one was asked to play a queen from the Chosun Dynasty.
또 다른 아이에게는 조선시대의 왕후를 연기하라고 했어.

forget
[fərgét]

v. 잊어버리다

Oh, what if I forget my lines?
아, 내가 대사를 잊어버리면 어떡하지?

• forgetful   a. 건망증이 있는, 잊기 쉬운

confident
[kánfidənt]

a. 자신만만한

Be confident!
자신감을 가져!

• confidence   n. 자신, 확신

semester
[siméstər]

n. 한 학기

Thanks. I really want to perform this semester.
고마워, 나는 정말로 이번 학기에 공연을 하고 싶어.

rush
[rʌʃ]

v. 서두르다
n. 분주함, 서두름

I'd better rush over to the administration office.
서둘러서 행정실로 가 봐야겠어.

Check Again!

A Translate each word into Korean.

1. administration .... 2. drama ....

3. inform .... 4. application ....

5. requirement .... 6. aptitude ....

7. performance .... 8. professor ....

9. confident .... 10. semester ....

B Translate each word into English.

1. 회원 ....

2. 왕조 ....

3. 녹화하다 ....

4. 면접 ....

5. 동년배 ....

C Fill in the blank with the appropriate word. Refer to the Korean.

1. Have you seen the new BB Jeans a⬚⬚⬚⬚⬚⬚⬚⬚ ?

   새로 나온 BB 청바지 광고를 봤어요?

2. Did you s⬚⬚⬚⬚⬚⬚⬚⬚ your book report?

   독후감을 제출했어요?

3. Ha! This p⬚⬚⬚⬚⬚⬚⬚⬚ that I was right.

   하! 이것은 내가 옳았었다는 것을 증명하는 거예요.

4. I only have two l⬚⬚⬚⬚⬚⬚⬚⬚ in the whole play.

   나는 연극 전체에서 대사가 두 마디 밖에 없어요.

5. The g⬚⬚⬚⬚⬚⬚⬚⬚ boy grabbed all the cookies.

   욕심 많은 남자 아이는 쿠키를 모두 움켜쥐었어요.

Chapter 3
Learning

Unit 8. We have a team project.

do an experiment

criticize others

make a summary report

Episode

Dear Diary,

We had an **assignment** in science class. ● It was a team **project**. ● We're learning about **electricity** right now. ● And we had to do an **experiment**. ● The experiment needed to show how electricity is **generated**. ● First, our team had a **discussion**. ● We decided to make a lemon **battery**. ● We needed a lemon and some **metal**. ● We decided to use some **coins** for the metal. ● The **principle** was quite simple. ● Lemon **acid** and metal will light a bulb. ● This is because of a **chemical reaction**. ● The experiment was a **success**. ● The **conversion** to electricity was interesting.

However, I didn't like Maria's **attitude** during the experiment. ● In a team project, everyone must **cooperate**. ● Maria **criticized** others but didn't do much work herself. ● I thought she was **selfish**. ● So I **intentionally** asked her to do something. ● I said, "Will you make a **summary** report? ● You will make our project **complete**." ● She liked the **thought** of that. ● I'm glad I got her to do her **share**.

다이어리에게,

우리는 과학 시간에 과제를 받았어. 그것은 팀 과제였어. 지금 전기에 대해 배우고 있거든. 그래서 우리는 실험을 해야 했어. 실험으로 전기가 어떻게 발생되는지를 보여 줘야 했어. 먼저 우리 팀은 의논했어. 우리는 레몬 배터리를 만들기로 했어. 레몬 한 개와 금속물이 필요했지. 우리는 동전을 금속으로 사용하기로 했어. 그 원리는 아주 간단했어. 레몬의 산과 금속물이 전구를 밝히는 거지. 이것은 화학적인 반응 때문이야. 실험은 성공이었어. 전기로의 전환이 재미있었어.

하지만 나는 실험하는 동안 마리아의 태도가 마음에 안 들었어. 팀 과제를 할 때는 모든 사람이 협력해야 돼. 마리아는 다른 사람들을 비난하면서 일은 별로 안 했어. 나는 그 애가 이기적이라고 생각했어. 그래서 나는 의도적으로 그녀에게 무언가를 부탁했어. "네가 요약 보고서를 만들어 줄래? 네가 우리의 과제를 완결시켜 주는 거야."라고 말했어. 그 애는 그 생각이 마음에 들었나 봐. 나는 그 애가 자기 역할을 하게 만들어서 기뻤어.

assignment
[əsáinmənt]

n. 숙제, 과제

We had an assignment in science class.
우리는 과학 시간에 과제를 받았어.

• assign v. 할당하다

project
[prədʒékt]

n. 과제

It was a team project.
그것은 팀 과제였어.

electricity
[ilèktrísəti]

n. 전기

We're learning about electricity right now.
우리는 지금 전기에 대해 배우고 있거든.

• electrical a. 전기의

experiment
[ikspérəmənt]

n. 실험
v. 실험을 하다

And we had to do an experiment.
그래서 우리는 실험을 해야 했어.

• do an experiment 실험을 하다

generate
[dʒénərèit]

v. 발생시키다

The experiment needed to show how electricity is generated.
실험으로 전기가 어떻게 발생되는지를 보여 줘야 했어.

• generation n. 발생

discussion
[diskʌ́ʃən]

n. 토론, 의논

First, our team had a discussion.
먼저 우리 팀은 의논했어.

• discuss v. 토론하다, 상의하다

battery
[bǽtəri]

n. 배터리, 전지

We decided to make a lemon battery.
우리는 레몬 배터리를 만들기로 했어.

metal
[métl]

n. 금속

We needed a lemon and some metal.
우리는 레몬 한 개와 금속물이 필요했지.

coin
[kɔin]

n. 동전

We decided to use some coins for the metal.
우리는 동전을 금속으로 사용하기로 했어.

principle
[prínsəpl]

n. 원리

The principle was quite simple.
그 원리는 아주 간단했어.

acid
[ǽsid]

n. 산

Lemon acid and metal will light a bulb.
레몬의 산과 금속물이 전구를 밝히는 거지.

• acidity n. 산도 • alkali n. 알칼리

chemical
[kémikəl]

a. 화학적인
n. 화학약품

This is because of a chemical reaction.
이것은 화학적인 반응 때문이야.

• chemistry n. 화학

reaction
[riːǽkʃən]

n. 반응

This is because of a chemical reaction.
이것은 화학적인 반응 때문이야.

• react v. 반응하다

success
[səksés]

n. 성공

The experiment was a success.
실험은 성공이었어.

• successful a. 성공적인 • succeed v. 성공하다

conversion
[kənvə́ːrʒən]

n. 전환

The conversion to electricity was interesting.
전기로의 전환이 재미있었어.

• convert v. 전환하다

attitude
[ǽtitjùːd]

n. 태도

However, I didn't like Maria's attitude during the experiment.
하지만 나는 실험하는 동안 마리아의 태도가 마음에 안 들었어.

cooperate
[kouápərèit]
v. 협력하다

In a team project, everyone must cooperate.
팀 과제를 할 때는 모든 사람이 협력해야 돼.

• cooperation n. 협력

criticize
[krítisàiz]
v. 비난하다, 흠잡다

Maria criticized others but didn't do much work herself.
마리아는 다른 사람들을 비난하면서 일은 별로 안 했어.

• criticism n. 비난, 비평   • critical a. 비판적인

selfish
[sélfiʃ]
a. 이기적인

I thought she was selfish.
나는 그 애가 이기적이라고 생각했어.

• selfishness n. 이기적임

intentionally
[inténʃənəli]
ad. 의도적으로

So I intentionally asked her to do something.
그래서 나는 의도적으로 그녀에게 무언가를 부탁했어.

• intention n. 의도, 목적   • intentional a. 의도적인

summary
[sʌ́məri]
n. 요약

I said, "Will you make a summary report? You will make our project complete."
"네가 요약 보고서를 만들어 줄래? 네가 우리의 과제를 완성시켜 주는 거야."라고 말했어.

• summarize v. 요약하다

complete
[kəmplíːt]
a. 완성된, 완결한
v. 완성하다

I said, "Will you make a summary report? You will make our project complete."
"네가 요약 보고서를 만들어 줄래? 네가 우리의 과제를 완결시켜 주는 거야."라고 말했어.

• completion n. 완성, 완결

thought
[θɔːt]
n. 생각

She liked the thought of that.
그 애는 그 생각이 마음에 들었나 봐.

• thoughtful a. 사려 깊은

share
[ʃɛər]
n. 몫, 역할
v. 공유하다

I'm glad I got her to do her share.
나는 그 애가 자기 역할을 하게 만들어서 기뻤어.

Check Again!

A Translate each word into Korean.

1. assignment ....
2. electricity ....
3. experiment ....
4. generate ....
5. principle ....
6. acid ....
7. chemical ....
8. conversion ....
9. cooperate ....
10. intentionally ....

B Translate each word into English.

1. 동전 ....
2. 금속 ....
3. 태도 ....
4. 완성된 ....
5. 몫, 역할 ....

C Fill in the blank with the appropriate word. Refer to the Korean.

1. We had a long d_____ about what to have for dinner.
   우리는 저녁 때 무엇을 먹을 건지에 대한 긴 토론을 벌였어요.

2. Our plan to surprise him was a s_____.
   그를 놀라게 해주기 위한 우리의 계획은 성공했어요.

3. The s_____ girl made everyone wait.
   그 이기적인 여자 아이는 모든 사람을 기다리게 만들었어요.

4. Please give a s_____ of your story.
   당신의 이야기를 요약해서 말해 줘요.

5. I just had a scary t_____.
   나는 방금 무서운 생각을 했어요.

Chapter 3
Learning

Unit 9. Hoony attends a science camp.

observe cells with a microscope

perform an operation

Episode

Last week Hoony attended a science camp and sent an email to Mom.

Dear Mom,

Mom, I like doing experiments at the camp. • Today we **observed** the **structure** of onions and fish. • During the first **session**, we experimented with onions. • First, we **peeled** the onions. • Then we sliced them into tiny **sections**. • We **dipped** the tiny sections into a pink colored **solution**. • Finally, we observed the cells with a **microscope**. • Our **instructor** said, "The cells will be **magnified** by 400 times." • "Who can **describe** how they look?" he asked us. • The cells were **stained** pink. • "They look beautiful," someone **replied**. • Another student answered, "The tiny cells have **complex** structures." • I learned that there are also **passages** for water and nutrients.

During the second session, our instructor brought a fish which was **alive**. • We had to cut open the body and **remove** its **organs**. • It was practically like performing an **operation**. • **Since** I was the captain of our team, I had to **grab** the knife. • Although I had a little **fear**, I had to **overcome** it. • I knew that no one else could **substitute** for me. • Mom, I will tell you more interesting stories tomorrow.

지난주에 후니가 과학 캠프에 참가해서 엄마에게 이메일을 보냈다.

엄마에게,
엄마, 전 캠프에서 실험하는 것이 좋아요. 오늘 우리는 양파와 물고기의 조직을 관찰했어요. 첫 시간에 우리는 양파를 가지고 실험했어요. 우선 우리는 양파의 껍질을 벗겼어요. 그리고 작은 조각으로 잘랐어요. 우리는 작은 조각을 핑크색 용액에 담가 두었어요. 마지막으로, 현미경으로 세포를 관찰했죠. 저희 선생님이 "세포가 400배 정도 확대될 거야."라고 말씀하셨어요. "누가 어떻게 생겼는지 묘사해 볼래?"하고 우리에게 물어보셨죠. 세포가 핑크색으로 물들어 있었어요. "예뻐요"라고 누군가가 대답했어요. 또 다른 학생은 "작은 세포가 복잡한 구조를 가지고 있어요."라고 대답했어요. 물과 영양분이 지나다니는 통로가 있다는 것도 배웠어요.

둘째 시간에는 선생님이 살아 있는 물고기를 가지고 오셨어요. 우리는 물고기 배를 갈라서 내장을 빼내야 했어요. 그건 사실상 수술하는 것과 같았죠. 내가 우리 팀의 조장이라서 칼을 잡아야 했어요. 좀 두려웠지만 그것을 극복해야만 했죠. 전 아무도 저를 대신할 사람이 없다는 것을 알았어요. 엄마, 내일 좀 더 재미있는 이야기를 해 드릴게요.

observe
[əbzə́:rv]

v. 관찰하다, 준수하다

Today we observed the structure of onions and fish.
오늘 우리는 양파와 물고기의 조직을 관찰했어요.

• observation n. 관찰 • observatory n. 관측소

structure
[strʌ́ktʃər]

n. 구조

Today we observed the structure of onions and fish.
오늘 우리는 양파와 물고기의 조직을 관찰했어요.

• structural a. 구조적인

session
[séʃən]

n. 기간, 회기

During the first session, we experimented with onions.
첫 시간에 우리는 양파를 가지고 실험했어요.

peel
[pi:l]

v. 껍질을 벗기다

First, we peeled the onions.
우선 우리는 양파의 껍질을 벗겼어요.

• peeler 껍질 벗기는 사람(기구)

section
[sékʃən]

n. 잘라낸 단면, 조각

Then we sliced them into tiny sections.
그리고 그것들을 작은 조각으로 잘랐어요.

• sectional a. 단면의

dip
[dip]

v. 담그다

We dipped the tiny sections into a pink colored solution.
우리는 작은 조각을 핑크색 용액에 담가 두었어요.

solution
[səljú:ʃən]

n. 용액, 해결(책)

We dipped the tiny sections into a pink colored solution.
우리는 작은 조각을 핑크색 용액에 담가 두었어요.

• solve v. 용해하다, 풀다

microscope
[máikrouskòup]

n. 현미경

Finally, we observed the cells with a microscope.
마지막으로, 현미경으로 세포를 관찰했죠.

instructor
[instrʌ́ktər]

n. 강사

Our instructor said, "The cells will be magnified by 400 times."

우리 선생님이 "세포가 400배 정도 확대될 거야."라고 말씀하셨어요.

• instruct v. 강의하다

magnify
[mǽgnəfài]

v. 확대하다

Our instructor said, "The cells will be magnified by 400 times."

우리 선생님이 "세포가 400배 정도 확대될 거야."라고 말씀하셨어요.

describe
[diskráib]

v. 묘사하다

"Who can describe how they look?" he asked us.

"누가 어떻게 생겼는지 묘사해 볼래?"하고 그가 우리에게 물어보셨죠.

• description n. 묘사 • descriptive a. 묘사적인

stain
[stein]

v. 물들게 하다
n. 얼룩

The cells were stained pink.

세포가 핑크색으로 물들어 있었어요.

• stained a. 물든, 얼룩진

reply
[riplái]

v. 대답하다
n. 대답

"They look beautiful," someone replied.

"예뻐요."라고 누군가가 대답했어요.

complex
[kəmpléks]

a. 복잡한, 복합의

Another student answered, "The tiny cells have complex structures."

또 다른 학생은 "작은 세포가 복잡한 구조를 가지고 있어요."라고 대답했어요.

passage
[pǽsidʒ]

n. 통로, 통과

I learned that there are also passages for water and nutrients.

나는 물과 영양분이 지나다니는 통로가 있다는 것도 배웠어요.

alive
[əláiv]

a. 살아 있는

During the second session, our instructor brought a fish which was alive.

둘째 시간에는 선생님이 살아 있는 물고기를 가지고 오셨어요.

remove
[rimúːv]

v. 제거하다

We had to cut open the body and remove its organs.
우리는 물고기 배를 갈라서 내장을 빼내야 했어요.

• removal   n. 제거

organ
[ɔ́ːrgən]

n. 장기, 기관

We had to cut open the body and remove its organs.
우리는 물고기 배를 갈라서 내장을 빼내야 했어요.

operation
[àpəréiʃən]

n. 수술, 작동

It was practically like performing an operation.
그건 사실상 수술하는 것과 같았죠.

• operate   v. 수술하다, 작동하다
• perform an operation   수술하다

since
[sins]

conj. ~이니까

Since I was the captain of our team, I had to grab the knife.
내가 우리 팀의 조장이라서 칼을 잡아야 했어요.

grab
[græb]

v. ~을 움켜잡다
n. 움켜잡기

Since I was the captain of our team, I had to grab the knife.
내가 우리 팀의 조장이라서 칼을 잡아야 했어요.

fear
[fiər]

n. 공포

Although I had a little fear, I had to overcome it.
좀 두려웠지만 그것을 극복해야만 했죠.

• fearful   a. 공포스러운

overcome
[òuvərkÁm]

v. 극복하다

Although I had a little fear, I had to overcome it.
좀 두려웠지만 그것을 극복해야만 했죠.

• overcome - overcame - overcome

substitute
[sÁbstitjùːt]

v. 대신하다
n. 대리인, 대용품

I knew that no one else could substitute for me.
난 아무도 나를 대신할 사람이 없다는 것을 알았죠.

• substitution   n. 대리, 대용
• substitute for   ~을 대신하다

Check Again!

A Translate each word into Korean.

1. overcome ....
2. substitute ....
3. alive ....
4. remove ....
5. reply ....
6. describe ....
7. organ ....
8. fear ....
9. instructor ....
10. session ....

B Translate each word into English.

1. 현미경 ....
2. 용액 ....
3. 복잡한 ....
4. 확대하다 ....
5. 물들게 하다 ....

C Fill in the blank with the appropriate word. Refer to the Korean.

1. S_____ the food at the restaurant was terrible, we asked for an apology.

   그 식당의 음식이 형편없어서, 우리는 사과를 요구했다.

2. The doctor performed an o_____ on the patient's leg.

   그 의사는 환자의 다리를 수술했다.

3. Astronauts can o_____ Venus with the Hubble space telescope.

   우주비행사들은 허블 우주 망원경으로 금성을 관찰할 수 있다.

4. Use the p_____ over there to reach the aquarium.

   수족관에 가려면 저기에 있는 통로를 이용하세요.

5. The s_____ of this tall building is unique.

   이 고층 건물의 구조는 독특하다.

✚ 명사 만들기 3

그 밖에 –th, –ence, –ance 등으로 끝나는 어휘 가운데는 명사가 많다.

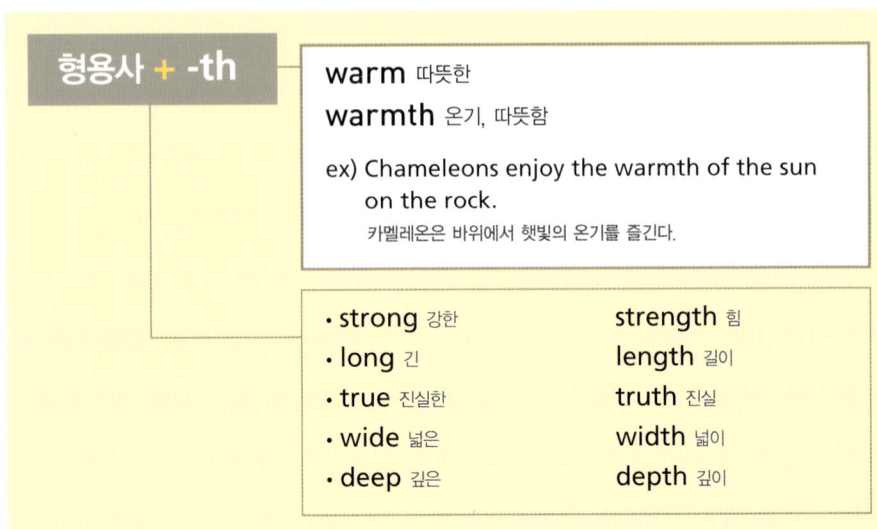

형용사 + -th

warm 따뜻한
warmth 온기, 따뜻함

ex) Chameleons enjoy the warmth of the sun on the rock.
카멜레온은 바위에서 햇빛의 온기를 즐긴다.

- **strong** 강한   **strength** 힘
- **long** 긴   **length** 길이
- **true** 진실한   **truth** 진실
- **wide** 넓은   **width** 넓이
- **deep** 깊은   **depth** 깊이

동사 + -ence -ance

enter 들어가다
entrance 입장

ex) Daniel paid the entrance fee to the park.
다니엘이 공원 입장료를 냈다.

- **exist** 존재하다   **existence** 존재
- **occur** 발생하다   **occurrence** 발생
- **appear** 나타나다. 등장하다   **appearance** 출현, 외관
- **hinder** 막다   **hindrance** 장애
- **maintain** 유지하다   **maintenance** 유지

Books & Literature

- fiction   소설
- non-fiction   논픽션(실화)
- romantic fiction   연애 소설
- historical fiction   역사 소설
- science fiction   공상과학 소설
- poetry   시
- biography   전기문

Culture Plus

Math 수학

+ algebra   대수학
+ add   더하다
+ subtract   빼다
+ multiply   곱하다
+ divide   나누나
+ natural number   자연수
+ fraction   분수

VOCA EDGE

EDGE

BLUE

Chapter 4. Trips and Entertainment

Chapter 4
Trips and Entertainment

Unit 10. There will be a talent show.

do magic tricks

be **enthusiastic**

Episode

Dear Diary,

Our school **festival** started today. ● We are going to have a **talent** show tomorrow. ● It is an **annual** event. ● The **admission** fee will be 3,000 won. ● All of the **profit** is going to be used to help the poor. ● The student hall can hold about 300 **audience** members.

I heard Junnie will do some **magic** tricks. ● This is because he belongs to the magic **community**. ● I **admit** his tricks are **excellent**. ● His card tricks are **particularly** great. ● They are not **amateur**. ● He can even **transform** a cane into a flower. ● The audience will be **enthusiastic**. ● Many girls hope he will **approach** them to give them the flower.

Sara is waiting for her prince **charming**, Juno. ● He belongs to the **literature** community. ● He plans to read a **poem**. ● Last year, we had an **opportunity** to listen to one of his poems. ● It was about crystal and **permanent** love. ● It **inspired** all the girls. ● I asked Sara, "Which **participant** will win first prize?" She **shrugged** and said, "**Probably** Juno." ● I knew that Sara **revealed** her wish.

다이어리에게,

우리 학교 축제가 오늘 시작됐어. 내일은 장기자랑 대회가 있을 거야. 장기자랑 대회는 해마다 열리는 행사야. 입장료는 3천원이야. 모든 수익은 가난한 사람들을 돕는 데 쓰일 거야. 학생회관에는 약 300명이 들어갈 수 있어

주니는 마술을 할 거라고 하던데. 그가 마술 동호회에 속해 있기 때문이야. 그의 묘기들이 우수한 것은 인정해. 그의 카드 묘기는 특히 멋져. 그의 묘기들은 아마추어의 수준이 아니야. 그는 심지어 지팡이를 꽃으로 변신시킬 수 있어. 관중들은 열광할 거야. 많은 여자 애들은 그 아이가 다가와서 꽃을 주기를 바라지.

사라는 그 아이의 매력적인 왕자님인 주노를 기다리고 있어. 그 아이는 문학동우회의 회원이지. 그는 시를 낭송할 계획이야. 작년에 우리는 그의 시 하나를 들어 볼 기회가 있었어. 시는 크리스털과 영원한 사랑에 관한 것이었어. 그 시는 모든 여자 아이들에게 영감을 줬어. 내가 사라에게 "어느 참가자가 대상을 차지할까?"라고 물었어. 그 애는 어깨를 으쓱하며, "아마, 주노가 타겠지."라고 하던데. 난 사라가 자기의 바람을 드러냈다는 것을 알았어.

festival
[féstəvəl]
n. 축제

Our school festival started today.
우리 학교 축제가 오늘 시작됐어.
• festive a. 축제적인

talent
[tǽlənt]
n. 재능

We are going to have a talent show tomorrow.
내일은 장기자랑 대회가 있을 거야.
• talented a. 재능이 있는

annual
[ǽnjuəl]
a. 해마다의

It is an annual event.
장기자랑 대회는 해마다 열리는 행사야.
• annually ad. 해마다

admission
[ædmíʃən]
n. 입장, 들어갈 권리

The admission fee will be 3,000 won.
입장료는 3천원이야.

profit
[práfit]
n. 수익, 이익

All of the profit is going to be used to help the poor.
모든 수익은 가난한 사람들을 돕는 데 쓰일 거야.
• profitable a. 이익이 되는

audience
[ɔ́ːdiəns]
n. 관객, 청중

The student hall can hold about 300 audience members.
학생회관에는 약 300명이 들어갈 수 있어.

magic
[mǽdʒik]
n. 마술

I heard Junnie will do some magic tricks.
주니는 마술을 할 거라고 하던대.
• magician n. 마술사 • do a magic trick 마술을 하다

community
[kəmjúːnəti]
n. 공동체

This is because he belongs to the magic community.
그가 마술 동호회에 속해 있기 때문이야.

admit
[ædmít]
v. 인정하다

I admit his tricks are excellent.
그의 묘기들이 우수한 것은 인정해.

• admission n. 인정, 자백

excellent
[éksələnt]
a. 우수한

I admit his tricks are excellent.
그의 묘기들이 우수한 것은 인정해.

• excellence n. 우수함 • excel v. 능가하다

particularly
[pərtíkjələrli]
ad. 특히

His card tricks are particularly great.
그의 카드 묘기는 특히 멋져.

• particular a. 특별한

amateur
[ǽmətʃùər]
a. 아마추어의
n. 아마추어

They are not amateur.
그의 묘기들은 아마추어의 수준이 아니야.

transform
[trænsfɔ́ːrm]
v. 변형시키다

He can even transform a cane into a flower.
그는 심지어 지팡이를 꽃으로 변신시킬 수 있어.

• transformation n. 변형 • transformer n. 변형시키는 것(사람)
• transform A into B A를 B로 변형시키다

enthusiastic
[enθúːziǽstik]
a. 열광적인

The audience will be enthusiastic.
관중들은 열광할 거야.

• enthusiasm n. 열광

approach
[əpróutʃ]
v. 다가가다, 접근하다
n. 접근

Many girls hope he will approach them to give them the flower.
많은 여자 애들은 그 아이가 다가와서 꽃을 주기를 바라지.

charming
[tʃáːrmiŋ]
a. 매력적인

Sara is waiting for her prince charming, Juno.
사라는 그 아이의 매력적인 왕자님인 주노를 기다리고 있어.

• charm n. 매력

literature
[lítərətʃər]
n. 문학

He belongs to the literature community.
그 아이는 문학동우회의 회원이지.

• literary a. 문학의

poem
[póuim]
n. 시

He plans to read a poem.
그는 시를 낭송할 계획이야.

• poet n. 시인 • poetry n. 시류

opportunity
[àpərtʃúːnəti]
n. 기회

Last year, we had an opportunity to listen to one of his poems.
작년에 우리는 그의 시 하나를 들어 볼 기회가 있었어.

permanent
[pə́ːrmənənt]
a. 영원한

It was about crystal and permanent love.
시는 크리스털과 영원한 사랑에 관한 것이었어.

• permanence n. 영원함 • permanently ad. 영원히

inspire
[inspáiər]
v. 영감을 주다

It inspired all the girls.
그 시는 모든 여자 아이들에게 영감을 줬어.

• inspiration n. 영감

participant
[pɑːrtísəpənt]
n. 참가자

I asked Sara, "Which participant will win first prize?"
내가 사라에게 "어느 참가자가 대상을 차지할까?"라고 물었어.

• participate v. 참가하다 • participation n. 참가

shrug
[ʃrʌg]
v. 어깨를 으쓱하다

She shrugged and said, "Probably Juno."
그 애는 어깨를 으쓱하며, "아마, 주노가 타겠지."라고 하던대.

probably
[prɑ́bəbli]
ad. 아마도

She shrugged and said, "Probably Juno."
그 애는 어깨를 으쓱하며, "아마, 주노가 타겠지."라고 하던대.

• probable a. 있음직한 • probability n. 있음직함

reveal
[rivíːl]
v. 드러내다

I knew that Sara revealed her wish.
난 사라가 자기의 바람을 드러냈다는 것을 알았어.

Check Again!

A Translate each word into Korean.

1. admission ....
2. amateur ....
3. community ....
4. audience ....
5. participant ....
6. literature ....
7. reveal ....
8. enthusiastic ....
9. opportunity ....
10. annual ....

B Translate each word into English.

1. 특히 ....
2. 수익 ....
3. 재능 ....
4. 시 ....
5. 마술 ....

C Fill in the blank with the appropriate word. Refer to the Korean.

1. I a   that the lion team will win first prize.

   사자팀이 일등을 할 것이라는 것을 인정해.

2. My brother likes the robot that t   into a motorcycle.

   나의 남동생은 오토바이로 변신하는 로봇을 좋아한다.

3. Our school f   is famous for having the best concerts.

   우리 학교 축제는 가장 훌륭한 콘서트를 여는 것으로 유명하다.

4. Every p   in the competition is only allowed to use one hand.

   대회의 모든 참가자들은 한 손만 사용할 수 있다.

5. Everyone likes to have conversations with Ryan because he is always

   e   .

   라이언은 항상 열광적이기 때문에 모두가 그와 대화하는 것을 좋아한다.

Chapter 4
Trips and Entertainment

Unit 11. We went on a safari tour.

join a package tour group

be quite **tame**

Episode

Dear Sara,

We **departed** early in the morning. ● Our **destination** was a deep forest. ● We joined a **package** tour group. ● It was my first time to see that kind of **wildlife**. ● We used a **local** bus. Last night, Mom was happy because the bus **fare** was **quite** low. ● She was right, but the **aisles** were horrible. ● They were so **narrow**. ● We could **barely** move. ● Also, the air conditioner did not **function** properly. ● Later, all the **tourists** got off the bus and got in a van. ● We arrived at an open **field** in a **rural** area. ● It was completely different from the **urban** areas I'm used to. ● It was a **tropical** place. ● I saw a **herd** of water buffalo and some lions. ● Five lions were **flocking** to a water puddle where there was a pregnant lioness. ● Their bodies were so long that the **length** of the lions surprised me. ● At one point I thought a lion was trying to **attack** me. ● I was scared and dropped some **raw** meat I had with me. ● However, they weren't very **aggressive**. ● They were quite **tame**. ● What we actually saw were just **enormous** cats.

사라에게.

우리는 이른 아침에 출발했단다. 우리의 목적지는 깊은 숲이었어. 우리는 단체관광단에 합류했어. 그런 야생 생물을 보는 것은 처음이었어. 우리는 시내 버스를 이용했어. 어젯밤 엄마는 버스 요금이 매우 저렴하다고 좋아하셨지. 엄마 말이 맞았지만, 통로가 끔찍했어. 너무 좁았거든. 거의 움직일 수가 없었어. 그리고 에어컨이 제대로 작동하지 않았어. 아주 불편했어. 나중에 모든 관광객들은 버스에서 내려서 봉고차를 탔어. 우리는 시골에 있는 넓은 들판에 도착했어. 그곳은 내가 익숙한 도시 지역과 완전히 달랐어. 열대 지역이었어. 나는 물소들과 몇몇 사자 무리를 봤어. 다섯 마리의 사자가 임신한 암컷 사자가 있는 물웅덩이로 무리지어 가고 있었어. 그 사자들의 몸이 너무 길어서 난 그 길이에 놀랐어. 어느 순간 나는 사자가 나를 공격하려는 줄 알았어. 나는 놀래서 가지고 있던 생고기를 떨어뜨렸어. 하지만 그것들은 별로 공격적이지 않았어. 상당히 길들여져 있었지. 우리가 실제로 만난 것은 아주 거대한 고양이라고 할 수 있었어.

depart
[dipá:rt]

v. 출발하다

We departed early in the morning.
우리는 이른 아침에 출발했단다.

• departure n. 출발

destination
[dèstənéiʃən]

n. 목적지

Our destination was a deep forest.
우리의 목적지는 깊은 숲이었어.

• destine v. 예정해 두다

package
[pǽkidʒ]

n. 패키지, 묶음

We joined a package tour group.
우리는 단체 관광단에 합류했어.

wildlife
[wáildlàif]

n. 야생 생물

It was my first time to see that kind of wildlife.
그런 야생 생물을 보는 것은 처음이었어.

local
[lóukəl]

a. 시내의, 지방의

We used a local bus.
우리는 시내 버스를 이용했어.

fare
[fɛər]

n. 요금

Last night, Mom was happy because the bus fare was quite low.
어젯밤 엄마는 버스 요금이 매우 저렴하다고 좋아하셨지.

quite
[kwait]

ad. 매우, 꽤

Last night, Mom was happy because the bus fare was quite low.
어젯밤 엄마는 버스 요금이 매우 저렴하다고 좋아하셨지.

aisle
[ail]

n. 통로

She was right, but the aisles were horrible.
엄마 말이 맞았지만, 통로가 끔찍했어.

narrow
[nǽrou]

a. 좁은
v. 좁히다

They were so narrow.
통로가 너무 좁았어.

barely
[bɛ́ərli]

ad. 거의 ~않다, 간신히

We could barely move.
우리는 거의 움직일 수가 없었어.

function
[fʌ́ŋkʃən]

v. 기능을 하다
n. 기능

Also, the air conditioner did not function properly.
그리고 에어컨이 제대로 작동하지 안했어.

•functional a. 기능의

tourist
[túərist]

n. 관광객

Later, all the tourists got off the bus and got in a van.
나중에 모든 관광객들은 버스에서 내려서 봉고차를 탔어.

•tourism n. 관광사업 •tour n. 관광

field
[fi:ld]

n. 들판

We arrived at an open field in a rural area.
우리는 시골에 있는 넓은 들판에 도착했어.

rural
[rúərəl]

a. 시골의

We arrived at an open field in a rural area.
우리는 시골에 있는 넓은 들판에 도착했어.

urban
[ə́ːrbən]

a. 도시의

It was completely different from the urban areas I'm used to.
그곳은 내가 익숙한 도시 지역과 완전히 달랐어.

tropical
[trápikəl]

a. 열대의

It was a tropical place.
그곳은 열대 지역이었어.

herd
[hə:rd]

n. 무리, 떼

I saw a herd of water buffalo and some lions.
나는 물소들과 몇몇 사자 무리를 봤어.

• a herd of 한 무리의 ~

flock
[flɔk]

v. 무리지어 가다
n. 무리

Five lions were flocking to a water puddle where there was a pregnant lioness.
다섯 마리의 사자가 임신한 암컷 사자가 있는 물웅덩이로 무리지어 가고 있었어.

length
[leŋkθ]

n. 길이

Their bodies were so long that the length of the lions surprised me.
그 사자들의 몸이 너무 길어 나는 그 길이에 놀았어.

• lengthen v. 길게 하다 • lengthy a. 긴

attack
[ətǽk]

v. 공격하다
n. 공격

At one point I thought a lion was trying to attack me.
어느 순간 나는 사자가 나를 공격하려는 줄 알았어.

raw
[rɔː]

a. 날 것의, 가공하지 않은

I was scared and dropped some raw meat I had with me.
나는 놀래서 가지고 있던 생고기를 떨어뜨렸어.

aggressive
[əgrésiv]

a. 공격적인

However, they weren't very aggressive.
하지만 그것들은 별로 공격적이지 않았어.

• aggress v. 공격하다 • aggression n. 공격

tame
[teim]

a. 길들여진
v. 길들이다

They were quite tame.
그것들은 상당히 길들여져 있었지.

• untamed 길들여지지 않은

enormous
[inɔ́ːrməs]

a. 거대한

What we actually saw were just enormous cats.
우리가 실제로 만난 것은 아주 거대한 고양이라고 할 수 있었어.

• enormously 막대하게, 엄청나게

Check Again!

A Translate each word into Korean.

1. fare ....
2. enormous ....
3. destination ....
4. narrow ....
5. aggressive ....
6. field ....
7. function ....
8. tropical ....
9. raw ....
10. herd ....

B Translate each word into English.

1. 통로 ....
2. 시골의 ....
3. 관광객 ....
4. 무리지어 가다 ....
5. 길들여진 ....

C Fill in the blank with the appropriate word. Refer to the Korean.

1. The time we have to d   is coming closer.

   우리가 출발해야 하는 시간이 점점 다가오고 있다.

2. He was so angry that he could b   smile.

   그는 너무 화가 나서 미소를 지을 수가 없었다.

3. You never know when an animal may a   you.

   동물이 너를 언제 공격할지 모른다.

4. The f   to the Bahamas was too expensive.

   바하마로 가는 요금은 너무 비쌌다.

5. The r   areas are losing their young people because they all move to urban areas.

   시골 지역은 젊은이들이 모두 도시로 이주하기 때문에 젊은이들이 줄고 있다.

Chapter 4
Trips and Entertainment

Unit 12. I pressed the send button.

be ignorant of what's happening

let the water overflow the sink

save a life with 1,000 won

Episode

Dear Diary,

I didn't realize how happy I was. • I didn't realize how ignorant I was of what was happening in the world. • From now on, I'll never say whole grain bread is not delicious. • I was watching a documentary program. • The program reflected our reality. • For example, it showed that there was nothing to eat in some regions. • Some kids were even looking through garbage for food. • At first I doubted my eyes. • But they really were looking in the trash for something to satisfy their hunger. • I felt sympathy for them. • Many of those kids die due to lack of medicine. • They also don't have any drinkable water. • It's because water in their land is polluted. • How miserable! • Isn't it incredible? • I felt so ashamed. • I often just let leftover food go to the landfill. • I even let the water overflow the sink. • I said to myself, "Hey, don't postpone helping. • You can become a real supporter right now." • I pressed a button on their web page. • The program gave me a message saying, "You can save a life with just 1,000 won!"

다이어리에게,

나는 내가 얼마나 행복한지 몰랐어. 내가 세상에 무슨 일이 일어나고 있는가에 대해 얼마나 무지했는가를 깨달았어. 앞으로는 통밀 빵이 맛이 없다고 안 할거야. 나는 다큐멘터리 프로그램을 보고 있었어. 그 프로그램은 우리의 현실을 반영해 주고 있었어. 예를 들면, 어떤 지역에서는 먹을 것이 없다는 것을 보여 주었어. 몇몇 아이들은 음식을 찾기 위해 쓰레기도 뒤지고 있었어. 처음에는 내 눈을 의심했어. 하지만 정말 그들은 허기를 채워 줄 무엇인가를 쓰레기에서 찾고 있었던 거야. 난 그들에게 연민을 느꼈지. 그 아이들 중 다수가 의약품 부족으로 죽는대. 그들은 마실 수 있는 물도 없어. 그들이 사는 땅의 물이 오염되었기 때문이지. 정말 비참하지. 정말 믿을 수 없지 않아? 난 너무 부끄러웠어. 종종 먹다 남은 음식이 쓰레기 매립지까지 가게 하거든. 심지어 자주 싱크대에 물이 넘쳐 흐르게도 하거든. 난 속으로, "돕는 것을 미루지 마. 지금 당장 진짜 후원자가 될 수 있어."라고 말을 했어. 난 웹사이트에 있는 버튼을 눌렀어. 그 프로그램은 "당신은 단돈 천 원으로 한 생명을 구할 수 있어요!"라는 메시지를 나에게 주었어.

realize
[ríːəlàiz]
v. 알아차리다, 깨닫다

I didn't realize how happy I was.
나는 내가 얼마나 행복한지 몰랐어.

• realization n. 깨달음, 이해

ignorant
[íɡnərənt]
a. 모르는, 무지한

I didn't realize how ignorant I was of what was happening in the world.
나는 내가 세상에 무슨 일이 일어나고 있는가에 대해 얼마나 무지했는가를 깨달았어.

• ignore v. 무시하다   • ignorance n. 무지

delicious
[dilíʃəs]
a. 맛있는

From now on, I'll never say whole grain bread is not delicious.
앞으로는 나는 통밀 빵이 맛이 없다고 안 할거야.

documentary
[dàkjuméntəri]
n. 다큐멘터리

I was watching a documentary program.
나는 다큐멘터리 프로그램을 보고 있었어.

reflect
[riflékt]
v. 반영하다

The program reflected our reality.
그 프로그램은 우리의 현실을 반영해 주고 있었어.

• reflection n. 반영

reality
[riǽləti]
n. 현실

The program reflected our reality.
그 프로그램은 우리의 현실을 반영해주고 있었어.

• realistic a. 현실적인

region
[ríːdʒən]
n. 지역

For example, it showed that there was nothing to eat in some regions.
예를 들면, 어떤 지역에서는 먹을 것이 없다는 것을 보여 주었어.

• regional a. 지역의

garbage
[ɡáːrbidʒ]
n. 쓰레기

Some kids were even looking through garbage for food.
몇몇 아이들은 음식을 찾기 위해 쓰레기를 뒤지고 있었어.

doubt
[daut]
v. 의심하다
n. 의심

At first I doubted my eyes.
처음에는 나는 내 눈을 의심했어.

• doubtful a. 의심스러운

hunger
[hʌ́ŋgər]
n. 배고픔, 기아

But they really were looking in the trash for something to satisfy their hunger.
하지만 정말 그들은 허기를 채워 줄 무엇인가를 쓰레기에서 찾고 있었던 거야.

• hungry a. 배고픈

sympathy
[símpəθi]
n. 동정, 연민

I felt sympathy for them.
난 그들에게 연민을 느꼈지.

• sympathize v. 동정하다 • sympathetic a. 동정심 있는

lack
[læk]
n. 부족
v. 부족하다

Many of those kids die due to lack of medicine.
그 아이들 중 다수가 의약품 부족으로 죽는대.

medicine
[médəsən]
n. 의약품

Many of those kids die due to lack of medicine.
그 아이들 중 다수가 의약품 부족으로 죽는대.

• medical a. 의학의, 의학적인

drinkable
[dríŋkəbl]
a. 마실 수 있는

They also don't have any drinkable water.
그들은 마실 수 있는 물도 없어.

• drink v. 마시다

pollute
[pəlúːt]
v. 오염시키다

It's because water in their land is polluted.
그들이 사는 땅의 물이 오염되었기 때문이지.

• pollution n. 오염 • polluted a. 오염된

miserable
[mízərəbl]
a. 비참한

How miserable!
정말 비참하지!

• misery n. 비참함

incredible
[inkrédəbl]

a. 놀라운, 믿기지 않는

Isn't it incredible?
놀랍지 않아?

• incredibility n. 믿어지지 않음   • credible a. 신뢰할 수 있는

ashamed
[əʃéimd]

a. 부끄러운

I felt so ashamed.
난 너무 부끄러웠어.

• shame n. 부끄러움, 치욕

landfill
[lǽndfil]

n. 쓰레기 매립지

I often just let leftover food go to the landfill.
나는 종종 먹다 남은 음식이 쓰레기 매립지까지 가게 하거든.

overflow
[òuvərflóu]

v. 넘쳐 흐르다

I even let the water overflow the sink.
나는 심지어 자주 싱크대에 물이 넘쳐 흐르게 하거든.

postpone
[poustpóun]

v. 미루다, 연기하다

I said to myself, "Hey, don't postpone helping.
You can become a real supporter right now."
난 속으로, "돕는 것을 미루지 마. 지금 당장 진짜 후원자가 될 수 있어."라고
말을 했지.

• postponement n. 연기

supporter
[səpɔ́:rtər]

n. 후원자

I said to myself, "Hey, don't postpone helping.
You can become a real supporter right now."
난 속으로, "돕는 것을 미루지 마. 지금 당장 진짜 후원자가 될 수 있어."라고
말을 했지.

• support v. 후원하다, 응원하다

press
[pres]

v. 누르다

I pressed a button on their web page.
난 웹사이트에 있는 버튼을 눌렀어.

save
[seiv]

v. 구하다, 절약하다

The program gave me a message saying, "You can
save a life with just 1,000 won!"
그 프로그램은 "당신은 단돈 천 원으로 한 생명을 구할 수 있어요!"라는 메시지를
나에게 주었어.

• safety n. 안전

Check Again!

A Translate each word into Korean.

1. realize ....
2. sympathy ....
3. garbage ....
4. documentary ....
5. supporter ....
6. region ....
7. miserable ....
8. ashamed ....
9. doubt ....
10. landfill ....

B Translate each word into English.

1. 구하다 ....
2. 의약품 ....
3. 부족 ....
4. 미루다 ....
5. 믿기지 않는 ....

C Fill in the blank with the appropriate word. Refer to the Korean.

1. Doctors warn that exposure to p   air is very dangerous.

   의사들은 오염된 공기에 노출되는 것이 매우 위험하다고 경고했다.

2. I feel s   for the people who are fired.

   나는 해고를 당하는 사람들에게 동정을 느낀다.

3. Could you p   down on these papers? They keep on flying away.

   이 서류들을 눌러 주시겠어요? 자꾸 날아가네요.

4. Having many s   helps in winning a game.

   많은 후원자들을 가지는 것은 경기를 이기는 데 도움이 된다.

5. The hospital says that there is a l   of type O blood.

   병원은 혈액형 O형이 부족하다고 말한다.

✚ 동사 만들기 1

명사나 형용사 뒤에 -ize 혹은 -ify를 붙여서 동사로 쓰이는 경우가 있다.
의미는 '~화하다 / ~하게 하다 / ~시키다' 등으로 풀이된다.

명사 + -ize
형용사

category 카테고리, 범주
categorize 범주에 넣다

ex) This music is categorized as classical music.
이 음악은 고전음악 범주에 든다.

- **general** 일반적인   **generalize** 일반화하다
- **summary** 요약, 개요   **summarize** 요점 정리하다
- **visual** 시각적인   **visualize** 시각화하다
- **critical** 비판적인   **criticize** 비평하다
- **drama** 희곡, 각본   **dramatize** 극화하다

명사 + -ify
형용사

justice 정의
justify 정당화시키다

ex) How can you justify your behavior?
당신은 어떻게 자신의 행동을 정당화시킬 수 있나요?

- **class** 분류, 등급   **classify** 등급으로 나누다
- **beauty** 아름다움   **beautify** 미화하다
- **notice** 통지   **notify** 통지하다
- **intense** 강한   **intensify** 강화시키다
- **diverse** 다양한   **diversify** 다양화하다

At an Airport

- book a flight 비행기 좌석을 예약하다
- reschedule a flight 비행기 시간을 재조정하다
- check in baggage 짐을 부치다
- go through security 검색대를 통과하다
- board a plane 비행기에 탑승하다
- fasten a seat belt 안전띠를 매다

Culture Plus

At a Contest 경시대회

+contestant 참가자
+competitor 경쟁자
+judge 심사위원, 심판
+lucky draw 행운권 추첨
+win a contest 대회에서 우승하다
+first prize 일등상
+runner up prize 이등상

VOCA EDGE

BLUE

love you, Kite We moved today. I want to join the drama club. We have a team project

he send button. Kite will attend the wonder dog championship. Relationships count most

! We made homemade pancakes. Hoony is taking taekwondo lessons. My dad's car is in

t an interesting festival! Sara's brother is running for president. Our school is doing an anti-

as skin trouble. Mom has become a regular customer of ABC Mart. Mom is impressed by

hy do floods and droughts alternate? Astronauts need to know special drills. Two whale

nt facilities. We love you, Kite We moved today. I want to join the drama club. We have c

safari tour. I pressed the send button. Kite will attend the wonder dog championship

c. Mud cookies are terrible! We made homemade pancakes. Hoony is taking taekwondc

d music for Brownie. What an interesting festival! Sara's brother is running for president. Ou

n art investment. Seri has skin trouble. Mom has become a regular customer of ABC Mart

y without sunlight. Why do floods and droughts alternate? Astronauts need to know specic

d boys use different facilities. We love you, Kite We moved today. I want to join the dramc

We went on a safari tour. I pressed the send button. Kite will attend the wonder dog

to a growth clinic. Mud cookies are terrible! We made homemade pancakes. Hoony i

Chapter 5. Hobbies

emorial. Sara composed music for Brownie. What an interesting festival! Sara's brothe

is horrible. Dad is interested in art investment. Seri has skin trouble. Mom has become

good and bad. Plants can grow without sunlight. Why do floods and droughts alterna

is puberty? Visit my blog Girls and boys use different facilities. We love you, Kite We movec

. There will be a talent show. We went on a safari tour. I pressed the send button. Kite wi

in the same boat. I go to a growth clinic. Mud cookies are terrible! We made homemade

trip to the War Memorial. Sara composed music for Brownie. What an interesting festival

Chapter 5
Hobbies

Unit 13. Kite will attend the wonder dog championship.

use **kitchen utensils**

tempt someone **with** sausages

Episode

Dear Diary,

Hoony and Seri are trying to find out something for my parents' 17th wedding anniversary. • "Look, there is an exciting **competition** in the paper. • And the first prize is **free** tickets to Hawaii," I said to Hoony and Seri. • It was a competition for talented pets. • Last year's **champion** was a wonder dog. • It could jump and **snap** two discs out of the air nearly at the same time. • Seri **registered** our dog. • Kite is **athletic**. • He can even stand on his **paws**. • Hoony and Seri are **training** him to move to the rhythm of music. • Right now, they are using kitchen **utensils** to make a rhythm. • When Hoony and Seri start making music, Kite is supposed to **stamp** his paw on the ground. • They started with **basic** skills. • First they **attempted** to get him to stand and walk around. • They made a video clip and **analyzed** it. • They kept **practicing**, but they kept on **failing**. • They were **exhausted**, and they were about to **surrender**. • Then, Seri asked me, "What about asking for help from an **expert**? • I mean your friend, Sara." • I said, "Hey, Sara said you can **tempt** him with sausages." • I **attached** some sausages to a stick and held it up in the air. • Finally, Kite was **encouraged** by the food and started stamping his paw.

다이어리에게,
후니와 세리는 부모님의 결혼 17주년 기념일을 위해 드릴 뭔가를 찾으려고 하고 있어. "봐, 재미있는 대회가 신문에 나왔어. 그리고 1등 상품은 하와이 무료 항공권이야."라고 내가 후니와 세리에게 말했어. 그것은 재능 있는 애완 동물을 선발하는 대회였어. 작년 챔피언은 신기한 개였어. 그 개는 원반 2개를 거의 동시에 공중에서 낚아챌 수 있었어. 세리는 우리 개를 등록시켰어. 카이트는 운동 감각이 있어. 앞발을 들고 서기도 해. 후니와 세리는 카이트가 음악의 리듬에 맞춰 움직이도록 훈련을 시키고 있어. 바로 지금 그들은 리듬을 내기 위해 주방기구를 이용하고 있어. 일단 후니와 세리가 음악 소리를 내기 시작하면 카이트는 발을 땅에 굴려야 하지. 두 사람은 기본적인 기술부터 시작했어. 먼저, 그들은 카이트가 서서 걸어다니게 하는 시도를 했어. 그들은 동영상을 만들어 분석했어. 그들은 계속 연습을 했지만 계속 실패했지. 그들이 지쳐서 막 포기하려던 찰나였어. 그때 세리가 나에게 물었어. "전문가에게 도움을 구하면 어떨까? 언니 친구 사라 말이야." "이봐, 사라가 카이트를 소시지로 유혹하래."라고 내가 말했어. 나는 소시지를 막대에 달아서 그것을 공중에 들어올렸어. 마침내 카이트는 먹을 것에 자극을 받아 앞발을 구르기 시작했어.

competition

[kὰmpətíʃən]

n. 대회, 경쟁

"Look, there is an exciting competition in the paper. And the first prize is free tickets to Hawaii," I said to Hoony and Seri.

"봐, 재미있는 대회가 신문에 나왔어. 그리고 1등 상품은 하와이 무료 항공권이야."라고 내가 후니와 세리에게 말했어.

• compete v. 경쟁하다 • competitive a. 경쟁력 있는

free

[fri:]

a. 무료의

"Look, there is an exciting competition in the paper. And the first prize is free tickets to Hawaii," I said to Hoony and Seri.

"봐, 재미있는 대회가 신문에 나왔어. 그리고 1등 상품은 하와이 무료 항공권이야."라고 내가 후니와 세리에게 말했어.

champion

[tʃǽmpiən]

n. 챔피언

Last year's champion was a wonder dog.

작년 챔피언은 신기한 개였어.

snap

[snǽp]

v. 잡아채다, 낚아채다

It could jump and snap two discs out of the air nearly at the same time.

그것은 원반 2개를 거의 동시에 공중에서 낚아챌 수 있었어.

register

[rédʒistər]

v. 등록하다

Seri registered our dog.

세리는 우리 개를 등록시켰어.

• registration n. 등록

athletic

[æθlétik]

a. 운동의, 운동을 잘하는

Kite is athletic.

카이트는 운동 감각이 있어.

• athlete n. 운동 선수

paw
[pɔː]
n. (동물의) 발

He can even stand on his paws.
그는 앞발을 들고 서기도 해.

train
[trein]
v. 훈련하다
n. 열차, 기차

Hoony and Seri are training him to move to the rhythm of music.
후니와 세리는 카이트가 음악의 리듬에 맞춰 움직이도록 훈련을 시키고 있어.

utensil
[juːténsəl]
n. 기구, 용구,
가정용품

Right now, they are using kitchen utensils to make a rhythm.
바로 지금 그들은 리듬을 내기 위해 주방기구를 사용하고 있지.

• kitchen utensil 주방 기구

stamp
[stæmp]
v. 발을 구르다

When Hoony and Seri start making music, Kite is supposed to stamp his paw on the ground.
일단 후니와 세리가 음악 소리를 내기 시작하면 카이트는 발을 땅에 굴러야 하지.

basic
[béisik]
a. 기초의

They started with basic skills.
그들은 기본적인 기술부터 시작했어.

• basically ad. 근본적으로

attempt
[ətémpt]
v. 시도하다
n. 시도

First they attempted to get him to stand and walk around.
그들은 카이트가 서서 걸어다니게 하는 시도를 했어.

• make an attempt 시도하다

analyze
[ǽnəlàiz]
v. 분석하다

They made a video clip and analyzed it.
그들은 동영상을 만들어 분석했어.

• analysis n. 분석   • analyst n. 분석가

practice
[prǽktis]

v. 연습하다 n. 연습

They kept practicing, but they kept on failing.
그들은 계속 연습을 했지만 계속 실패했지.

• keep -ing 계속 ~하다

fail
[feil]

v. 실패하다

They kept practicing, but they kept on failing.
그들은 계속 연습을 했지만 계속 실패했지.

• failure n. 실패

exhausted
[igzɔ́ːstid]

a. 지친

They were exhausted, and they were about to surrender.
그들은 지쳐서 막 포기하려던 찰나였어.

• exhaust v. 지치게 하다

surrender
[səréndər]

v. 포기하다, 양도하다
n. 포기, 양도

They were exhausted, and they were about to surrender.
그들은 지쳐서 막 포기하려던 찰나였어.

• be about to + V 막 ~하려고 하다

expert
[ékspəːrt]

n. 전문가

Then Seri asked me, "What about asking for help from an expert? I mean your friend, Sara."
그때 세리가 나에게 물었어. "전문가에게 도움을 구하면 어떨까? 언니 친구 사라 말이야."

• expertise n. 전문기술

tempt
[tempt]

v. 유혹하다

I said, "Hey, Sara said you can tempt him with sausages."
"이봐, 사라가 카이트를 소시지로 유혹하래." 라고 내가 말했어.

• temptation n. 유혹

attach
[ətǽtʃ]

v. 부착하다

I attached some sausages to a stick and held it up in the air.
나는 소시지를 막대에 달아서 그것을 공중에 들어올렸어.

• attachment n. 부착, 첨부 • attach A to B A를 B에 붙이다

encourage
[enkə́ːridʒ]

v. 격려하다

Finally, Kite was encouraged by the food and started stamping his paw.
마침내 카이트는 먹을 것에 자극을 받아 앞발을 구르기 시작했어.

• encouragement n. 격려

Check Again!

A Translate each word into Korean.

1. attach ....
2. snap ....
3. utensil ....
4. athletic ....
5. fail ....
6. practice ....
7. analyze ....
8. surrender ....
9. expert ....
10. train ....

B Translate each word into English.

1. 발을 구르다 ....
2. 유혹하다 ....
3. (동물의) 발 ....
4. 준비하다 ....
5. 격려하다 ....

C Fill in the blank with the appropriate word. Refer to the Korean.

1. The professor is an e   in computer graphics.

   교수는 컴퓨터 그래픽에 전문가이다.

2. I am always ready for a c   .

   나는 항상 경쟁할 준비가 되어 있다.

3. Children below 8 years old need to be e   .

   8살 이하의 아이들은 격려받는 것을 필요로 한다.

4. The magician a   to make the lady disappear.

   그 마술사는 여성을 사라지게 하는 시도를 했다.

5. The couple looks e   from fighting.

   그 커플은 싸우는 데 지친 것 같다.

Chapter 5
Hobbies

Unit 14. Relationships count most.

important **elements** to succeed in the workplace

be the first one **to be recruited**

Episode

Dear Mom,

Don't say **mid-term** grades are everything. • Do you really trust **statistics**? • What **element** is most important to succeed in the workplace? • Do you think **academic** performance is the best? • It is **significant**, but not of **utmost** importance. • According to the statistics, 66.8% of college **graduate**s get a job. • That means 66.8% are **employed**. • But some do not get employed even with high grades on their **resumes**. • In the workplace, people usually get a **promotion** in 8 years. • Some get promoted faster. This is because they are **devoted** workers, not good students. • They **retire** within 30 years. • At an interview, some people talked about why they **quit**. • They **responded** with various reasons. • Some quit due to poor **pay**. • However, most of them quit because of poor work **relationships**. • Having **hardships** with **colleagues** can be a big problem. • **Likewise**, having difficulties with **supervisors** was another major concern. • All of this means, I should find my **passion** and work on relationships. • Mom, you know how passionate I am in many different **fields**. • You know how talented I am at **maintaining** good relationships with people. • Mom, I will be the first one to be **recruited**.

엄마에게,
중간고사 성적이 전부라고 말씀하지 마세요. 엄마는 통계를 정말 믿으세요? 직장에서 가장 중요한 요소가 무엇일까요? 학업 성적이 최고라고 생각하세요? 중요하긴 하지만 제일 중요하지는 않아요. 통계에 따르면, 대학 졸업생의 66.8%가 취업을 해요. 대학생의 66.8%만 직업이 생기는 거죠. 하지만 몇몇은 이력서에 높은 성적이 적혀 있어도 취업을 못해요. 직장에서 사람들은 대개 8년 만에 승진을 해요. 몇몇은 승진을 더 빨리 해요. 성적이 좋은 학생들이었기 때문이 아니라 헌신적인 직원이기 때문이에요. 그들은 30년 안에 은퇴를 해요. 인터뷰에서, 어떤 사람들은 왜 일을 그만두는지에 대해 얘기했어요. 그들은 다양한 이유를 댔어요. 몇몇은 급료가 낮아 그만둬요. 그러나 대부분은 업무상의 관계가 원만하지 않아 그만둔대요. 동료들과 어려움이 큰 문제일 수 있어요. 마찬가지로 상사와의 어려움이 또 다른 주요 사유지요. 이 모든 것이 의미하는 것은 내가 열정을 찾아내 사람들과의 관계에 노력해야 한다는 거예요. 엄마, 제가 여러 다양한 분야에 얼마나 열정적인지 아시잖아요. 제가 사람들과 관계를 얼마나 잘 유지하는지도 아시고요. 엄마, 전 취직을 하는 첫 번째 사람이 될 거예요.

mid-term
[mid-tə:rm]
a. 중간고사의

Don't say mid-term grades are everything.
엄마, 중간고사 성적이 전부라고 말씀하지 마세요.

statistics
[stətístiks]
n. 통계

Do you really trust statistics?
엄마는 통계를 정말 믿으세요?

• statistical a. 통계적인

element
[éləmənt]
n. 요소

What element is most important to succeed in the workplace?
직장에서 가장 중요한 요소는 무엇일까요?

• elemental a. 요소의 • elementary a. 초보의, 기본이 되는

academic
[æ̀kədémik]
a. 학문의

Do you think academic performance is the best?
학업 성적이 최고라고 생각하세요?

• academy n. 학원, 전문학교

significant
[signífikənt]
a. 중요한

It is significant, but not of utmost importance.
중요하긴 하지만 제일 중요하지는 않아요.

• significance n. 중요성 • significantly ad. 두드러지게

utmost
[ʌ́tmòust]
a. 최상의

It is significant, but not of utmost importance.
중요하긴 하지만 제일 중요하지는 않아요.

graduate
[grǽdʒuèit]
n. 졸업생
v. 졸업하다

According to the statistics, 66.8% of college graduates get a job.
통계에 따르면, 대학 졸업생의 66.8%가 취업을 해요.

• graduation n. 졸업

employ
[emplɔ́i]
v. 고용하다

That means 66.8% are employed.
대학생의 66.8%만 직업이 생기는 거죠.

• employment n. 고용 • employer n. 고용주

resume
[rézúmèi]]
n. 이력서
v. 다시 시작하다

But some do not get employed even with high grades on their resumes.
하지만 몇몇은 이력서에 높은 성적이 적혀 있어도 취업을 못해요.

promotion
[prəmóuʃən]
n. 승진

In the workplace, people usually get a promotion in 8 years.
직장에서 사람들은 대개 8년 만에 승진을 해요.

• promote v. 승진하다

devoted
[divóutid]
a. 헌신적인

This is because they are devoted workers, not good students.
성적이 좋은 학생들이었기 때문이 아니라 헌신적인 직원이기 때문이에요.

• devote v. 헌신하다 • devotion n. 헌신

retire
[ritáiər]
v. 은퇴하다

They retire within 30 years.
그들은 30년 안에 은퇴를 해요.

• retirement n. 은퇴

quit
[kwit]
v. 그만두다, 포기하다

At an interview, some people talked about why they quit. 인터뷰에서, 어떤 사람들은 왜 일을 그만두는지 이야기했어요.

• quit - quit - quit

respond
[rispánd]
v. 답변하다

They responded with various reasons.
그들은 다양한 이유를 댔어요.

• response n. 답변

pay
[pei]
n. 급료, 급여

Some quit due to poor pay.
몇몇은 급료가 낮아 그만둬요.

relationship
[riléiʃənʃìp]
n. 관계

However, most of them quit because of poor work relationships. 그러나 대부분은 업무상의 관계가 원만하지 않아 그만둔대요.

• relate v. 관련시키다

hardship
[háːrdʃìp]
n. 어려움

Having hardships with colleagues can be a big problem.
동료들과 어려움이 큰 문제일 수 있어요.

colleague
[káliːg]
n. 동료 (=coworker)

Having hardships with colleagues can be a big problem.
동료들과 어려움이 큰 문제일 수 있어요.

likewise
[láikwàiz]
ad. 마찬가지로

Likewise, having difficulties with supervisors was another major concern.
마찬가지로 상사와의 어려움이 또 다른 주요 사유지요.

supervisor
[súːpərvàizər]
n. 감독자, 상사

Likewise, having difficulties with supervisors was another major concern.
마찬가지로 상사와의 어려움이 또 다른 주요 사유지요.

• supervise v. 감독하다

passion
[pǽʃən]
n. 열정

All of this means, I should find my passion and work on relationships.
이 모든 것이 의미하는 것은 내가 열정을 찾아내 사람들과의 관계에 노력해야 한다는 거예요.

• passionate a. 열정 있는 • passionately ad. 열렬히

field
[fiːld]
n. 분야

Mom, you know how passionate I am in many different fields.
엄마, 제가 여러 다양한 분야에 얼마나 열정적인지 아시잖아요.

maintain
[meintéin]
v. 유지하다

You know how talented I am at maintaining good relationships with people.
당신은 제가 사람들과 관계를 얼마나 잘 유지하는지 아시죠.

• maintenance n. 유지, 보수

recruit
[rikrúːt]
v. 직원을 모집하다

Mom, I will be the first one to be recruited.
엄마, 전 취직을 하는 첫 번째 사람이 될 거예요.

• recruitment n. 모집

Check Again!

A Translate each word into Korean.

1. academic ....
2. graduate ....
3. relationship ....
4. devoted ....
5. quit ....
6. mid-term ....
7. statistics ....
8. employ ....
9. hardship ....
10. likewise ....

B Translate each word into English.

1. 유지하다 ....
2. 요소 ....
3. 은퇴하다 ....
4. 분야 ....
5. 동료 ....

C Fill in the blank with the appropriate word. Refer to the Korean.

1. I am making a perfect r................ to be employed.

   나는 취직하기 위해 완벽한 이력서를 만들고 있다.

2. There are 3 main e................ in writing a story.

   글을 쓰는 데 3가지의 주된 요소가 있다.

3. The s................ of the camp was so strict.

   캠프의 감독자는 매우 엄격했다.

4. Can you give me any hints about the p................ this year?

   올해의 승진에 대해 힌트 좀 줄 수 있나요?

5. Love can be felt when two people show their p................ .

   두 사람이 서로의 열정을 보일 때 사랑은 느껴질 수 있다.

Chapter 5
Hobbies

Unit 15. Finally, I got accepted.

be restless

pretend to be a frog

Episode

Dear Diary,

Oh, thank god! I went to **hell** and heaven. ● I was late for the **audition**. ● It was the **final** audition for the play, *The Frog and the Princess.* ● There was **fierce** competition because only one person can be chosen. ● I did not wear any **fancy** clothes. ● I even left my **self-introduction** at home. ● I was very **restless**. ● **Despite** these feelings, I tried to be **calm**. ● The **judges** asked questions nonstop. ● We had to answer in **detail**. ● And we didn't have much time to **figure out** the answers. ● One student did not give the **proper** answers. ● They were quite **inappropriate**, and not **logical** at all. ● There was another **candidate**, who looked **perfect**. ● She looked like a princess from a **fantasy**. ● But her acting was not **outstanding** at all. ● Then it was my **turn**. ● I jumped and **pretended** to be a frog which hopped out of a well. ● When the results came out, I **passed**! ● Did they think I had **potential**? ● My **positive** attitude helped a lot. ● It's one of my natural **assets**.

다이어리에게,

아, 살았다! 난 지옥과 천국을 다녀왔어. 내가 오디션에 늦었지 뭐야. 그것은 '개구리와 공주' 라는 연극의 최종 오디션 이었어. 단 한 명만 뽑히기 때문에 경쟁이 치열했지. 나는 화려한 옷을 입지 않았어. 심지어 자기소개서도 집에 놓고 왔 어. 나는 매우 안절부절했어. 이러한 감정에도 불구하고 나는 침착하려고 애썼어. 심사위원들은 끊임없이 질문을 해댔 어. 우리는 자세하게 답변해야 했지. 그런데 우리는 답변을 생각할 시간이 별로 없었어. 한 학생은 적절한 답변을 하지 못했어. 대답이 부적절하고 전혀 논리적이지 않았지. 또 다른 후보가 있었는데, 완벽해 보였어. 그 애는 환상 소설 속에 나오는 공주 같았어. 그러나 연기는 전혀 뛰어나지 않았어. 그러고 나서 내 차례였어. 나는 점프를 해서 연못에서 뛰어 나온 개구리인 척 했어. 결과가 나왔는데, 내가 합격했어! 그들은 내가 잠재력이 있다고 생각하는 것일까? 나의 긍정적 인 태도가 많은 도움이 됐어. 그게 내 자산 중 하나야.

hell
[hel]

n. 지옥

Oh, thank god! I went to hell and heaven.
아, 살았다! 난 지옥과 천국을 다녀왔어.

audition
[ɔːdíʃən]

n. 오디션
v. 오디션을 하다

I was late for the audition.
내가 오디션에 늦었지 뭐야.

final
[fáinəl]

a. 최종의

It was the final audition for the play, *The Frog and the Princess.*
그것은 '개구리와 공주' 라는 연극의 최종 오디션이었어.

• finally ad. 드디어, 마지막으로

fierce
[fiərs]

a. 치열한, 사나운

There was fierce competition because only one person can be chosen.
단 한 명만 뽑히기 때문에 경쟁이 치열했지.

• fiercely ad. 치열하게, 사납게

fancy
[fǽnsi]

a. 화려한
v. 공상하다

I did not wear any fancy clothes.
나는 화려한 옷을 입지 않았어.

self-introduction
[self-intrədʌ́kʃən]

n. 자기소개서

I even left my self-introduction at home.
나는 심지어 자기소개서도 집에 놓고 왔어.

restless
[réstlis]

a. 불안한

I was very restless.
나는 매우 안절부절했지.

• rest n. 휴식

despite
[dispáit]

prep. ~에도 불구하고

Despite these feelings, I tried to be calm.
이러한 감정에도 불구하고 나는 침착하려고 애썼어.

calm
[kɑ:m]
a. 침착한, 고요한

Despite these feelings, I tried to be calm.
이러한 감정에도 불구하고 나는 침착하려고 애썼어.

• calmness n. 침착함, 고요함

judge
[dʒʌdʒ]
n. 심사위원, 재판장
v. 재판하다

The judges asked questions nonstop.
심사위원들은 끊임없이 질문을 해댔어.

detail
[díːteil]
n. 세부사항

We had to answer in detail.
우리는 자세하게 답변해야 했지.

• in detail 세부적으로, 상세히

figure out
[fígjər aut]
v. 생각해 내다,
   이해하다

And we didn't have much time to figure out the answers.
그런데 우리는 답변을 생각할 시간이 별로 없었어.

proper
[prápər]
a. 적절한

One student did not give the proper answers.
한 학생은 적절한 답변을 하지 못했어.

• properly ad. 적절하게

inappropriate
[ìnəpróupriət]
a. 부적절한

They were quite inappropriate, and not logical at all.
대답이 부적절하고 전혀 논리적이지 않았지.

• inappropriately ad. 부적절하게   • appropriate a. 적절한

logical
[lɔ́dʒikəl]
a. 논리적인

They were quite inappropriate, and not logical at all.
대답이 부적절하고 전혀 논리석이지 않았어.

• logic n. 논리

candidate
[kǽndədèit]
n. 후보

There was another candidate, who looked perfect.
또 다른 후보가 있었는데, 완벽해 보였어.

perfect
[pə́:rfikt]
a. 완벽한

There was another candidate, who looked perfect.
또 다른 후보가 있었는데, 완벽해 보였어.

• perfectly ad. 완벽하게

fantasy
[fǽntəsi]
n. 환상(작품), 공상

She looked like a princess from a fantasy.
그 애는 환상 소설 속에 나오는 공주 같았어.

• fantastic a. 환상적인

outstanding
[àutstǽndiŋ]
a. 뛰어난, 눈에 띄는

But her acting was not outstanding at all.
그러나 그녀의 연기는 전혀 뛰어나지 않았어.

• outstand v. 눈에 띄다

turn
[tə:rn]
n. 차례
v. 돌다, 돌리다

Then it was my turn.
그러고 나서 내 차례였어.

pretend
[priténd]
v. ~인 체하다,
흉내를 내다

I jumped and pretended to be a frog which hopped out of a well.
나는 점프를 해서 연못에서 뛰어나온 개구리인 척 했어.

pass
[pæs]
v. 통과하다, 합격하다

When the results came out, I passed!
결과가 나왔는데, 내가 합격했어!

potential
[poutén∫əl]
n. 잠재력
a. 잠재적인

Did they think I had potential?
그들은 내가 잠재력이 있다고 생각하는 것일까?

• potentially ad. 잠재적으로

positive
[pázətiv]
a. 긍정적인

My positive attitude helped a lot.
나의 긍정적인 태도가 많은 도움이 됐어.

• positively ad. 긍정적으로 • negative a. 부정적인

asset
[ǽset]
n. 자산

It's one of my natural assets.
그게 내 자산 중 하나야.

Check Again!

A Translate each word into Korean.

1. audition ....
2. proper ....
3. asset ....
4. potential ....
5. outstanding ....
6. despite ....
7. hell ....
8. positive ....
9. self-introduction ....
10. judge ....

B Translate each word into English.

1. 후보 ....
2. 불안한 ....
3. 부적절한 ....
4. 치열한 ....
5. 논리적인 ....

C Fill in the blank with the appropriate word. Refer to the Korean.

1. Today's f_____ performance will be made by Yuna Kim.
   오늘의 마지막 공연은 김연아가 할 것이다.

2. We sometimes wear more f_____ clothes when we feel insecure.
   우리는 때때로 불안할 때 더 화려한 옷을 입는다.

3. My teacher explained the theory in d_____.
   나의 선생님께서는 그 이론에 관해 아주 자세하게 설명해 주셨다.

4. A teacher that can develop students' p_____ is the best.
   학생들의 잠재력을 발달시킬 수 있는 교사가 최고이다.

5. A p_____ attitude would make you into a better person.
   긍정적인 사고가 너를 더 나은 사람으로 만들어 줄 것이다.

✚ 동사 만들기 2

형용사나 명사 뒤에 -en을 붙이거나 명사나 형용사 앞에 en-를 붙여서 동사로 쓰이는 경우가 있다. '~하게 하다'의 의미로 풀이되는 경우가 많다.

형용사 + -en 명사

sharp 날카로운
sharpen 날카롭게 하다

ex) Sharpen your pencils with this pencil sharpener.
이 연필깎기로 연필을 깎아라.

- **deep** 깊은   **deepen** 깊게 하다, 심화시키다
- **short** 짧은   **shorten** 짧게 하다
- **wide** 넓은   **widen** 넓히다
- **deaf** 귀가 먼   **deafen** 귀머거리로 만들다
- **fright** 공포   **frighten** 놀라게 하다

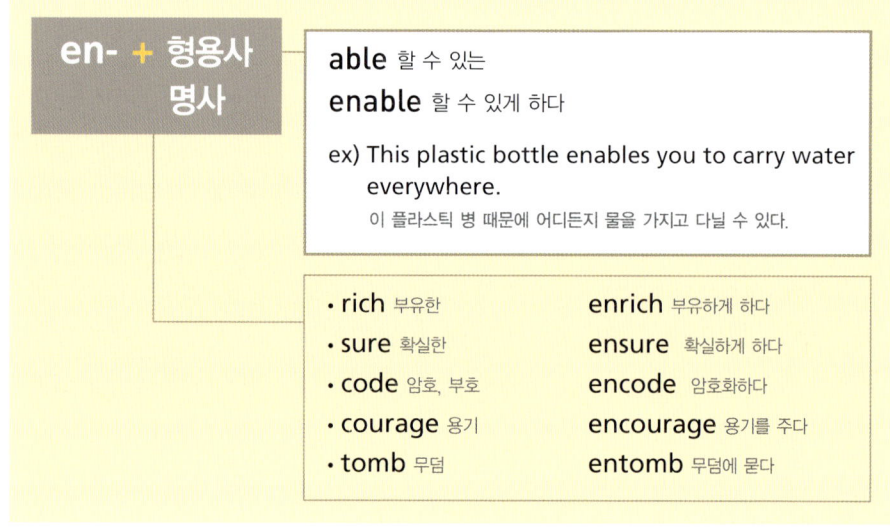

en- + 형용사 명사

able 할 수 있는
enable 할 수 있게 하다

ex) This plastic bottle enables you to carry water everywhere.
이 플라스틱 병 때문에 어디든지 물을 가지고 다닐 수 있다.

- **rich** 부유한   **enrich** 부유하게 하다
- **sure** 확실한   **ensure** 확실하게 하다
- **code** 암호, 부호   **encode** 암호화하다
- **courage** 용기   **encourage** 용기를 주다
- **tomb** 무덤   **entomb** 무덤에 묻다

Free Time Activities

- go to a concert 콘서트에 가다
- go to the gym 체육관에 가다
- go for a walk 산책하러 가다
- have friends over 친구를 초대하다
- hang out with sb ~와 어울려 다니다
- have a party 파티를 열다

Culture Plus

Films 영화

+ director 감독
+ character 등장 인물
+ part 역할
+ plot 줄거리
+ theme 주제
+ special effect 특수 효과
+ soundtrack 영화 음악
+ subtitle 자막
+ dubbing 더빙, 재녹음

VOCA
EDGE
BLUE

love you, Kite We moved today. I want to join the drama club. We have a team projec

the send button. Kite will attend the wonder dog championship. Relationships count mos

e! We made homemade pancakes. Hoony is taking taekwondo lessons. My dad's car is i

at an interesting festival! Sara's brother is running for president. Our school is doing an ant

has skin trouble. Mom has become a regular customer of ABC Mart. Mom is impressed b

Why do floods and droughts alternate? Astronauts need to know special drills. Two whale

nt facilities. We love you, Kite We moved today. I want to join the drama club. We have

safari tour. I pressed the send button. Kite will attend the wonder dog championship

ic. Mud cookies are terrible! We made homemade pancakes. Hoony is taking taekwond

d music for Brownie. What an interesting festival! Sara's brother is running for president. Ou

in art investment. Seri has skin trouble. Mom has become a regular customer of ABC Mar

without sunlight. Why do floods and droughts alternate? Astronauts need to know specic

d boys use different facilities. We love you, Kite We moved today. I want to join the drama

. We went on a safari tour. I pressed the send button. Kite will attend the wonder dog

to a growth clinic. Mud cookies are terrible! We made homemade pancakes. Hoony

Chapter 6. Health

emorial. Sara composed music for Brownie. What an interesting festival! Sara's brothe

Unit 16. We're in the same boat.

is horrible. Dad is interested in art investment. Seri has skin trouble. Mom has become

Unit 17. I go to a growth clinic.

good and bad. Plants can grow without sunlight. Why do floods and droughts alterna

Unit 18. Mud cookies are terrible!

is puberty? Visit my blog Girls and boys use different facilities. We love you, Kite We moved

. There will be a talent show. We went on a safari tour. I pressed the send button. Kite wi

in the same boat. I go to a growth clinic. Mud cookies are terrible! We made homemade

trip to the War Memorial. Sara composed music for Brownie. What an interesting festival

Chapter 6
Health

Unit 16. We're in the same boat.

get an eye infection

not **victims,** but **beneficiaries**

promise to keep it a secret

Episode

Dear Diary,

Sometimes we welcome **germs**. • It's because they spread quickly like **rumors** do. • Do you know what **triggers** them to spread at school?

Sara hasn't been **present** at school for two days. • She got an eye **infection**. • Her seat is **unoccupied**. • Some classmates **whisper** to each other. • They tried to guess who would be the next **victim**. • In reality they are not victims, but **beneficiaries**. • We talked about how we could **unite**. • Sujin and Hyeonbin are **determined** to be next. • They will use Sara's handkerchief. What a **brilliant** idea!

We **estimate** that 10% of our class already got the eye infection. • At this **rate**, the **majority** of our class will get infected soon. • **Eventually**, we'll all get a break from school. • Our class president **warned** us. • "Hey, don't feel too **guilty**. • But make sure your teachers don't find the **truth** out." • We made a **resolution**. • And we **promised** to keep it a secret. • **Otherwise**, our plan will be ruined. • **Consequently**, we're all **in the same boat**.

다이어리에게,

때때로 우리는 세균을 환영해. 세균들이 소문처럼 빨리 퍼지기 때문이야. 무엇 때문에 학교에 그것들이 퍼지고 있는지 아니?

사라는 이틀째 학교에 결석했어. 눈병에 걸렸어. 그 아이의 자리는 비어 있지. 몇몇 학급 친구들은 서로 귓속말을 하지. 그들은 누가 다음 희생자가 될지 추측해 보려고 했어. 사실은 희생자가 아니라 수혜자야. 우리는 어떻게 하면 단결할 수 있을지에 대해 이야기했어. 수진이와 현빈이가 다음 차례가 되기로 결정이 되었어. 그 아이들은 사라의 손수건을 사용할 거야. 얼마나 멋진 생각이야!

우리 반의 10%가 벌써 눈병에 걸린 걸로 추산하고 있어. 이 속도라면 곧 우리 반의 대다수가 감염될 거야. 결국, 학교를 쉴 수 있을 거야. 우리 반 회장은 우리에게 경고를 했어. "이봐, 너무 죄책감을 느끼지 마. 하지만 선생님들이 진실을 알아내지 못하도록 해야 해." 우리는 결의를 했고 비밀을 지키기로 약속했지. 그렇지 않으면 우리 계획은 수포로 돌아갈 거야. 결과적으로, 우리는 모두 한 배를 탄 거지.

germ
[dʒəːrm]

n. 세균

Sometimes we welcome germs.
때때로 우리는 세균을 환영해.

---

rumor
[rúːmər]

n. 소문

It's because they spread quickly like rumors do.
세균들이 소문처럼 빨리 퍼지기 때문이야.

---

trigger
[trígər]

v. 유발하다,
방아쇠를 당기다

n. 방아쇠

Do you know what triggers them to spread at school?
무엇 때문에 학교에 그것들이 퍼지고 있는지 아니?

---

present
[prézənt]

a. 출석한, 현재의
n. 현재

Sara hasn't been present at school for two days.
사라는 이틀째 학교에 결석했어.

• absent a. 결석한

---

infection
[infékʃən]

n. 감염

She got an eye infection.
그녀는 눈병에 걸렸어.

• infect v. 감염시키다   • infectious a. 전염병의, 전염성의

---

unoccupied
[ʌnákjəpàid]

a. 자리를 차지하지 않
은, 소유자가 없는

Her seat is unoccupied.
그녀의 자리는 비어 있어.

• occupy v. 차지하다

---

whisper
[hwíspər]

v. 귓속말을 하다
n. 귓속말

Some classmates whisper to each other.
몇몇 학급 친구들은 서로 귓속말을 하지.

---

victim
[víktim]

n. 희생자

They tried to guess who would be the next victim.
그들은 누가 다음 희생자가 될지 추측해 보려고 했어.

• victimize v. 희생시키다

beneficiary
[bènəfíʃièri]

n. 수익자, 수혜자

In reality they are not victims, but beneficiaries.

사실은 희생자가 아니라 수혜자야.

• beneficial a. 유익한

unite
[juːnáit]

v. 단결하다

We talked about how we could unite.

우리는 어떻게 하면 단결할 수 있을지에 대해 이야기했어.

• unity n. 단결

determine
[ditə́ːrmin]

v. 결심하다, 결정하다

Sujin and Hyeonbin are determined to be next.

수진이와 현빈이가 다음 차례가 되기로 결정이 되었어.

• determination n. 결심, 결정

brilliant
[bríljənt]

a. 훌륭한, 뛰어난

What a brilliant idea!

정말 멋진 생각이야!

• brilliance n. 탁월함, 뛰어남

estimate
[éstəmèit]

v. 추산하다, 추정하다

We estimate that 10% of our class already got the eye infection.

우리 반의 10%가 벌써 눈병에 걸린 걸로 추산하고 있어.

• estimation n. 판단

rate
[reit]

n. 속도, 비율

At this rate, the majority of our class will get infected soon.

이 속도라면 곧 우리 반의 대다수가 감염될 거야.

• at this rate 이 속도(비율)로

majority
[mədʒɔ́(ː)rəti]

n. 대다수

At this rate, the majority of our class will get infected soon.

이 속도라면 곧 우리 반의 대다수가 감염될 거야.

• major a. 주요의 • minority 소수

eventually
[ivéntʃuəli]

ad. 결국

Eventually, we'll all get a break from school.

결국, 학교를 쉴 수 있을 거야.

• eventual a. 최후의

warn
[wɔ:rn]

v. 경고하다

Our class president warned us.
우리 반 회장이 우리에게 경고를 했어.

• warning n. 경고

guilty
[gílti]

a. 죄책감을 느끼는, 유죄인

"Hey, don't feel too guilty. But make sure your teachers don't find the truth out."
"이봐, 너무 죄책감을 느끼지 마. 하지만 선생님들이 진실을 알아내지 못하도록 해야 해."

• guilt n. 유죄

truth
[tru:θ]

n. 진실

"Hey, don't feel too guilty. But make sure your teachers don't find the truth out."
"이봐, 너무 죄책감을 느끼지 마. 하지만 선생님들이 진실을 알아내지 못하도록 해야 해."

• true a. 진실의

resolution
[rèzəlú:ʃən]

n. 결의

We made a resolution.
우리는 결의를 했어.

• resolve v. 결심하다 • resolute a. 굳게 결심한
• make a resolution 결의를 하다

promise
[prámis]

v. 약속하다
n. 약속, 전망

And we promised to keep it a secret.
그리고 우리는 비밀을 지키기로 약속했지.

• promising a. 전망 있는

otherwise
[ʌðərwàiz]

ad. 그렇지 않으면

Otherwise, our plan will be ruined.
그렇지 않으면 우리 계획은 수포로 돌아갈 거야.

consequently
[kánsikwəntli]

ad. 결과적으로

Consequently, we're all in the same boat.
결과적으로, 우리는 모두 한 배를 탄 거지.

• consequence n. 결과 • consequent a. 결과의, 결과로서 생기는

in the same boat
[in ðə seim bout]

한 배를 탄, 같은 운명인

Consequently, we're all in the same boat.
결과적으로, 우리는 한 배를 탄 거지.

Check Again!

A Translate each word into Korean.

1. infection ....   2. brilliant ....

3. eventually ....   4. present ....

5. whisper ....   6. germ ....

7. promise ....   8. warn ....

9. estimate ....   10. rate ....

B Translate each word into English.

1. 다수 ....

2. 수혜자 ....

3. 희생자 ....

4. 소문 ....

5. 결정하다 ....

C Fill in the blank with the appropriate word. Refer to the Korean.

1. We need to hurry. O__________ , we will be late for the movie.

   우리는 서둘러야 해. 그렇지 않으면 영화에 늦을 거야.

2. My friends didn't know that I was p_________ when they were talking about me.

   내 친구들은 나에 대해 이야기하고 있을 때 내가 그 자리에 참석해 있는지 몰랐다.

3. Some people forget to w_______ when they are in a library.

   어떤 사람들은 도서관에서는 귓속말로 말해야 하는 것을 잊는다.

4. The government e________ that our economy will rise by only 5%.

   정부는 우리 경제가 겨우 5% 성장할 것이라고 추산한다.

5. Finally, they admitted that they were in the same b_______ .

   결국, 그들은 자신들이 같은 운명이라는 사실을 인정했다.

Chapter 6
Health

Unit 17. I go to a growth clinic.

have a **regular** check-up

reach the handles on the subway

get a hormone injection

Episode

Dear Mom,

Mom, why am I so short? ● We had a regular check-up at school. ● And I had to measure my height and weight. ● My height was much shorter than average. ● Before bed, I drink a big size glass of milk. ● On weekends, I play basketball. ● But, what's the result?

The only advantage of being short is that sometimes bus drivers think I'm an elementary student. ● I only have a few humble wishes. ● I just want to be able to reach the handles on the subway. ● I want to roll up my new jeans just once rather than two or three times. ● Today, Mom took me to a growth clinic.

What affects height? ● The doctor said there are various factors: nutrition, stress, genes, etc. ● After a few medical check-ups, the doctor asked about my parents' height. ● His conclusion was as follows. ● My height is due to my genes. ● The doctor suggests getting some special treatment. ● He is talking about a hormone injection. ● I hate needles, but it seems inevitable. ● Isn't there any alternative to this hormone therapy?

엄마에게,

엄마, 나는 왜 이렇게 키가 작을까요? 우리는 학교에서 정기 검진을 받았어요. 그래서 키와 몸무게를 재야 했어요. 내 키는 평균보다 꽤 작았어요. 잠자기 전에 나는 큰 사이즈의 우유를 마셔요. 주말에는 농구를 해요. 하지만 결과가 뭐죠?

키 작은 것의 유일한 정점은 버스 기사분들이 나를 초등학생으로 본다는 것이죠. 나는 소박한 바람을 갖고 있어요. 나는 단지 지하철 손잡이에 손이 닿고 싶을 뿐이에요. 단지 새 청바지를 2번이나 3번 접기보다는 1번만 접고 싶을 뿐이에요. 오늘 엄마가 나를 성장 클리닉에 데리고 가셨어요.

무엇이 키에 영향을 줄까요? 의사선생님은 다양한 요소들이 있다고 말씀하셨어요. 영양, 스트레스, 유전자 등등. 몇 가지 검사 후에 의사선생님은 부모님의 키를 물으셨죠. 그분의 결론은 다음과 같았어요. 내 키는 유전자 때문이래요. 의사는 특별 치료를 받으라고 제안했어요. 그분은 호르몬 주사를 말씀하시는 거예요. 나는 주사가 싫지만 피할 수 없는 것 같아요. 이 호르몬 치료법에 대한 대안은 없을까요?

regular
[régjulər]

a. 정기적인, 규칙적인

We had a regular check-up at school.
우리는 학교에서 정기 검진을 받았어요.

• regularly ad. 정기적으로, 규칙적으로

weight
[weit]

n. 무게, 체중

And I had to measure my height and weight.
그래서 나는 키와 몸무게를 재야 했어요.

• weigh v. 측정하다, 재다

average
[ǽvəridʒ]

n. 평균

My height was much shorter than average.
내 키는 평균보다 꽤 작았어요.

result
[rizʌ́lt]

n. 결과
v. 결과가 되다

But, what's the result?
하지만 결과가 뭐죠?

advantage
[ədvǽntidʒ]

n. 이익

The only advantage of being short is that sometimes bus drivers think I'm an elementary student.
키 작은 것의 유일한 장점은 버스 기사분들이 나를 초등학생으로 본다는 것이죠.

• advantageous a. 이익이 되는   • disadvantage n. 불이익

humble
[hʌ́mbl]

a. 소박한, 겸손한

I only have a few humble wishes.
나는 소박한 바람을 갖고 있어요.

• humbleness n. 소박함, 겸손함

reach
[riːtʃ]

v. 도달하다
n. 미치는 범위

I just want to be able to reach the handles on the subway.
나는 단지 지하철 손잡이에 손이 닿고 싶을 뿐이에요.

• reachable a. 도달할 수 있는

handle
[hǽndl]

n. 손잡이

I just want to be able to reach the handles on the subway.
나는 단지 지하철 손잡이에 손이 닿고 싶을 뿐이에요.

roll
[roul]
v. 둥글게 말다

I want to roll up my new jeans just once rather than two or three times.
나는 단지 새 청바지를 2번이나 3번 접기보다는 1번만 접고 싶을 뿐이에요.

• roll up 말아 올리다

growth
[grouθ]
n. 성장

Today, Mom took me to a growth clinic.
오늘 엄마가 나를 성장 클리닉에 데리고 가셨어요.

• grow v. 성장하다

affect
[əfékt]
v. 영향을 미치다,
   ~인 체하다

What affects height?
무엇이 키에 영향을 줄까요?

• affection n. 가장함

various
[vέəriəs]
a. 다양한

The doctor said there are various factors: nutrition, stress, genes, etc.
의사선생님은 다양한 요소들이 있다고 말씀하셨어요. 영양, 스트레스, 유전자 등등.

• vary v. 바꾸다, 다양하게 하다   • variety n. 다양성

factor
[fǽktər]
n. 요소

The doctor said there are various factors: nutrition, stress, genes, etc.
의사선생님은 다양한 요소들이 있다고 말씀하셨어요. 영양, 스트레스, 유전자 등등.

nutrition
[njuːtríʃən]
n. 영양

The doctor said there are various factors: nutrition, stress, genes, etc.
의사선생님은 다양한 요소들이 있다고 말씀하셨어요. 영양, 스트레스, 유전자 등등.

• nutritious a. 영양의   • malnutrition n. 엉양실조

medical
[médikəl]
a. 의학의

After a few medical check-ups, the doctor asked about my parents' height.
몇 가지 검사 후에 의사는 부모님의 키를 물으셨죠.

• medicine n. 약, 의학

conclusion
[kənklúːʒən]

n. 결론

His conclusion was as follows.
의사의 결론은 다음과 같았어요.

• conclude v. 결론을 내리다   • conclusive a. 결정적인

gene
[dʒiːn]

n. 유전자

My height is due to my genes.
내 키는 유전자 때문이래요.

• genetic a. 유전의

suggest
[sədʒést]

v. 제안하다, 암시하다

The doctor suggests getting some special treatment.
의사는 특별 치료를 받으라고 제안했어요.

• suggestion n. 제안

treatment
[tríːtmənt]

n. 치료, 처리

The doctor suggests getting some special treatment.
의사는 특별 치료를 받으라고 제안했어요.

• treat v. 치료하다

injection
[indʒékʃən]

n. 주사

He is talking about a hormone injection.
그 분은 호르몬 주사를 말씀하시는 거예요.

• inject v. 주사하다

inevitable
[inévitəbl]

a. 피할 수 없는

I hate needles, but it seems inevitable.
나는 주사가 싫지만 피할 수 없는 것 같아요.

• inevitably ad. 불가피하게, 부득이   • evitable a. 피할 수 있는

alternative
[ɔːltə́ːrnətiv]

n. 대안

Isn't there any alternative to this hormone therapy?
이 호르몬 치료법에 대한 대안은 없을까요?

• alternate v. 교대로 하다

therapy
[θérəpi]

n. 치료법

Isn't there any alternative to this hormone therapy?
이 호르몬 치료법에 대한 대안은 없을까요?

• therapist n. 치료사

Check Again!

A Translate each word into Korean.

1. affect ....
2. humble ....
3. inevitable ....
4. conclusion ....
5. gene ....
6. various ....
7. medical ....
8. reach ....
9. nutrition ....
10. factor ....

B Translate each word into English.

1. 이익 ....
2. 결과 ....
3. 성장 ....
4. 대안 ....
5. 주사 ....

C Fill in the blank with the appropriate word. Refer to the Korean.

1. We need a r   check-up to stay healthy.
   건강을 유지하기 위해서 정기적인 검진이 필요하다.

2. Some teenagers have white hair because white hair comes from
   g   .
   흰 머리는 유전이기 때문에 흰 머리가 난 청소년들이 있다.

3. The g   of a tree can be seen by its annual rings.
   나무의 성장은 나무의 나이테를 보면 알 수 있다.

4. There is a TV program on why mental t   is not something
   to be ashamed of.
   정신 치료를 받는 것이 왜 부끄러운 것이 아닌지에 관한 TV 프로그램이 있다.

5. Did he s   taking a walk along the lake?
   그가 호숫가를 따라서 산책하자고 제안했나요?

Chapter 6
Health

Unit 18. Mud cookies are terrible!

material made of dirt and water

suffer from indigestion

live in much better conditions

Episode

Sara: Bomi, have you heard of mud cookies?

Bomi: Mud? Are you talking about the material made of dirt and water?

Sara: Yes. Actually, in some countries mud cookies are snacks for kids.

Bomi: How can kids digest them? ● Aren't they harmful?

Sara: The truth is, they end up suffering from indigestion. ● They also have severe stomachaches.

Bomi: Why do manufacturers bake these cookies? ● That's really cruel. ● And what is the government doing? ● One of their main jobs is to protect people.

Sara: Right. Our food should be guaranteed to be safe. ● But kids there eat these cookies and feel some satisfaction. ● There is a food crisis there.

Bomi: Food crisis? Even so, this situation is unacceptable. ● They need reliable food.

For a moment, I couldn't say anything. ● I was stricken dumb. ● It was quite a depressing story. ● I realized that we're living in much better conditions. ● It's a blessing that we don't have to eat mud cookies.

사라: 보미야, 진흙 과자에 대해 들어 봤어?
보미: 진흙이라고? 흙과 물로 만들어진 물질을 말하는 거야?
사라: 맞아. 사실 어떤 나라에서는 진흙 과자가 아이들 간식이야.
보미: 어떻게 아이들이 그걸 소화시키니? 해롭지 않아?
사라: 사실은, 아이들이 결국 소화불량으로 고통받게 돼. 그들은 심각한 복통에도 시달리지.
보미: 왜 제조업자들이 이런 과자를 굽는 거야? 정말 잔인하다. 그리고 정부는 뭘 하고 있는 거야? 그들이 해야 하는 중요한 일 중 하나가 국민을 지키는 것이잖아.
사라: 맞아. 우리가 먹는 음식은 안전이 보장되어야 해. 하지만 그곳의 아이들은 이런 쿠키를 먹고 포만감을 느끼지. 그곳은 식량난을 겪고 있거든.
보미: 식량난이라고? 그렇더라도 이 상황은 용납이 되지 않아. 그 사람들은 믿을 수 있는 음식이 필요하잖아.

잠시 동안, 나는 아무 말도 할 수 없었다. 말문이 막혔다. 그것은 꽤 우울한 이야기였다. 나는 우리가 훨씬 더 나은 조건에서 살아간다는 것을 깨달았다. 우리가 진흙 과자를 먹지 않아도 된다는 것은 축복이다.

mud
[mʌ́d]
n. 진흙

Bomi, have you heard of mud cookies?
보미야, 진흙 과자에 대해 들어 봤어?

material
[mətíəriəl]
n. 재료, 물질

Mud? Are you talking about the material made of dirt and water?
진흙이라고? 흙과 물로 만들어진 물질을 말하는 거야?

actually
[ǽktʃuəli]
ad. 실제로

Actually, in some countries mud cookies are snacks for kids.
사실 어떤 나라에서는 진흙 과자가 아이들 간식이야.

•actual a. 실제인

snack
[snæk]
n. 간식

Actually, in some countries mud cookies are snacks for kids.
사실 어떤 나라에서는 진흙 과자가 아이들 간식이야.

digest
[didʒést]
v. 소화하다

How can kids digest them?
어떻게 아이들이 그걸 소화시키니?

•digestion n. 소화 •digestive a. 소화력 있는

harmful
[háːrmfəl]
a. 위험한

Aren't they harmful?
해롭지 않아?

•harm n. 위험 v. 해를 입히다

indigestion
[ìndidʒéstʃən]
n. 소화불량

The truth is, they end up suffering from indigestion.
사실은, 아이들이 결국 소화불량으로 고통받게 돼.

severe
[sivíər]
a. 심한

They also have severe stomachaches.
그들은 심각한 복통에도 시달리지.

•severely ad. 심하게

manufacturer
[mæ̀njufǽktʃərər]

n. 제조업자

Why do manufacturers bake these cookies?
왜 제조업자들이 이런 과자를 굽는 것일까?

• manufacture v. 제조하다 n. 제조업

cruel
[krúːəl]

a. 잔인한

That's really cruel.
정말 잔인하다.

• cruelty n. 잔인함, 무자비

government
[gʌ́vərnmənt]

n. 정부

And what is the government doing?
그럼 정부는 뭘 하고 있는 거야?

• govern v. 다스리다 • governing a. 다스리는

main
[mein]

a. 주요한

One of their main jobs is to protect people.
그들이 해야 하는 중요한 일 중 하나가 국민을 지키는 것이잖아.

• mainly ad. 주로

protect
[prətékt]

v. 보호하다

One of their main jobs is to protect people.
그들이 해야 하는 중요한 일 중 하나가 국민을 지키는 것이잖아.

• protection n. 보호 • protective a. 보호하는

guarantee
[gæ̀rəntíː]

v. 보장하다
n. 보장, 보증

Our food should be guaranteed to be safe.
우리가 먹는 음식은 안전이 보장되어야 해.

satisfaction
[sæ̀tisfǽkʃən]

n. 만족감

But kids there eat these cookies and feel some satisfaction.
하지만 그곳의 아이들은 이런 쿠키를 먹고 포만감을 느끼지

• satisfactory a. 만족스러운, 더할나위 없는
• satisfy v. 만족시키다

crisis
[kráisis]

n. 위기

There is a food crisis there.
그곳은 식량난을 겪고 있거든.

situation
[sìtʃuéiʃən]
n. 상황

Even so, this situation is unacceptable.
그렇더라도 이런 상황은 용납이 되지 않아.

• situational a. 상황의

unacceptable
[ʌ̀nəkséptəbəl]
a. 용납되지 않는

Even so, this situation is unacceptable.
그렇더라도 이런 상황은 용납이 되지 않아.

• accept v. 용납하다, 수용하다

reliable
[riláiəbəl]
a. 믿을 만한

They need reliable food.
그 사람들은 믿을 수 있는 음식이 필요하잖아.

• rely v. 의존하다

moment
[móumənt]
n. 순간

For a moment, I couldn't say anything.
잠시 동안, 나는 아무 말도 할 수 없었다.

• momentary a. 순간의

dumb
[dʌm]
a. 말을 못하는,
   말문이 막히는

I was stricken dumb.
나는 말문이 막혔다.

• be stricken dumb 말문이 막히다

depressing
[diprésiŋ]
a. 우울한

It was quite a depressing story.
그것은 꽤 우울한 이야기였다.

• depress v. 낙담시키다

condition
[kəndíʃən]
n. 조건

I realized that we're living in much better conditions.
나는 우리가 훨씬 더 나은 조건에서 살아간다는 것을 깨달았다.

• conditional a. 조건부의

blessing
[blésiŋ]
n. 축복

It's a blessing that we don't have to eat mud cookies.
우리가 진흙 과자를 먹지 않아도 된다는 것은 축복이다.

• bless v. 축복하다

Check Again!

A Translate each word into Korean.

1. moment ....
2. manufacturer ....
3. material ....
4. snack ....
5. reliable ....
6. harmful ....
7. indigestion ....
8. unacceptable ....
9. guarantee ....
10. satisfaction ....

B Translate each word into English.

1. 심한 ....
2. 잔인한 ....
3. 주요한 ....
4. 말문이 막히는 ....
5. 우울한 ....

C Fill in the blank with the appropriate word. Refer to the Korean.

1. The s_____ I saw proved that he was guilty.

   내가 본 상황은 그가 유죄라는 것을 증명했다.

2. It is said that people are given three m_____ to change their lives.

   사람들에게 인생을 바꿀 세 번의 순간이 주어진다는 얘기가 있다.

3. Pigs seem to like to roll in m_____.

   돼지들은 진흙 속에서 구르는 것을 좋아하는 것 같다.

4. The tofu is easy to d_____.

   그 두부는 소화하기 쉽다.

5. A bodyguard's job is to p_____ their clients.

   경호원의 임무는 자신의 고객을 보호하는 것이다.

✚ 형용사 만들기

명사 뒤에 -ful 혹은 -less를 붙여서 형용사로 쓰일 수 있다. 의미는 -ful은
'~이 가득한'으로, -less는 '~이 없는'으로 해석된다.

명사 + -ful

care 주의, 조심
careful 조심스러운

ex) Be careful. There is hot chocolate in the mug.
조심해. 머그 잔에 핫 초코가 있어.

• **help** 도움	**helpful** 도움이 되는
• **sorrow** 슬픔	**sorrowful** 슬픔에 젖은
• **thank** 고마움	**thankful** 고마운
• **faith** 신뢰, 믿음	**faithful** 충실한
• **joy** 즐거움	**joyful** 기쁜, 즐거운

명사 + -less

regard 고려
regardless 부주의한, 고려하지 않는

ex) Regardless of age, everyone is equal.
나이에 관계없이 모든 사람들은 평등하다.

• **help** 도움	**helpless** 무력한
• **thank** 고마움	**thankless** 감사할 줄 모르는
• **faith** 신뢰, 믿음	**faithless** 신의가 없는
• **joy** 즐거움	**joyless** 즐거움이 없는
• **penny** 1페니	**penniless** 무일푼의
• **mercy** 자비심	**merciless** 자비심이 없는

At a Clinic

- make an appointment with a doctor
  의사와 예약을 하다

- consult a doctor 의사와 상담하다

- have one s temperature taken 체온을 재다

- have one s pulse taken 맥박을 재다

- have one s blood pressure taken 혈압을 재다

- prescribe medicine for sb ~의 약을 처방하다

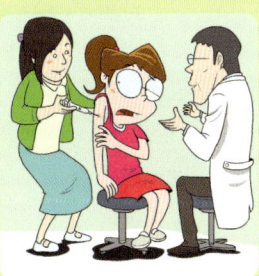

Culture Plus

Hospital 병원

+ clinic 진료소, 의원

+ hospital 종합 병원

+ dental clinic 치과

+ doctor s office 의원

+ emergency room 응급실

+ surgery 외과, 수술

+ treatment 치료

+ injection 주사

VOCA EDGE

BLUE

Chapter 7. People

Unit 19. We made homemade pancakes.

Unit 20. Hoony is taking taekwondo lessons.

Unit 21. My dad's car is in the garage.

Chapter 7
People

Unit 19. We made homemade pancakes.

measure the ingredients precisely

beat the eggs

start to smoke

mistake salt **for** sugar

Episode

Dear Diary,

Seri and I are making homemade pancakes. ● Seri says they are healthier than store-bought pancakes. ● She also says she has experience with pancakes at school, so she is the chef. ● And I am her assistant.

She shows me the recipe. ● We get the ingredients together. ● I put the flour on the scale. ● Seri makes me measure the ingredients precisely. ● She puts some ingredients together then beats two eggs and puts them in. ● Then she adds the milk and oil. ● I heat the frying pan and spread some butter on it. ● Seri pours too much batter on the pan and the pan starts to smoke. ● Oh no! Seri hurriedly turns over the pancake. ● But it's hopeless. ● In the end, both sides are burnt. ● And the inside is slightly undercooked. ● Seri failed to control the heat. ● "Seri, what happened? ● It tastes bitter and salty." ● She mistook salt for sugar. ● I don't trust her now. ● She can't blame me for her mistakes.

다이어리에게,

세리와 나는 팬케이크를 손수 만들고 있어. 세리는 그것들이 가게에서 파는 팬케이크보다 건강에 더 좋다고 해. 그 아이는 또한 학교에서 팬케이크를 만든 경험도 있다고 해. 그래서 그 아이가 요리사야. 그리고 나는 그 아이의 조수야.

그 아이는 내게 조리법을 보여 줘. 우리는 함께 재료를 모아. 나는 밀가루를 저울 위에 올려놓아. 세리는 나에게 재료들을 정확하게 재라고 해. 세리는 몇 가지 재료를 합치고는 달걀 두 개를 세게 휘저은 다음 안에 넣어. 그리고 그 아이는 우유와 식용유를 첨가해. 나는 후라이팬을 뜨겁게 달구고 나서 그 위에 버터를 얇게 발라. 세리가 후라이팬에 반죽을 너무 많이 부어서 후라이팬에서 연기가 나기 시작해. 오 이런! 세리는 서둘러서 팬케이크를 뒤집어. 하지만 어쩔 수가 없어. 결국 양쪽이 다 탔어. 그리고 안쪽은 약간 덜 익었어. 세리가 불을 잘 조절하지 못했던 거야. "세리, 어떻게 된 거야? 맛이 쓰고 짜잖아." 그 애는 소금을 설탕으로 잘못 알았던 거야. 나는 이제 그 애를 믿지 못하겠어. 그 애가 자기 실수를 내 탓이라 할 수는 없어.

homemade
[hóumméid]
a. 손수 만든

Seri and I are making homemade pancakes.
세리와 나는 팬케이크를 손수 만들고 있어.

healthier
[hélθiər]
a. 더 건강한
(healthy의 비교급)

Seri says they are healthier than store-bought pancakes.
세리는 그것들이 가게에서 파는 팬케이크보다 건강에 더 좋다고 해.

• healthy a. 건강한   • health n. 건강

chef
[ʃef]
n. 요리사

She also says she has experience with pancakes at school, so she is the chef.
그 아이는 또한 학교에서 팬케이크를 만든 경험이 있다고 해요. 그래서 그 아이가 요리사예요.

assistant
[əsístənt]
n. 조수

And I am her assistant.
그리고 나는 그 아이의 조수야.

• assist v. 돕다, 조수를 하다

recipe
[résəpì:]
n. 조리법

She shows me the recipe.
그 아이는 내게 조리법을 보여 줘.

ingredient
[ingríːdiənt]
n. 재료

We get the ingredients together.
우리는 함께 재료를 모아.

scale
[skeil]
n. 저울, 계량기

I put the flour on the scale.
나는 밀가루를 저울 위에 올려놓아.

measure
[méʒər]
v. 재다, 측정하다

Seri makes me measure the ingredients precisely.
세리는 나에게 재료들을 정확하게 재라고 해.

• measurement n. 측량, 계량

precisely
[prisáisli]

ad. 정확하게

Seri makes me measure the ingredients precisely.

세리는 나에게 재료들을 정확하게 재라고 해.

• precise a. 정확한

beat
[bi:t]

v. (달걀 등을) 세게 휘젓다

She puts some ingredients together then beats two eggs and puts them in.

세리는 몇 가지 재료를 합치고는 달걀 두 개를 세게 휘저은 다음 안에 넣어.

• beat-beat-beaten

add
[æd]

v. 더하다, 보태다

Then she adds the milk and oil.

그리고 그 아이는 우유와 식용유를 첨가해.

• addition n. 추가, 더하기   • additional a. 추가적인

heat
[hi:t]

v. 뜨겁게 하다, 가열하다
n. 열, 더위

I heat the frying pan and spread some butter on it.

나는 후라이팬을 뜨겁게 달구고 나서 그 위에 버터를 얇게 발라.

batter
[bǽtər]

n. 반죽

Seri pours too much batter on the pan and the pan starts to smoke.

세리가 후라이팬에 반죽을 너무 많이 부어서 후라이팬에서 연기가 나기 시작해.

smoke
[smouk]

v. 연기를 내다
n. 연기

Seri pours too much batter on the pan and the pan starts to smoke.

세리가 후라이팬에 반죽을 너무 많이 부어서 후라이팬에서 연기가 나기 시작해.

hurriedly
[hə́:ridli]

ad. 급하게

Oh no! Seri hurriedly turns over the pancake.

오 이런! 세리는 서둘러서 팬케이크를 뒤집어.

• hurry v. 서두르다

hopeless
[hóuplis]

a. 절망적인, 어찌할 수 없는

But it's hopeless.

하지만 어쩔 수가 없어.

• hope v. 바라다, 희망하다

burn
[bə:rn]

v. 불에 타다

In the end, both sides are burnt.
결국 양쪽이 다 탔어.

• burnt a. 불에 탄 • burn - burnt - burnt

slightly
[sláitli]

ad. 약간

And the inside is slightly undercooked.
그리고 안쪽은 약간 덜 익었어.

• slight a. 약간의

undercook
[ʌ́ndərkuk]

v. 덜 익히다

And the inside is slightly undercooked.
그리고 안쪽은 약간 덜 익었어.

• undercooked a. 덜 익은 • cook v. 요리하다

control
[kəntróul]

v. 조절하다
n. 조절

Seri failed to control the heat.
세리가 불을 잘 조절하지 못했던 거야.

• fail to+ V ~하는 것을 실패하다

salty
[sɔ́:lti]

a. 짠

Seri, what happened? It tastes bitter and salty.
세리, 어떻게 된 거야. 맛이 쓰고 짜잖아.

• salt n. 소금

mistake
[mistéik]

v. 착각하다
n. 실수

She mistook salt for sugar.
그 애는 소금을 설탕으로 잘못 알았던 거야.

• mistake A for B A를 B로 착각하다
• mistake - mistook - mistaken

trust
[trʌst]

v. 믿다
n. 신뢰

I don't trust her now.
나는 이제 그 애를 믿지 못하겠어.

• trusty a. 믿음직한 • trustworthy a. 신뢰할 수 있는

blame
[bleim]

v. 나무라다, 탓하다
n. 비난, 나무람

She can't blame me for her mistakes.
그 애가 자기 실수를 내 탓이라 할 수는 없어.

• blameful a. 비난할 만한, 나무랄 만한

Check Again!

A Translate each word into Korean.

1. precisely ....   2. chef ....

3. assistant ....   4. recipe ....

5. ingredient ....   6. scale ....

7. measure ....   8. batter ....

9. hurriedly ....   10. slightly ....

B Translate each word into English.

1. 건강한 ....

2. 짠 ....

3. 달걀 등을 세게 휘젓다 ....

4. 뜨겁게 하다 ....

5. 연기를 내다 ....

C Fill in the blank with the appropriate word. Refer to the Korean.

1. Are these muffins h   ?

   이 머핀들은 집에서 만든 건가요?

2. Should I a   a bit more salt?

   소금을 조금 더 첨가할까요?

3. All our efforts were h   .

   우리의 모든 노력에도 어쩔 수가 없었어요.

4. The chicken was a bit u   .

   닭고기가 약간 덜 익었어요.

5. Don't blame me. You m   oil for vinegar.

   나를 탓하지 말아요. 당신이 식용유를 식초로 착각했잖아요.

Chapter 7
People

Unit 20. Hoony is taking taekwondo lessons.

have one's hand **in a bandage**

walk through **the cemetery**

demonstrate one's skill

Episode

Bomi: What's wrong? • You look serious and a little gloomy.

Hoony: I've made a crucial decision. • I'm going to take taekwondo lessons as part of my extracurricular activities. • I'll show my friends that I can break even 15 layers of bricks.

Bomi: Then you have to join the summer camp. • You know, the one all the kids call "horror camp."

Hoony: Do they call it that because the teacher is so stern?

Bomi: He is more than just stern. • He is like a drill sergeant • Moreover, he makes all the kids walk through the cemetery at night.

Hoony: No problem. • I'm still going to join and develop my skills.

Hoony has his right hand in a bandage. • It was injured. • Hoony and Jaejin have been friends since they graduated from the same kindergarten. • He tends to think that he is superior to Jaejin in most areas. • Today Hoony and Jaejin had a bet to see who could break ten layers of bricks. • Hoony told Jaejin that it was unlikely that he'd be able to do it. • But Jaejin demonstrated his skill and broke all ten. • All their friends were overwhelmed. • Hoony also tried, but what a disgrace! • He failed. He probably felt insulted • I could tell he was also offended by his friends' laughter. • Hoony kept saying Jaejin's bricks must have been hollow. • He really wanted to believe that Jaejin deceived him. • But, from now on, Hoony will have to work hard to achieve his goals.

보미: 왜 그러니? 심각하고 좀 우울해 보이는데.

후니: 난 중요한 결심을 했어. 과외 활동으로 태권도 수업을 들을 거야. 내 친구들에게 내가 벽돌 15장도 깰 수 있다는 걸 보여 줄 거야.

보미: 그럼 넌 여름 캠프에 참가해야겠구나. 아이들이 "공포의 캠프"라고 부르는 거 있잖니.

후니: 선생님이 아주 엄격하시기 때문에 아이들이 그렇게 부르는 거야?

보미: 그냥 엄격한 정도가 아니야. 훈련 담당 하사관 같아. 더군다나 모든 아이들에게 밤에 공동묘지를 걷도록 시킨대.

후니: 괜찮아. 난 그래도 참가해서 실력을 쌓을 거야.

후니는 오른손에 밴드를 감고 있다. 손을 다쳤기 때문이다. 후니와 재진이는 같은 유치원을 졸업할 때부터 친구였다. 그 아이는 자신이 모든 면에서 재진이보다 우수하다고 생각하곤 한다.

오늘 후니와 재진이는 누가 벽돌 열 장을 깰 수 있는지를 놓고 내기를 했다. 후니는 재진이에게 그가 벽돌을 깰 수 없을 것 같다고 말했다. 그러나 재진이는 열 장 모두를 깨면서 자신의 실력을 보여 주었다. 모든 친구들이 압도되었다. 후니도 시도해 봤지만 무슨 망신이람! 그는 실패했다. 후니는 아마 모욕감을 느꼈을 것이다. 친구들이 웃었기 때문에 후니가 감정도 상했다는 것을 알 수 있었다. 후니는 재진이가 깬 벽돌은 틀림없이 속이 비었을 거라고 계속 말했다. 후니는 재진이가 자신을 속인 거라고 진심으로 믿고 싶어 했다. 그러나 지금부터 후니는 자신의 목표를 달성하기 위해 열심히 연습해야 한다.

gloomy
[glú:mi]
a. 우울한

What's wrong? You look serious and a little gloomy.
왜 그러니? 심각하고 좀 우울해 보이는데.

• gloomily ad. 어둡게 • gloominess n. 우울

crucial
[krú:ʃəl]
a. 중요한

I've made a crucial decision.
난 중요한 결심을 했어.

extracurricular activity
[èkstrəkəríkjulər æktívəti]
n. 과외 활동

I'm going to take taekwondo lessons as part of my extracurricular activities.
과외 활동으로 태권도 수업을 들을 거야.

layer
[léiər]
n. 층
v. 층으로 만들다

I'll show my friends that I can break even 15 layers of bricks.
내 친구들에게 내가 벽돌 15장도 깰 수 있다는 걸 보여 줄 거야.

horror
[hɔ́:rər]
n. 공포

You know, the one all the kids call "horror camp."
아이들이 "공포의 캠프"라고 부르는 거 있잖니.

• horrible a. 공포스러운 • horrifying a. 무서운

stern
[stə́:rn]
a. 엄격한

Do they call it that because the teacher is so stern?
선생님이 아주 엄격하시기 때문에 아이들이 그렇게 부르는 거야?

drill sergeant
[dril sá:rdʒənt]
n. 훈련 담당 하사관

He is like a drill sergeant.
그 사람은 훈련 담당 하사관 같아.

moreover
[mɔ:róuvər]
ad. 더군다나

Moreover, he makes all the kids walk through the cemetery at night.
더군다나 모든 아이들에게 밤에 공동묘지를 걷도록 시킨대.

cemetery
[sémətèri]
n. 공동묘지

Moreover, he makes all the kids walk through the cemetery at night.
더군다나 모든 아이들에게 밤에 공동묘지를 걷도록 시킨대.

develop
[divéləp]
v. 발전시키다

I'm still going to join and develop my skills.
난 그래도 참가해서 실력을 쌓을 거야.

• development n. 발전 • developed a. 발전된

injure
[índʒər]
v. 상처를 입히다

Hoony has his right hand in a bandage. It was injured.
후니는 오른손에 밴드를 감고 있다. 손을 다쳤기 때문이다.

• injury n. 부상, 상처 • injured a. 다친, 상처 입은

kindergarten
[kíndərgàːrtn]
n. 유치원

Hoony and Jaejin have been friends since they graduated from the same kindergarten.
후니와 재진이는 같은 유치원을 졸업할 때부터 친구였다.

tend
[tend]
v. 경향이 있다

He tends to think that he is superior to Jaejin in most areas.
그 아이는 자신이 모든 면에서 재진이보다 우수하다고 생각하곤 한다.

• tendency n. 경향 • tend to + V ~한 경향이 있다

superior
[supíəriər]
a. 우수한, 뛰어난

He tends to think that he is superior to Jaejin in most areas.
그 아이는 자신이 모든 면에서 재진이보다 우수하다고 생각하곤 한다.

• superiority n. 우월함, 우세 • inferior a. 열등한

bet
[bet]
n. 내기
v. 내기하다

Today Hoony and Jaejin had a bet to see who could break ten layers of bricks.
오늘 후니와 재진이는 누가 벽돌 열 장을 깰 수 있는지를 놓고 내기를 했다.

unlikely
[ʌnláikli]
a. ~일 것 같지 않은

Hoony told Jaejin that it was unlikely that he'd be able to do it.
후니는 재진이에게 그가 벽돌을 깰 수 없을 것 같다고 말했다.

demonstrate
[démənstrèit]

v. 실지로 해 보이다,
증명하다

But Jaejin demonstrated his skill and broke all ten.
그러나 재진이는 열 장 모두를 깨면서 자신의 실력을 보여 주었다.

• demonstration n. 시범

overwhelm
[òuvərhwélm]

v. 압도하다

All their friends were overwhelmed.
모든 친구들이 압도되었다.

disgrace
[disgréis]

n. 불명예, 망신
v. 수치가 되다

Hoony also tried, but what a disgrace! He failed!
후니도 시도해 봤지만 무슨 망신이람! 그는 실패했다.

• disgraceful a. 수치스러운

insulted
[ínsʌltid]

a. 모욕을 받은

He probably felt insulted.
후니는 아마 모욕감을 느꼈을 것이다.

• insult v. 모욕하다   n. 모욕
• insulting a. 모욕적인, 무례한

offend
[əfénd]

v. 감정을 상하게 하다

I could tell he was also offended by his friends' laughter.
친구들이 웃었기 때문에 후니는 감정도 상했다는 것을 알 수 있었다.

• offensive a. 불쾌한

hollow
[hálou]

a. 속이 빈
v. 속이 비게 하다

Hoony kept saying Jaejin's bricks must have been hollow
후니는 재진이가 깬 벽돌은 틀림없이 속이 비었을 거라고 계속 말했다.

deceive
[disíːv]

v. 속이다

He really wanted to believe that Jaejin deceived him.
후니는 재진이가 자신을 속인 거라고 진심으로 믿고 싶어 했다.

• deception n. 속임   • deceptive a. 사람을 속이는, 현혹시키는

achieve
[ətʃíːv]

v. 달성하다

But, from now on Hoony will have to work hard to achieve his goals.
그러나 지금부터 후니는 자신의 목표를 달성하기 위해 열심히 연습해야 한다.

• achievement n. 달성   • achievable a. 달성 가능한

Check Again!

A Translate each word into Korean.

1. hollow ....
2. gloomy ....
3. moreover ....
4. deceive ....
5. achieve ....
6. stern ....
7. cemetery ....
8. disgrace ....
9. insulted ....
10. overwhelm ....

B Translate each word into English.

1. 공포 ....
2. 시범을 보이다 ....
3. ~일 것 같지 않은 ....
4. 우수한 ....
5. 감정을 상하게 하다 ....

C Fill in the blank with the appropriate word. Refer to the Korean.

1. Danny's left arm was i

   대니는 왼쪽 팔을 다쳤다.

2. The girl t to chat in class.

   그 여자아이는 수업 시간에 수다를 떠는 경향이 있다.

3. Yesterday my dad and I had a b on the World Series.

   어제 아빠와 나는 월드시리즈를 놓고 내기를 했다.

4. Don't touch the table. There is a thick l of dust on it.

   테이블에 손대지 말아요. 두껍게 쌓인 먼지 층이 있잖아.

5. Finally she made a c decision and left for America.

   드디어 그녀는 중대한 결정을 내리고 미국으로 떠났다.

Chapter 7
People

Unit 21. My dad's car is in the garage.

be in the **garage**

suffer from some **nausea** and **dizziness**

Episode

Dear Diary,

My father's car is in the garage. • His car had a breakdown. • According to the mechanic, it will take 10 days to mend. • It was drizzling yesterday. • My parents were out shopping and my father stopped his car at an intersection. • Incidentally a car was right behind his. • The other driver tried in vain to stop his car but it was hopeless. • Bang! There was a crash. • The damage to Dad's car was severe. • After the accident, Dad was about to start roaring at the other driver. • But he discovered that the other driver was just a young boy trembling with fear. • Later, he found out that the boy was just a minor. • He was driving his dad's car drunk without a driver's license. • Dad said the boy would have to stand trial. • I wonder what misled him into thinking he could drive a car while drunk.

This morning Mom went to a clinic and the doctor prescribed her some pills. • She was suffering from some nausea and dizziness. • At first she just tried home remedies like hot baths and massages. • She thought it just a trivial matter. • But now, she has a lot of pain because the muscles around her neck are strained. • Seri made a special type of rice with a lot of fluid for her. • She doesn't think Mom should be eating solid food. • Although Mom says she has been experiencing nightmares, she seems to enjoy reading books lying in bed.

다이어리에게.

우리 아빠 차는 차 수리공장에 있어. 아빠 차가 고장이 났어. 정비사는 차를 고치는 데 열흘이 걸린다고 해. 어제 보슬비가 내리고 있었어. 부모님은 쇼핑하러 나가셨는데 아버지가 교차로에서 차를 세우셨어. 우연히 아빠 차 바로 뒤에 차가 한 대 있었어. 그 상대편 운전자는 차를 세우려고 했으나 허사였어. 꽝! 충돌사고가 났지. 아빠 차가 심하게 피손되었어. 사고가 난 후에 아빠는 상대 운전자에게 막 소리를 지르려고 하셨어. 하지만 아빠는 상대 운전자가 두려움에 떨고 있는 어린 소년이란 것을 발견하셨어. 나중에 그 운전자가 미성년자라는 것을 아셨어. 그는 자기 아버지 차를 면허도 없이 술에 취해서 운전하고 있었던 거야. 아빠는 그 소년이 재판을 받아야 할 것이라고 하셨어. 난 무엇 때문에 그 아이가 술 취한 상태로 운전을 할 수 있다고 생각했는지가 궁금해.

오늘 아침 엄마는 병원에 가셨고 의사 선생님이 알약을 처방하셨어. 엄마는 메스꺼움과 어지러움 때문에 고생을 하셨어. 처음에 엄마는 집에서 하는 치료법으로 뜨거운 물로 목욕을 하거나 마사지만 하셨어. 대수롭지 않은 일이라고 생각하셨던 거야. 하지만 지금은 목 주위의 근육이 긴장되어 있기 때문에 많은 통증을 느끼셔. 세리는 엄마를 위해서 수분이 많은 특별한 죽을 끓였어. 그 아이는 엄마가 고형식을 드시면 안 된다고 생각하지. 엄마가 비록 악몽처럼 끔찍한 일을 경험하셨지만, 엄마는 자리에 누워서 책을 읽는 것을 즐기시는 것 같아.

garage
[gərάːʒ]
n. 자동차 수리공장, 차고

My father's car is in the garage
우리 아빠 차는 차 수리공장에 있어.

breakdown
[bréikdàun]
n. 고장

His car had a breakdown
아빠 차가 고장이 났어.

• break down v. 고장 나다 • broken-down a. 박살 난, 망가진

mechanic
[məkǽnik]
n. 정비사, 수리공

According to the mechanic, it will take 10 days to mend.
정비사는 차를 고치는 데 열흘이 걸린다고 해.

• mechanical a. 기계적인

mend
[mend]
v. 고치다

According to the mechanic, it will take 10 days to mend.
정비사는 차를 고치는 데 10일이 걸린다고 해.

drizzle
[drízl]
v. 이슬비가 내리다
n. 이슬비, 보슬비

It was drizzling yesterday.
어제 보슬비가 내리고 있었어.

intersection
[intərsékʃən]
n. 교차로

My parents were out shopping and my father stopped his car at an intersection.
부모님은 쇼핑하러 나가셨는데 아버지가 교차로에서 차를 세우셨어.

• intersect v. 교차하다

incidentally
[ìnsədéntʃəli]
ad. 우연히

Incidentally a car was right behind his.
우연히 아빠 차 바로 뒤에 차가 한 대 있었어.

• incident n. 우발적인 사건 • incidental a. 우연히 일어나는

vain
[vein]
a. 헛된, 쓸데없는

The other driver tried in vain to stop his car but it was hopeless.
그 상대편 운전자는 차를 세우려고 했지만 허사였어.

• in vain 헛되게, 쓸데없이

crash
[kræʃ]

n. (차량의) 충돌,
   (비행기 등의) 추락
v. 충돌하다

Bang! There was a crash.

쾅! 충돌사고가 났지.

---

damage
[dǽmidʒ]

n. 피해, 파손
v. 피해를 주다

The damage to Dad's car was severe.

아빠 차가 심하게 파손되었어.

• damaged a. 피해를 입은, 파손된

---

roar
[rɔːr]

v. 고함치다, 으르렁거리다
n. 고함, 으르렁거림

After the accident, Dad was about to start roaring at the other driver.

사고가 난 후에 아빠는 상대 운전자에게 막 소리를 지르려고 하셨어.

---

tremble
[trémbl]

v. 떨다, 진동하다

But he discovered that the other driver was just a young boy trembling with fear.

하지만 아빠는 상대 운전자가 공포로 떨고 있는 어린 소년이란 것을 발견하셨어.

---

minor
[máinər]

n. 미성년자, 부전공(자)

Later, he found out that the boy was just a minor.

나중에 그 운전자가 미성년자라는 것을 아셨어.

---

drunk
[drʌŋk]

a. 술 취한

He was driving his dad's car drunk without a driver's license.

그는 자기 아버지 차를 면허도 없이 술에 취해서 운전하고 있었던 거야.

• drink v. 술 취하다   • drink - drank - drunk

---

license
[láisəns]

n. 면허

He was driving his dad's car drunk without a driver's license.

그는 자기 아버지 차를 면허도 없이 술에 취해서 운전하고 있었던 거야.

• licensed a. 면허를 받은   • driver's license 운전 면허증

---

trial
[tráiəl]

n. 재판

Dad said the boy would have to stand trial.

아빠는 그 소년이 재판을 받아야 할 것이라고 하셨어.

• try v. 재판하다   • stand trial 재판을 받다

mislead
[mislíːd]

v. 잘못 이끌다, 오도하다

I wonder what misled him into thinking he could drive a car while drunk.

난 무엇 때문에 그 아이가 술 취한 상태로 운전을 할 수 있다고 생각했는지가 궁금해.

• misleading a. 잘못 이끄는　• mislead - misled - misled

prescribe
[priskráib]

v. 처방하다

This morning Mom went to a clinic and the doctor prescribed her some pills.

오늘 아침 엄마는 병원에 가셨고 의사 선생님이 알약을 처방하셨어.

• prescription n. 처방, 처방약

nausea
[nɔ́ːziə]

n. 메스꺼움, 구토

She was suffering from some nausea and dizziness.

엄마는 메스꺼움과 어지러움 때문에 고생을 하셨어.

• nauseous a. 구토가 나는

dizziness
[dízinis]

n. 어지러움

She was suffering from some nausea and dizziness.

엄마는 메스꺼움과 어지러움 때문에 고생을 하셨어.

• dizzy a. 어지러운

remedy
[rémədi]

n. 치료법　v. 치료하다

At first she just tried home remedies like hot baths and massages.

처음에 엄마는 집에서 하는 치료법으로 뜨거운 물로 목욕을 하거나 마사지만 하셨지.

trivial
[tríviəl]

a. 사소한, 하찮은

She thought it just a trivial matter.

엄마는 대수롭지 않은 일이라고 생각하셨어.

strain
[strein]

v. 긴장시키다

But now, she has a lot of pain because the muscles around her neck are strained.

하지만 지금은 목 주위의 근육이 긴장되어 있기 때문에 많은 통증을 느끼셔.

• strained a. 긴장된

fluid
[flúːid]

n. 수분, 수액
a. 유동성의

Seri made a special type of rice with a lot of fluid for her.

세리는 엄마를 위해서 수분이 많은 특별한 죽을 끓였어.

solid
[sálid]

a. 고체의　n. 고체

She doesn't think Mom should be eating solid food.

그 아이는 엄마가 고형식을 드시면 안 된다고 생각해.

• solidify v. 굳히다

Check Again!

A Translate each word into Korean.

1. breakdown ....
2. damage ....
3. drizzle ....
4. intersection ....
5. roar ....
6. fluid ....
7. nausea ....
8. drunk ....
9. license ....
10. garage ....

B Translate each word into English.

1. 우연히 ....
2. 미성년자 ....
3. 어지러움 ....
4. 오도하다 ....
5. 사소한 ....

C Fill in the blank with the appropriate word. Refer to the Korean.

1. Did the doctor p_____ you cough medicine?

   의사선생님이 당신에게 기침약을 처방해 주셨나요?

2. Soon the criminal will stand t_____ for kidnapping.

   조만간 그 범인은 유괴에 대해 재판을 받을 것이다.

3. The boy was seriously injured in a car c_____.

   그 소년은 자동차 충돌사고로 심하게 다쳤다.

4. We need more f_____ to make it softer.

   우리는 그것을 부드럽게 하기 위해서 좀 더 많은 액체가 필요하다.

5. I can't trust my grandma's home r_____. They seem to lack scientific basis.

   나는 할머니가 집에서 해 주시는 치료법들을 믿을 수가 없다. 과학적인 근거가 부족해 보인다.

+ 사람을 나타내는 말

명사나 동사 뒤에 -er, -or, -ist 등을 붙여서 그 일을 하는 사람을 나타내는 경우가 많다.
또한 성별을 나타내기 위해서 여성인 경우 -ess 등을 붙이기도 한다.

**동사 +
-er/-or/-ist**

edit 편집하다
editor 편집자

ex) The publisher is looking for editors.
그 출판사는 편집자를 구하고 있다.

- **publish** 편집하다   **publisher** 편집자
- **invent** 발명하다   **inventor** 발명가
- **extinguish** 불을 끄다   **extinguisher** 불을 끄는 사람, 소화기
- **ministry** 목회   **minister** 목회자
- **arson** 방화   **arsonist** 방화자

**남성을 나타내는 말
+ -ess**

남성	여성
• **actor** 남자 배우	**actress** 여자 배우
• **waiter** 남자 종업원	**waitress** 여자 종업원
• **steward** 남자 승무원	**stewardess** 여자 승무원
• **god** 신	**goddess** 여신
• **emperor** 황제	**empress** 황후

Describing People

A: What does he look like? 그 사람은 외모가 어때요?

B: He is tall and slim. 그는 키가 크고 날씬해요.

Positive

- plump 통통한
- chubby 토실토실한
- slim 날씬한
- slender 날씬한

Negative

- overweight 과체중의
- obese 비만인
- bony 뼈만 남은
- skinny 바싹 마른, 앙상한

Culture Plus

Characters 성격

+ arrogant 거만한
+ selfish 이기적인
+ warm-hearted 마음이 따뜻한
+ cold-hearted 냉정한
+ sociable 사교적인
+ decisive 결단력이 있는
+ indecisive 우유부단한

+ modest 겸손한
+ generous 관대한

VOCA EDGE

BLUE

love you, Kite We moved today. I want to join the drama club. We have a team projec

the send button. Kite will attend the wonder dog championship. Relationships count mos

e! We made homemade pancakes. Hoony is taking taekwondo lessons. My dad's car is i

at an interesting festival! Sara's brother is running for president. Our school is doing an ant

has skin trouble. Mom has become a regular customer of ABC Mart. Mom is impressed b

Why do floods and droughts alternate? Astronauts need to know special drills. Two whale

nt facilities. We love you, Kite We moved today. I want to join the drama club. We have a

safari tour. I pressed the send button. Kite will attend the wonder dog championship

c. Mud cookies are terrible! We made homemade pancakes. Hoony is taking taekwonda

d music for Brownie. What an interesting festival! Sara's brother is running for president. Ou

in art investment. Seri has skin trouble. Mom has become a regular customer of ABC Mar

without sunlight. Why do floods and droughts alternate? Astronauts need to know specia

boys use different facilities. We love you, Kite We moved today. I want to join the drama

We went on a safari tour. I pressed the send button. Kite will attend the wonder dog

to a growth clinic. Mud cookies are terrible! We made homemade pancakes. Hoony i

Chapter 8. History, Art and Culture

emorial. Sara composed music for Brownie. What an interesting festival! Sara's brothe

Unit 22. Hoony went on a trip to the War Memorial.

is horrible. Dad is interested in art investment. Seri has skin trouble. Mom has become

Unit 23. Sara composed music for Brownie.

good and bad. Plants can grow without sunlight. Why do floods and droughts alterna

Unit 24. What an interesting festival!

is puberty? Visit my blog Girls and boys use different facilities. We love you, Kite We moved

. There will be a talent show. We went on a safari tour. I pressed the send button. Kite wi

in the same boat. I go to a growth clinic. Mud cookies are terrible! We made homemade

trip to the War Memorial. Sara composed music for Brownie. What an interesting festival

Chapter 8
History, Art and Culture

Unit 22. Hoony went on a trip to the War Memorial.

play with **diverse** models

under one's command

be compared to the god of the sea

Episode

Hoony is playing with a turtle ship model **floating** in a bath tub. ● He has **diverse** models such as **shields** and swords displayed in his room. ● He bought the models at a **souvenir** shop.

Bomi: How was your field trip to the War **Memorial** today?

Hoony: It was great! ● I liked the **exhibit** of the turtle ship, **Admiral** Yi Sunshin's invention.

Bomi: Admiral Yi and his armies were pretty **legendary**. ● The turtle ship was very effective at destroying enemy **vessels**. ● Most enemy vessels that came up against it were **wrecked**. ● Soldiers that were on wrecked ships were usually **drowned** or seriously **wounded**. ● Because of the turtle ship's effectiveness Korea's enemies had to **retreat**.

Hoony: Under Admiral Yi's **command**, enemy armies were worn down and **weakened**.

Bomi: Exactly. ● If he had been born in Scandinavia, he may well have been respected as one of the greatest military **conquerors**. ● He could **foresee** what was going to happen at sea. ● He can even be compared to the god of the sea in Greek **myths**, Poseidon.

Hoony: Yeah, but it would have been even better if he had **supplemented** the ship with a part on the **rear** that could shoot out like the head of a turtle. ● I think that would have really **terrified** his enemies.

Bomi: Actually, seeing Admiral Yi in command against them was already quite a **dreaded** sight for enemies.

Hoony is interested in attending an **institute** to study the turtle ship. ● As a war hero, Admiral Yi was not **ambitious**. ● He was humble and **loyal** to our country.

후니는 욕조에 거북선 모형을 띄워 놓고 놀고 있다. 그 아이는 방패나 칼 등 다양한 모형들을 방에 진열해 놓았다. 그 아이는 기념품 가게에서 그 모형을 샀다.

보미: 오늘 전쟁기념관에 소풍 간 것은 어땠어?

후니: 정말 좋았어. 난 이순신 장군의 발명품인 거북선이 전시된 것이 좋았어.

보미: 이순신 장군과 그의 군대는 정말 전설적이었지. 거북선은 적의 전함을 파괴시키는 데 효과적이었어. 거북선에 대적한 대부분의 적의 전함은 난파되었지. 난파선에 있었던 군사들은 대부분 물에 빠져 죽거나 심하게 부상을 당했어. 거북선의 효능 때문에 한국에 대항한 적군들은 퇴각해야만 했지.

후니: 이순신 장군의 지휘 아래, 적군은 지쳤고 전력이 약해졌지.

보미: 맞아. 만일 그가 스칸디나비아에서 태어났더라면 가장 위대한 정복자 중 하나로 존경을 받았을 거야. 그분은 해상에서 어떤 일이 일어날지를 예측할 수 있었던 거야. 그리스 신화에 나오는 바다의 신 포세이돈과도 비교될 수 있지.

후니: 맞아, 하지만 거북선의 머리처럼 꼬리에서도 화포를 쏠 수 있도록 보완을 했으면 더 나았을 거라고 생각해. 그러면 적들을 겁나게 했을 거야.

보미: 사실, 이순신 장군이 지휘를 하는 것을 보는 것만도 적들에게는 이미 겁을 먹게 하는 광경이었지.

후니는 거북선을 연구하는 연구소에 다니는 것에 관심이 있다. 전쟁 영웅으로서 이순신 장군은 야심이 있지는 않았다. 그분은 겸손하고 우리나라에 충성을 다했다.

float

[flout]

v. 뜨다

Hoony is playing with a turtle ship model floating in a bath tub.

후니는 욕조에 거북선 모형을 띄워 놓고 놀고 있다.

diverse

[divə́ːrs]

a. 다양한

He has diverse models such as shields and swords displayed in his room.

그 아이는 방패나 칼 등 다양한 모형들을 방에 진열해 놓았다.

• diversify v. 다양화하다   • diversity n. 다양성

shield

[ʃiːld]

n. 방패

v. 방패로 막다, 보호하다

He has diverse models such as shields and swords displayed in his room.

그 아이는 방패나 칼 등 다양한 모형들을 방에 진열해 놓았다.

souvenir

[sùːvəníər]

n. 기념품

He bought the models at a souvenir shop.

그 아이는 기념품 가게에서 그 모형을 샀다.

memorial

[mimɔ́ːriəl]

n. 기념물, 기념관

How was your field trip to the War Memorial today?

오늘 전쟁기념관에 소풍 간 것은 어땠어?

• memorialize v. 기념하다, 기념식을 거행하다

exhibit

[igzíbit]

n, 전시, 전시품

v. 전시하다

It was great! I liked the exhibit of the turtle ship, Admiral Yi Sunshin's invention.

정말 좋았어. 난 이순신 장군의 발명품인 거북선이 전시된 것이 좋았어.

• exhibition n. 전람회

admiral

[ǽdmərəl]

n. 해군 대장, 제독

It was great! I liked the exhibit of the turtle ship, Admiral Yi Sunshin's invention.

정말 좋았어. 난 이순신 장군의 발명품인 거북선이 전시된 것이 좋았어.

legendary

[lédʒəndèri]

a. 전설적인

Admiral Yi and his armies were pretty legendary.

이순신 장군과 그의 군대는 정말 전설적이었지.

• legend n. 전설

vessel

[vésəl]

n. 선박, 배

The turtle ship was very effective at destroying enemy vessels.

거북선은 적의 전함을 파괴시키는 데 효과적이었어.

wreck
[rek]
v. 난파시키다
n. 난파

Most enemy vessels that came up against it were wrecked. 거북선에 대적한 대부분의 적의 전함은 난파되었지.
• wrecked a. 난파된

drown
[draun]
v. 익사하다,
  익사시키다

Soldiers that were on wrecked ships were usually drowned or seriously wounded.
난파선에 있었던 군사들은 대부분 물에 빠져 죽거나 심하게 부상을 당했어.
• drowned a. 익사한

wound
[wúːnd]
v. 부상을 입히다
n. 부상

Soldiers that were on wrecked ships were usually drowned or seriously wounded.
난파선에 있었던 군사들은 대부분 물에 빠져 죽거나 심하게 부상을 당했어.
• wounded a. 부상을 당한

retreat
[riːtríːt]
v. 물러나다, 퇴각하다
n. 퇴각

Because of the turtle ship's effectiveness Korea's enemies had to retreat.
거북선의 효능때문에 한국에 대항한 적군들은 퇴각해야만 했지.

command
[kəmǽnd]
n. 명령, 지휘
v. 명령하다, 지휘하다

Under Admiral Yi's command, enemy armies were worn down and weakened.
이순신 장군의 지휘 아래, 적군은 지쳤고 전력이 약해졌지.
• under one's command ~의 지휘(통솔) 아래

weaken
[wíːkən]
v. 약화시키다

Under Admiral Yi's command, enemy armies were worn down and weakened.
이순신 장군의 지휘 아래, 적군은 지쳤고 전력이 약해졌지.
• weak a. 약한 • weakened a. 약화된

conqueror
[kάŋkərər]
n. 정복자

If he had been born in Scandinavia, he may well have been respected as one of the greatest military conquerors.
만일 그가 스칸디나비아에서 태어났더라면 가장 위대한 정복자 중 하나로 존경을 받았을 거야.
• conquer v. 정복하다 • conquered a. 정복된

foresee
[fɔːrsíː]
v. 예견하다

He could foresee what was going to happen at sea.
그분은 해상에서 어떤 일이 일어날지를 예측할 수 있었던 거야.
• foresight n. 선견지명, 통찰력 • foresee - foresaw - foreseen

myth
[miθ]

n. 신화

He can even be compared to the god of the sea in Greek myths, Poseidon.
그리스 신화에 나오는 바다의 신 포세이돈과도 비교될 수 있지.

• mythical a. 신화의

supplement
[sʌ́plmənt]

v. 보충하다
n. 추가, 보충

Yeah, but it would have been even better if he had supplemented the ship with a part on the rear that could shoot out like the head of a turtle.
맞아, 하지만 거북선의 머리처럼 꼬리에서도 화포를 쏠 수 있도록 보완을 했으면 더 나았을 거라고 생각해.

• supplementary a. 추가의 n. 추가된 것(사람)

rear
[riər]

n. 뒷부분, 후미

Yeah, but it would have been even better if he had supplemented the ship with a part on the rear that could shoot out like the head of a turtle.
맞아, 하지만 거북선의 머리처럼 꼬리에서도 화포를 쏠 수 있도록 보완을 했으면 더 나았을 거라고 생각해.

terrify
[térəfài]

v. 무섭게 하다, 겁을 주다

I think that would have really terrified his enemies.
그러면 적들을 겁나게 했을 거야.

• terrified a. 겁을 먹은

dreaded
[drédid]

a. 겁먹게 하는

Actually, seeing Admiral Yi in command against them was already quite a dreaded sight for enemies.
사실, 이순신 장군이 지휘를 하는 것을 보는 것만도 적들에게는 이미 겁을 먹게 하는 광경이었지.

• dread v. 겁나게 하다 n. 공포, 불안

institute
[ínstətjùːt]

n. 연구소

Hoony is interested in attending an institute to study the turtle ship.
후니는 거북선을 연구하는 연구소에 다니는 것에 관심이 있다.

ambitious
[æmbíʃəs]

a. 야심 있는

As a war hero, Admiral Yi was not ambitious.
전쟁 영웅으로서 이순신 장군은 야심이 있지는 않았다.

• ambition n. 야심, 야망

loyal
[lɔ́iəl]

a. 충실한

He was humble and loyal to our country.
그분은 겸손하고 우리나라에 충성을 다했다.

• loyalty n. 충성

Check Again!

A Translate each word into Korean.

1. memorial ....
2. ambitious ....
3. wreck ....
4. terrify ....
5. souvenir ....
6. vessel ....
7. exhibit ....
8. myth ....
9. drown ....
10. diverse ....

B Translate each word into English.

1. 정복자 ....
2. 뒷부분 ....
3. 예견하다 ....
4. 퇴각하다 ....
5. 보충하다 ....

C Fill in the blank with the appropriate word. Refer to the Korean.

1. This language i_____ was established to teach foreign languages to orphans.

   이 언어 연구소는 고아들에게 외국어를 가르쳐 주기 위해서 설립되었다.

2. The earthquake w_____ the structure of the building.

   지진이 그 건물의 구조를 약화시켰다.

3. They became united under his c_____.

   그의 통솔 하에 그들은 하나가 되었다.

4. He found a d_____ body risen to the surface of the river.

   그는 익사한 시체가 강 위로 떠오른 것을 보았다.

5. According to the doctor who treated people, ten soldiers were seriously w_____.

   사람들을 치료한 의사에 따르면, 군인 열 명이 심하게 부상을 입었다고 한다.

Chapter 8
History, Art and Culture

Unit 23. Sara composed music for Brownie.

be against wearing fur coats

take someone **for a walk**

be due in five weeks

Episode

I encountered Sara on my way home.

Bomi: Did you finish composing some music for Brownie? • You said you were going to combine Bach, Beethoven, and Mozart.

Sara: Not yet. • It's hard to combine music and keep it in harmony. • I've been revising it constantly.

Bomi: Why don't you just randomly cut and paste some of their music together? • All of their work is so beautiful.

Sara: I can't. It's for my beloved Brownie. • You know I became sort of an animal rights activist since I got her. • I'm even against wearing fur coats and things like that.

Bomi: Oh, sorry. • I fully understand you. • By the way, what kinds of symptoms do dogs have during pregnancy? • Does she crave sour food like humans sometimes do? • Does she get moody?

Sara: She gets tired really easily. • That's easy to recognize. • She also seems more sensitive than usual. • And, her belly has enlarged quite a bit.

Bomi: So can you still take her for walks up that steep hill by your house?

Sara: No, but she still needs to work out regularly. • My mom is going to sew Brownie some new paw coverings to protect her feet.

Bomi: When are the puppies due?

Sara: The vet says in exactly five weeks.

Sara is busy composing music for Brownie. • I hope Brownie likes her music.

난 집에 오는 길에 사라를 우연히 만났다.

보미: 브라우니를 위한 작곡 마쳤니? 넌 바하, 베토벤과 모짜르트를 결합시킬 거라고 했잖아.
사라: 아직. 음악을 결합시켜서 조화를 이루게 하는 건 힘든 작업이야. 계속 수정하고 있어.
보미: 그 사람들의 음악 중에서 몇 가지를 임의로 잘라서 붙이는 건 어때? 모든 곡이 정말 아름답잖아.
사라: 그럴 수 없어. 내가 가장 사랑하는 브라우니를 위한 거잖아. 내가 브라우니를 얻은 후에 일종이 동물 권이 운동가가 된 거 너 알지. 난 털 코트와 그런 종류의 옷을 입는 것도 반대해.
보미: 아, 미안해. 널 충분히 이해해. 그건 그렇고, 개들은 임신했을 때 어떤 증상이 있지? 사람들이 가끔 그러는 것 처럼 신 음식을 먹고 싶어 하니? 침울해지니?
사라: 브라우니가 정말 쉽게 피로해져. 척 보면 알아. 평소보다 더 민감해 보이기도 해. 그리고 배가 꽤 부풀었어.
보미: 그래서 아직도 집 옆에 있는 경사진 언덕을 오르도록 산책시키니?
사라: 아니야, 그렇지만 그녀는 아직도 규칙적으로 운동을 할 필요가 있어. 우리 엄마가 브라우니의 발을 보호하는 새로운 발싸개를 바느질해 주실 거야.
보미: 강아지는 언제가 예정일이지?
사라: 수의사가 정확하게 5주면 태어난다고 말했어.

사라는 브라우니를 위해서 곡을 만드느라고 바쁘다. 난 브라우니가 사라의 음악을 좋아하기를 바란다.

encounter
[enkáuntər]
v. (우연히) 만나다, 마주치다
n. 마주침

I encountered Sara on my way home.
난 집에 오는 길에 우연히 사라를 만났다.

compose
[kəmpóuz]
v. 작곡하다

Did you finish composing some music for Brownie?
브라우니를 위한 작곡 마쳤니?

• composition n. 작곡, 작문 • composer n. 작곡가

combine
[kəmbáin]
v. 결합시키다, 조합하다

You said you were going to combine Bach, Beethoven, and Mozart.
넌 바하, 베토벤과 모짜르트를 결합시킬 거라고 했잖아.

• combination n. 결합, 조합

harmony
[háːrməni]
n. 조화

Not yet. It's hard to combine music and keep it in harmony. 아직. 음악을 결합시키면서 조화를 이루게 하는 건 힘든 작업이야.

• harmonize v. 조화시키다 • harmonious a. 조화로운
• harmoniously ad. 조화롭게 • keep ~ in harmony ~을 조화롭게 하다

revise
[riváiz]
v. 수정하다

I've been revising it constantly.
계속 수정하고 있어.

• revision n. 수정 • revised a. 수정된

constantly
[kánstəntli]
ad. 지속적으로

I've been revising it constantly.
계속 수정하고 있어.

• constant a. 지속적인

randomly
[rǽndəmli]
ad. 임의로

Why don't you just randomly cut and paste some of their music together?
그 사람들의 음악 중에서 몇 가지를 임의로 잘라서 붙이는 건 어때?

• randomize v. 무작위로 뽑다 • random a. 임의의, 무작위의

beloved
[bilʌ́vd]
a. 소중한, 가장 사랑하는

It's for my beloved Brownie.
내가 가장 사랑하는 브라우니를 위한 거잖아.

activist
[ǽktəvist]

n. 행동주의자

You know I became sort of an animal rights activist since I got her.
내가 브라우니를 얻은 후에 일종의 동물 권익 운동가가 된 거 너 알지.

• activism n. 행동주의

fur
[fəːr]

n. 털, 모피

I'm even against wearing fur coats and things like that.
난 털 코트와 그런 종류의 옷을 입는 것도 반대해.

• furry a. 털의, 모피의

fully
[fúli]

ad. 충분히

I fully understand you.
난 널 충분히 이해해.

• full a. 충분한

symptom
[símptəm]

n. 증상

By the way, what kinds of symptoms do dogs have during pregnancy?
그건 그렇고, 개들은 임신했을 때 어떤 증상이 있지?

pregnancy
[préɡnənsi]

n. 임신

By the way, what kinds of symptoms do dogs have during pregnancy?
그건 그렇고, 개들은 임신했을 때 어떤 증상이 있지?

• pregnant a. 임신한

crave
[kreiv]

v. 갈망하다,
간절히 원하다

Does she crave sour food like humans sometimes do?
사람들이 가끔 그러는 것처럼 브라우니도 신 음식을 먹고 싶어 하니?

• craving n. 갈망

sour
[sáuər]

a. 신
v. 시게 하다

Does she crave sour food like humans sometimes do?
사람들이 가끔 그러는 것처럼 브라우니도 신 음식을 먹고 싶어 하니?

moody
[múːdi]

a. 침울한, 변덕스러운

Does she get moody?
침울해지니?

recognize
[rékəgnàiz]

v. 알아보다, 인식하다

She gets tired really easily. That's easy to recognize.

브라우니가 정말 쉽게 피로해져. 그건 척 보면 알아.

• recognition n. 인식

sensitive
[sénsətiv]

a. 민감한

She also seems more sensitive than usual.

평소보다 더 민감해 보이기도 해.

• sensitivity n. 민감성   • sensible a. 분별력 있는

enlarge
[enláːrdʒ]

v. 확대하다

And, her belly has enlarged quite a bit.

그리고 배가 꽤 부풀었어.

• enlarged a. 확대된   • enlargement n. 확대

steep
[stiːp]

a. 경사진, 가파른

So can you still take her for walks up that steep hill by your house?

그래서 아직도 집 옆에 있는 경사진 언덕을 오르도록 산책시키니?

work out
[wə́ːrkàut]

v. 운동하다

No, but she still needs to work out regularly.

아니야, 그렇지만 그녀는 아직도 규칙적으로 운동을 할 필요가 있어.

• workout n. 운동

sew
[sou]

v. 바느질하다

My mom is going to sew Brownie some new paw coverings to protect her feet.

우리 엄마가 브라우니의 발을 보호하는 새로운 발싸개를 바느질해 주실거야.

due
[djuː]

a. ~하기로 되어 있는

When are the puppies due?

강아지는 언제가 예정일이지?

exactly
[igzǽktli]

ad. 정확하게

The vet says in exactly five weeks.

수의사가 정확하게 5주면 태어난다고 말했어.

• exact a. 정확한

Check Again!

A Translate each word into Korean.

1. encounter ....
2. fully ....
3. symptom ....
4. activist ....
5. fur ....
6. constantly ....
7. beloved ....
8. sew ....
9. enlarge ....
10. crave ....

B Translate each word into English.

1. 작곡하다 ....
2. 수정하다 ....
3. 임의로 ....
4. 민감한 ....
5. 운동하다 ....

C Fill in the blank with the appropriate word. Refer to the Korean.

1. We haven't met before. How can I r   you?

   저희는 전에 만난 적이 없어요. 제가 어떻게 알아볼 수 있을까요?

2. During my p   I was careful about food.

   임신 중에 나는 음식을 먹는 것에 조심했다.

3. There is a s   decline in the world economy.

   세계 경제에 가파른 하강세가 있다.

4. There is an excellent c   of colors in this picture.

   이 그림에는 탁월한 색의 조합이 있다.

5. A person with depression easily gets m   .

   우울증이 있는 사람은 쉽게 침울해진다.

Chapter 8
History, Art and Culture

Unit 24. What an interesting festival!

do belly dancing

perform in a **dynamic** break dance competition

Episode

Dear Diary,

In two weeks there will be a school festival. ● The **motto** of the festival is freedom and **independence**. ● I happened to **overhear** a conversation between some teachers. ● Even the teachers are going to have **special** performances at the festival. ● I heard some of the teachers will do **belly dancing**. ● Our history teacher will **undertake** the task of leading the dance team. ● The girls are **hilarious** because they can see the tight **muscles** of the history teacher. ● The boys are also **anxious** to watch the show. ● One of the **highlights** of the festival is going to be a street performance.

On the street, some students will perform in a **dynamic** break dance competition. ● It will be **terrific**. ● All the **pedestrians** walking by will get to see. ● Our new principal is very **liberal**. ● He seems to know what **freedom** means to students. ● He doesn't **condemn** us just because our ears are **pierced**. ● **Unfortunately**, our **previous** principal was different. ● For example, during **assemblies**, he always talked about dress **codes**. ● He also talked about the **duty** of students. ● That's why some students called his speeches **sermons**. ● Nowadays we feel as if a new **era** of freedom has begun. ● I expect this year's festival to be really fun.

다이어리에게,

두 주 후에 학교 축제가 있어. 축제의 표어는 자유와 독립이야. 난 우연히 몇몇 선생님들의 대화를 엿듣게 되었어. 선생님들도 축제에서 특별 공연을 할 거라고 해. 난 몇몇 선생님들이 밸리 댄스를 출 거라고 들었어. 우리 역사 선생님은 댄스 팀을 이끌 임무를 맡을 거야. 여학생들은 역사 선생님의 탄탄한 근육을 볼 수 있기 때문에 즐거울 거야. 남학생도 쇼를 보기를 기대하고 있어. 축제의 가장 중요한 부분 중 하나는 거리 공연이 될 거야.

거리에서 몇몇 학생들이 역동적인 브레이크 댄스 경연대회를 선보일 거야. 정말 멋질 거야. 지나가는 모든 행인들이 보게 될 거야. 우리 학교에 새로 오신 교장 선생님은 매우 개방적이셔. 그분은 자유가 학생들에게 어떤 의미인지 아시는 것 같아. 교장 선생님은 귀를 뚫었다는 이유만으로 우리를 혼내지 않으셔. 불행하게도 우리 학교의 전 교장 선생님은 달랐어. 예를 들면, 조회 중에 그분은 항상 복장 규정에 대해 언급하셨어. 그분은 또한 학생들의 의무에 대해 말씀하셨어. 그래서 몇몇 학생들은 그분의 연설을 설교라고 불렀어. 요즘 우리는 새로운 자유의 시대가 시작된 것 같은 느낌이야. 올해의 축제는 정말 재미있을 거라고 기대해.

motto
[mátou]
n. 표어, 모토

The motto of the festival is freedom and independence.
축제의 표어는 자유와 독립이야.

independence
[ìndipéndəns]
n. 독립

The motto of the festival is freedom and independence.
축제의 표어는 자유와 독립이야.

• independent a. 독립적인 • dependent a. 의존적인

overhear
[òuvərhíər]
v. 우연히 듣다

I happened to overhear a conversation between some teachers.
난 우연히 몇몇 선생님들의 대화를 엿듣게 되었어.

special
[spéʃəl]
a. 특별한

Even the teachers are going to have special performances at the festival.
선생님들도 축제에서 특별 공연을 할 거라고 해.

• specialty n. 전문, 전공

belly dancing
[béli dǽnsiŋ]
n. 밸리 댄스

I heard some of the teachers will do belly dancing.
난 몇몇 선생님들이 밸리 댄스를 출거라는 거라고 들었어.

undertake
[ʌ̀ndərtéik]
v. 책임을 맡다

Our history teacher will undertake the task of leading the dance team.
우리 역사 선생님은 댄스 팀을 이끌 임무를 맡을 거야.

hilarious
[hilέəriəs]
a. 유쾌한, 즐거운

The girls are hilarious because they can see the tight muscles of the history teacher.
여학생들은 역사 선생님의 탄탄한 근육을 볼 수 있기 때문에 즐거울 거야.

• hilariously ad. 즐겁게

muscle
[mʌ́səl]
n. 근육

The girls are hilarious because they can see the tight muscles of the history teacher.
여학생들은 역사 선생님의 탄탄한 근육을 볼 수 있기 때문에 즐거울 거야.

• muscular a. 근육의

anxious
[ǽŋkʃəs]
a. 열망하는, 걱정하는

The boys are also anxious to watch the show.
남학생도 쇼를 보기를 기대하고 있어.

• anxiety n. 열망, 근심 • be anxious to+V ~하기를 갈망하다

highlight
[háilàit]
n. 가장 중요한 부분
v. 강조하다

One of the highlights of the festival is going to be a street performance.
축제의 가장 중요한 부분 중 하나는 거리 공연이 될 거야.

dynamic
[dainǽmik]
a. 역동적인

On the street, some students will perform in a dynamic break dance competition.
거리에서 몇몇 학생들이 역동적인 브레이크 댄스 경연대회를 선보일 것거야.

terrific
[tərífik]
a. 굉장한, 멋진

It will be terrific.
정말 멋질 거야.

pedestrian
[pədéstriən]
n. 보행자, 행인
a. 도보의, 보행의

All the pedestrians walking by will get to see.
지나가는 모든 행인들이 보게 될 거야.

liberal
[líbərəl]
a. 개방적인, 자유주의의
n. 자유주의자

Our new principal is very liberal.
우리 학교에 새로 오신 교장 선생님은 매우 개방적이셔.

• liberate v. 자유롭게 만들다 • liberation n. 해방

freedom
[fríːdəm]
n. 자유

He seems to know what freedom means to students.
그분은 자유가 학생들에게 어떤 의미인지 아시는 것 같아.

• free a. 자유스러운

condemn
[kəndém]
v. 비난하다

He doesn't condemn us just because our ears are pierced.
교장 선생님은 귀를 뚫었다는 이유만으로 우리를 혼내지 않으셔.

• condemnation n. 비난 • condemnable a. 비난할 만한

pierce
[piərs]

v. ~에 구멍을 뚫다, 관통하다

He doesn't condemn us just because our ears are pierced.
교장 선생님은 귀를 뚫었다는 이유만으로 우리를 혼내지 않으셔.

• pierced a. 구멍이 난

unfortunately
[ʌnfɔ́:rtʃənitli]

ad. 불행하게도

Unfortunately, our previous principal was different.
불행하게도 우리 학교의 전 교장 선생님은 달랐어.

• unfortunate a. 불행한 • fortunately ad. 운 좋게도, 다행히도

previous
[prí:viəs]

a. 이전의

Unfortunately, our previous principal was different.
불행하게도 우리 학교의 전 교장 선생님은 달랐어.

• previously ad. 이전에

assembly
[əsémbli]

n. 집회

For example, during assemblies, he always talked about dress codes.
예를 들면, 조회 중에 그분은 항상 복장 규정에 대해 언급하셨어.

• assemble v. 모이다

code
[koud]

n. 규정

For example, during assemblies, he always talked about dress codes.
예를 들면, 조회 중에 그분은 항상 복장규정에 대해 언급하셨어.

duty
[djú:ti]

n. 의무

He also talked about the duty of students.
그분은 또한 학생들의 의무에 대해 말씀하셨어.

• dutiful a. 의무를 다하는

sermon
[sə́:rmən]

n. 설교

That's why some students called his speeches sermons.
그래서 몇몇 학생들은 그분의 연설을 설교라고 불렀어.

era
[íərə]

n. 시대

Nowadays we feel as if a new era of freedom has begun.
요즘 우리는 새로운 자유의 시대가 시작된 것 같은 느낌이야.

Check Again!

A Translate each word into Korean.

1. motto ....
2. highlight ....
3. assembly ....
4. muscle ....
5. overhear ....
6. era ....
7. hilarious ....
8. sermon ....
9. code ....
10. dynamic ....

B Translate each word into English.

1. 독립 ....
2. 이전의 ....
3. 개방적인 ....
4. 보행자 ....
5. 비난하다 ....

C Fill in the blank with the appropriate word. Refer to the Korean.

1. Laura will u_____ the task of monitoring the kids.

   로라는 아이들을 관리하는 일을 맡게 될 것이다.

2. The couple are a_____ to adopt a child.

   그 부부는 아이를 입양하고 싶어 한다.

3. Cindy wants to have her ears p_____.

   신디는 귀를 뚫고 싶어 한다.

4. U_____ his debut was not successful.

   불행하게도 그의 데뷔는 성공적이지 못했다.

5. The audience was impressed by the magician's t_____ skills.

   관객들은 마술사의 굉장한 기술에 감명받았다.

✚ 형용사나 부사로 쓰이는 -ly

형용사 뒤에 –ly가 붙어서 부사로 쓰이는 경우가 많으며 명사 뒤에 –ly가 붙어서
형용사로 사용되기도 한다.

형용사 + -ly

arrogant 거만한
arrogantly 거만하게

ex) Sometimes Sally behaves arrogantly.
가끔씩 샐리는 너무 거만하게 군다.

• **absolute** 완벽한	**absolutely** 완벽하게
• **rapid** 빠른	**rapidly** 빠르게
• **gradual** 점차적인	**gradually** 점진적으로
• **increasing** 증가하는	**increasingly** 더욱 더
• **immediate** 즉각적인	**immediately** 즉시

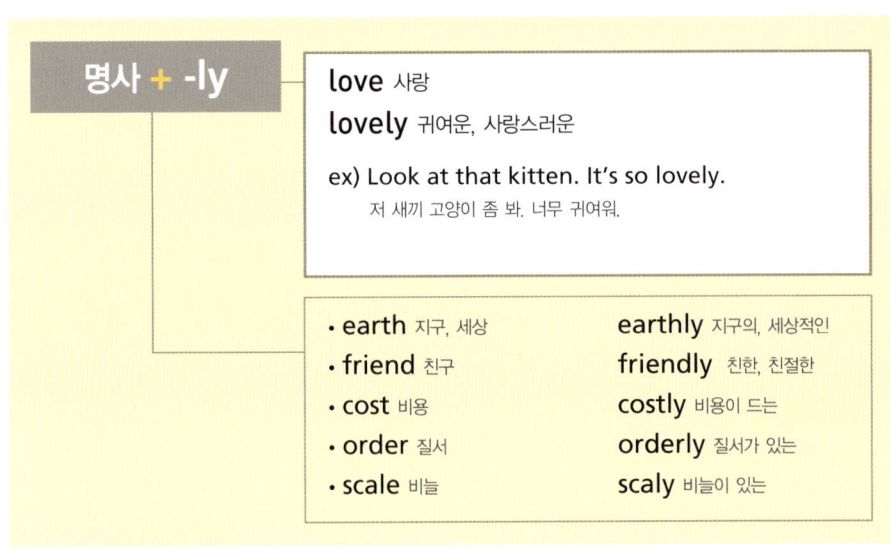

명사 + -ly

love 사랑
lovely 귀여운, 사랑스러운

ex) Look at that kitten. It's so lovely.
저 새끼 고양이 좀 봐. 너무 귀여워.

• **earth** 지구, 세상	**earthly** 지구의, 세상적인
• **friend** 친구	**friendly** 친한, 친절한
• **cost** 비용	**costly** 비용이 드는
• **order** 질서	**orderly** 질서가 있는
• **scale** 비늘	**scaly** 비늘이 있는

Art

- take a photo 사진을 찍다
- draw a picture 그림을 그리다
- mold the clay 진흙으로 형태를 만들다
- have an exhibition 전시회를 가지다
- build a statue 동상을 세우다

Culture Plus

Musical Instrument 악기

+ string(ed) instrument 현악기
+ percussion instrument 타악기
+ wind instrument 관악기
+ brass instrument 금관 악기
+ woodwind instrument 목관 악기
+ keyboard instrument 건반 악기

VOCA EDGE
BLUE

love you, Kite We moved today. I want to join the drama club. We have a team project

the send button. Kite will attend the wonder dog championship. Relationships count most

e! We made homemade pancakes. Hoony is taking taekwondo lessons. My dad's car is in

at an interesting festival! Sara's brother is running for president. Our school is doing an anti

has skin trouble. Mom has become a regular customer of ABC Mart. Mom is impressed by

Why do floods and droughts alternate? Astronauts need to know special drills. Two whale

nt facilities. We love you, Kite We moved today. I want to join the drama club. We have a

safari tour. I pressed the send button. Kite will attend the wonder dog championship

c. Mud cookies are terrible! We made homemade pancakes. Hoony is taking taekwondo

d music for Brownie. What an interesting festival! Sara's brother is running for president. Our

in art investment. Seri has skin trouble. Mom has become a regular customer of ABC Mart

v without sunlight. Why do floods and droughts alternate? Astronauts need to know specia

d boys use different facilities. We love you, Kite We moved today. I want to join the drama

. We went on a safari tour. I pressed the send button. Kite will attend the wonder dog

e to a growth clinic. Mud cookies are terrible! We made homemade pancakes. Hoony i

Chapter 9. Politics and Social Issues

emorial. Sara composed music for Brownie. What an interesting festival! Sara's brother

Unit 25. Sara's brother is running for president.

is horrible. Dad is interested in art investment. Seri has skin trouble. Mom has become

Unit 26. Our school is doing an anti-suicide campaign.

good and bad. Plants can grow without sunlight. Why do floods and droughts alterna

Unit 27. The recent food scandal is horrible.

is puberty? Visit my blog Girls and boys use different facilities. We love you, Kite We moved

e. There will be a talent show. We went on a safari tour. I pressed the send button. Kite wa

in the same boat. I go to a growth clinic. Mud cookies are terrible! We made homemade

trip to the War Memorial. Sara composed music for Brownie. What an interesting festiva

Chapter 9
Politics and Social Issues

Unit 25. Sara's brother is running for president.

suggest that the school **install a lift**

be not sufficient

Episode

Seri: Sara's brother, Dongwoo, is **running** for school president. • He is quite **capable** of doing a good job. • His speeches were very **distinctive**. • And, they were also a bit **radical**. • Most other speeches were about how to **conform** to school **regulations**. • But Dongwoo explains why **specific** things should be done. • He suggested that the school **install** a lift. • He said that there should be one to help **disabled** students.

Bomi: Are you going to **vote** for him?

Seri: Sure. • Dongwoo knows what is **necessary** to make **improvements**. • One of my classmates has **trouble** moving his wheelchair to the fifth floor. • He can't use the stairs, so he uses a **ramp**. • Once his wheelchair **slipped** and he broke his arm. • Also for the girls' **sake**, he suggested that the school install more toilets in the girls' restroom. • **Compared** to the boys' restroom, the number of toilets we have is not **sufficient**.

Bomi: Interesting!

Last week, Sara showed me Dongwoo's **manuscript**. • It was great but it was full of boy's **stuff**. • There wasn't much for the **female** students. • Sara and I **recollected** our elementary school days. • We thought we could help him become a **desirable** candidate if we gave him some information **relevant** to female students' needs. • We hope it will make a difference, even if it is just a **subtle** difference. • Sara and I hope Dongwoo is elected president.

세리: 사라 언니 동생, 동우가 학생회장에 출마한대. 그 아이는 정말 학생회장에 적임자야. 그 아이가 하는 연설은 정말로 독창적이고 약간은 획기적이었지. 대부분의 다른 연설들은 학교 규정을 따르는 법에 관한 것이었어. 하지만 동우는 왜 구체적인 일들이 이루어져야 하는지를 설명해 주지. 그 아이는 학교에서 엘리베이터를 설치해 줄 것을 제안했어. 그 아이는 장애우들을 도와줄 엘리베이터 하나가 있어야 한다고 말했어.

보미: 넌 그 아이에게 투표할 거니?

세리: 물론이지. 동우는 상황을 개선하려면 무엇이 필요한지를 알아. 우리 반 아이 중 한 명은 5층까지 휠체어를 옮기느라 어려움을 겪지. 계단을 이용할 수 없기 때문에 경사로를 이용해. 한번은 휠체어가 미끄러져서 팔이 부러졌어. 게다가 여학생들을 위해서 그 애는 학교가 여학생 화장실에 변기를 좀 더 설치해 줄 것을 제안했지. 남학생 화장실에 비교해 볼 때, 변기 숫자가 충분하지 않거든.

보미: 흥미로운데!

지난주에 사라는 나에게 동우가 쓴 원고를 보여 주었다. 그것은 훌륭했지만 온통 남자애들에 관한 내용이었다. 여학생에 관한 것은 많지 않았다. 사라와 나는 우리 초등학교 시절을 생각해 보았다. 우리가 그 아이에게 여학생에 관련된 정보를 준다면 동우가 바람직한 후보가 되는 데 도움을 줄 수 있다고 생각했다. 우리는 그것이 비록 미세한 차이일지라도 변화를 가져올 수 있기를 바란다. 사라와 나는 동우가 학생회장에 뽑히기를 바란다.

run
[rʌn]
v. 출마하다

Sara's brother, Dongwoo, is running for school president.
사라 언니의 동생, 동우가 학생회장에 출마한대.

capable
[kéipəbl]
a. ~할 수 있는

He is quite capable of doing a good job.
그 아이는 정말 학생회장에 적임자야.

• capability n. 능력 • be capable of ~을 할 수 있다

distinctive
[distíŋktiv]
a. 특유의, 특색있는

His speeches were very distinctive.
그 아이가 하는 연설은 정말로 독창적이었어.

• distinction n. 구별 • distinct a. 뚜렷한, 구별되는

radical
[rǽdikəl]
a. 급진적인, 획기적인

And, they were also a bit radical.
그리고 그 아이가 한 연설문은 약간은 획기적이었지.

conform
[kənfɔ́ːrm]
v. 따르다, 순응하다

Most other speeches were about how to conform to school regulations.
대부분의 다른 연설들은 학교 규정을 따르는 법에 관한 것이었어.

• conformity n. 준수 • conform to ~을 따르다

regulation
[règjuléiʃən]
n. 규정

Most other speeches were about how to conform to school regulations.
대부분의 다른 연설들은 학교 규정을 따르는 법에 관한 것이었어.

• regulate v. 규제하다

specific
[spisífik]
a. 구체적인, 특정한

But Dongwoo explains why specific things should be done.
하지만 동우는 왜 구체적인 일들이 이루어져야 하는지를 설명해 주지.

• specify v. 구체적으로 실명하다 • specification n. 열거

install
[instɔ́ːl]
v. 설치하다

He suggested that the school install a lift.
그 아이는 학교에서 엘리베이터를 설치해 줄 것을 제안했어.

• installation n. 설치

disabled
[diséibld]
a. 장애가 있는, 불구가 된

He said that there should be one to help disabled students.
그 아이는 장애우들을 도와줄 엘리베이터 하나가 있어야 한다고 말했어.

• disable v. 무력화 하다, 불구로 만들다 • disability n. 장애, 무능

vote
[vout]

v. 투표하다 n. 투표

Are you going to vote for him?
넌 그 아이에게 투표할 거니?

• vote for ~에게 투표하다

necessary
[nésəsèri]

a. 필요한

Dongwoo knows what is necessary to make improvements. 동우는 상황을 개선하려면 무엇이 필요한지를 알아.

• necessity n. 필요

improvement
[imprúːvmənt]

n. 향상

Dongwoo knows what is necessary to make improvements. 동우는 상황을 개선하려면 무엇이 필요한지를 알아.

• improve v. 향상시키다 • make an improvement 향상시키다

trouble
[trʌ́bəl]

n. 문제
v. 괴롭히다, 걱정시키다

One of my classmates has trouble moving his wheelchair to the fifth floor.
우리 반 아이 중 한 명은 5층까지 휠체어를 옮기느라 어려움을 겪지.

• have trouble -ing ~하느라 어려움을 겪다

ramp
[ræmp]

n. 경사로

He can't use the stairs, so he uses a ramp.
그 아이는 계단을 이용할 수 없기 때문에 경사로를 이용해.

• ramped a. 비탈진

slip
[slip]

v. 미끄러지다

Once his wheelchair slipped and he broke his arm.
한번은 휠체어가 미끄러져서 팔이 부러졌어.

• slippery a. 미끄러운

sake
[seik]

n. 위함, 이익

Also, for the girls' sake, he suggested that the school install more toilets in the girls' restroom.
게다가 여학생들을 위해서 그 애는 학교가 여학생 화장실에 변기를 좀 더 설치해 줄 것을 제안했지.

• for one's sake ~를 위해서

compare
[kəmpέər]

v. 비교하다

Compared to the boys' restroom, the number of toilets we have is not sufficient.
남학생 화장실에 비교해 볼 때, 변기 숫자가 충분하지 않거든.

• comparison n. 비교 • comparable a. 비교할 수 있는
• compared to ~에 비교해 볼 때

sufficient
[səfíʃənt]
a. 충분한

Compared to the boys' restroom, the number of toilets we have is not sufficient.
남학생 화장실에 비교해 볼 때, 변기 숫자가 충분하지 않거든.

• suffice v. 만족시키다, 충족시키다

manuscript
[mǽnjuskrìpt]
n. 원고

Last week, Sara showed me Dongwoo's manuscript.
지난주에 사라는 나에게 동우가 쓴 원고를 보여 주었다.

stuff
[stʌf]
n. 물질, 재료

It was great but it was full of boy's stuff.
그것은 훌륭했지만 온통 남자애들에 관한 내용이었다.

female
[fíːmeil]
a. 여성의 n. 여성

There wasn't much for the female students.
여학생에 관한 것은 많지 않았다.

• male a. 남성의 n. 남성

recollect
[rèkəlékt]
v. 회상하다

Sara and I recollected our elementary school days.
사라와 나는 우리 초등학교 시절을 생각해 보았다.

• recollection n. 회상, 회고

desirable
[dizáiərəbl]
a. 바람직한

We thought we could help him become a desirable candidate if we gave him some information relevant to female students' needs. 우리가 그 아이에게 여학생에 관련된 정보를 준다면 동우가 바람직한 후보가 되는 데 도움을 줄 수 있다고 생각했다.

• desire v. 바라다 • desirability n. 바람직함

relevant
[réləvənt]
a. 관련된, 적절한

We thought we could help him become a desirable candidate if we gave him some information relevant to female students' needs. 우리가 그 아이에게 여학생에 관련된 정보를 준다면 동우가 바람직한 후보가 되는 데 도움을 줄 수 있다고 생각했다.

• relevantly ad. 적절하게 • irrelevant a. 관련이 없는

subtle
[sʌ́tl]
a. 미묘한, 미세한

We hope it will make a difference, even if it is just a subtle difference.
우리는 그것이 비록 미세한 차이일지라도 변화를 가져올 수 있기를 바란다.

• subtlety n. 미묘, 민감

Check Again!

A Translate each word into Korean.

1. radical ....
2. slip ....
3. regulation ....
4. disabled ....
5. distinctive ....
6. stuff ....
7. desirable ....
8. recollect ....
9. female ....
10. subtle ....

B Translate each word into English.

1. 원고 ....
2. 출마하다 ....
3. 경사로 ....
4. 구체적인 ....
5. 설치하다 ....

C Fill in the blank with the appropriate word. Refer to the Korean.

1. C_____ to fresh vegetables, canned vegetables are not delicious.
   신선한 야채와 비교할 때, 통조림으로 된 야채는 맛이 없다.

2. There has been a big i_____ in my brother's behavior.
   내 남동생의 행동에는 많은 발전이 있어 왔다.

3. Could you give Laura some advice for her s_____?
   로라를 위해서 그녀에게 조언을 해 줄 수 있겠니?

4. They tried to c_____ to safety standards.
   그들은 안전 수칙을 따르려고 노력했다.

5. Your answer is not r_____ to my point.
   당신의 대답은 제 요지와 관련이 없어요.

be astonished by the tragic news

take a survey

Episode

Dear Diary,
My classmates were talking about the death of another star. ● One of the nation's top stars committed suicide. ● People were astonished by the tragic news of her death.

She looked so elegant and happy on TV. ● She seemed so mentally tough. ● No one expected she would perish so easily. ● It turns out that her personal life was quite the opposite of her public life. ● There was a debate about the cause of her death. ● People were trying to make a connection between her death and her personal problems. ● Some people say her sudden death was due to depression derived from problems in her personal life. ● Others say she was becoming very distressed about family matters. ● She must have been suppressing her personal anguish whenever she was in public. ● She must have had such a hard time.

After lunch, all the students took a survey. ● It was conducted by a committee called "Teens' Happy Life." ● The aim of "Teens' Happy Life" is to prevent teen suicides. ● Most of the questions in the survey were related to our psychological condition. ● The questions were as follows: ● If you have problems, who is the first person you consult? ● Have you ever attempted suicide? ● What is the best method for preventing suicide among teens? ● Do you think anti-suicide campaigns are effective?
I hope all the teens live a happy life.

다이어리에게,
우리 반 아이들이 또 다른 스타의 죽음에 관해서 이야기하고 있었어. 우리나라의 유명 스타 중 한 사람이 자살을 했거든. 사람들은 그녀가 죽었다는 비극적인 소식에 충격을 받았어.

TV에서 본 그녀는 너무나 우아하고 행복해 보였지. 그녀는 정신적으로 강인해 보였어. 어느 누구도 그녀가 그렇게 쉽게 죽을 것이라고 생각하지 못했어. 그녀의 개인적인 삶은 공인으로서의 삶과 완전히 반대라는 것이 드러난 거야. 그녀의 죽음을 둘러싼 원인을 놓고 토론이 벌어졌어. 사람들은 그녀의 죽음과 개인적인 문제를 연관시키려 하고 있었어. 어떤 사람들은 그녀의 갑작스런 죽음이 그녀의 개인적인 삶에서 생겨난 우울증 탓이었다고 말해. 다른 사람들은 그녀가 가족 문제로 너무나 괴로워했다고 해. 그녀가 대중 앞에 설 때마다 그녀는 자신의 개인적인 고통을 억눌러 왔음이 틀림없어. 그녀는 정말로 힘든 시간을 보냈을 거야.

점심을 먹고 나서 모든 학생들이 설문조사를 받아. 그것은 "십대의 행복한 삶"이라는 한 위원회에서 실시한 거야. "십대의 행복한 삶"의 목적은 십대의 자살을 예방하는 거야. 설문지의 질문들은 대체로 우리의 심리적인 상황과 관련된 것이었어. 질문은 다음과 같았어. 만일 문제가 있으면 당신은 누구에게 가장 처음으로 의논을 합니까? 자살을 시도해 본 적이 있습니까? 십대의 자살을 예방하기 위한 최선의 방법은 무엇입니까? 자살 반대 캠페인이 효과가 있다고 생각합니까? 나는 십대 모두가 행복한 삶을 살기를 바래.

commit
[kəmít]
v. 저지르다

One of the nation's top stars committed suicide.
우리나라의 유명 스타 중 한 사람이 자살을 했어.
• commitment n. 수행, 범행

suicide
[súːəsàid]
n. 자살

One of the nation's top stars committed suicide.
우리나라의 유명 스타 중 한 사람이 자살을 했어.
• suicidal a. 자살의 • commit suicide 자살하다

astonish
[əstániʃ]
v. 놀라게 하다

People were astonished by the tragic news of her death. 사람들은 그녀가 죽었다는 비극적인 소식에 충격을 받았어.
• astonishment n. 놀람 • astonished a. 놀란, 충격을 받은

tragic
[trǽdʒik]
a. 비극적인

People were astonished by the tragic news of her death. 사람들은 그녀가 죽었다는 비극적인 소식에 충격을 받았어.
• tragedy n. 비극

elegant
[éləgənt]
a. 우아한

She looked so elegant and happy on TV.
TV에서 본 그녀는 너무나 우아하고 행복해 보였지.
• elegance n. 우아함

tough
[tʌf]
a. 강인한

She seemed so mentally tough.
그녀는 정신적으로 강인해 보였어.
• toughness n. 강인함

perish
[périʃ]
v. 사라지다, 죽다

No one expected she would perish so easily.
어느 누구도 그녀가 그렇게 쉽게 죽을 것이라고 생각하지 못했어.
• perishable a. 죽기 쉬운, 썩기 쉬운

opposite
[ápəzit]
n. 정반대
a. 정반대인

It turns out that her personal life was quite the opposite of her public life.
그녀의 개인적인 삶은 공인으로서의 삶과 완전히 반대라는 것이 드러난 거야.

debate
[dibéit]
n. 토론 v. 토론하다

There was a debate about the cause of her death.
그녀의 죽음을 둘러싼 원인을 놓고 토론이 벌어졌어.

connection
[kənékʃən]

n. 연관, 관련

People were trying to make a connection between her death and her personal problems.

사람들은 그녀의 죽음과 개인적인 문제를 연관시키려 하고 있었어.

• connect v. 연관시키다, 연결하다
• make a connection between A and B A와 B를 연관시키다

depression
[dipréʃən]

n. 우울증

Some people say her sudden death was due to depression derived from problems in her personal life.

어떤 사람들은 그녀의 갑작스런 죽음이 개인적인 삶에서 생겨난 우울증 탓이었다고 말해.

• depress v. 우울하게 하다 • depressed a. 낙담한, 우울한

derive
[diráiv]

v. 끌어내다, 유래하다

Some people say her sudden death was due to depression derived from problems in her personal life.

어떤 사람들은 그녀의 갑작스런 죽음이 그녀의 개인적인 삶에서 생겨난 우울증 탓이었다고 말해.

• derived a. 유래된 • derivation n. 유래, 파생

distressed
[distrést]

a. 괴로워하는

Others say she was becoming very distressed about family matters.

다른 사람들은 그녀가 가족 문제로 너무나 괴로워했다고 말해.

• distress v. 괴롭히다 n. 괴로움

suppress
[səprés]

v. 억누르다

She must have been suppressing her personal anguish whenever she was in public.

그녀가 대중 앞에 설 때마다 무엇인가가 그녀의 개인적인 고통을 억눌러 왔음이 틀림없어.

• suppression n. 억압, 탄압

anguish
[æŋgwiʃ]

n. 고뇌, 번민

She must have been suppressing her personal anguish whenever she was in public.

그녀가 대중 앞에 설 때마다 무엇인가가 그녀의 개인적인 고통을 억눌러 왔음이 틀림없어.

survey
[səːrvéi]

n. 설문조사
v. 설문조사를 하다

After lunch, all the students took a survey.

전신을 먹고 나서 모든 착생들이 설문조시를 받았이.

• take a survey 설문조사를 받다

conduct
[kəndʌ́kt]

v. 실시하다, 행하다
n. 행위, 행실

It was conducted by a committee called "Teens' Happy Life."

그것은 "십대의 행복한 삶"이라는 위원회에서 실시한 거야.

• conducted a. 행해진, 실시된

committee
[kəmíti]

n. 위원회

It was conducted by a committee called "Teens' Happy Life."
그것은 "십대의 행복한 삶"이라는 한 위원회에서 실시한 거야.

aim
[eim]

n. 목표
v. 목표로 삼다

The aim of "Teens' Happy Life" is to prevent teen suicides.
"십대의 행복한 삶"의 목적은 십대의 자살을 예방하는 거야.

• aimed a. 겨누어진

prevent
[privént]

v. 예방하다

The aim of "Teens' Happy Life" is to prevent teen suicides.
"십대의 행복한 삶"의 목적은 십대의 자살을 예방하는 거야.

• prevention n. 예방 • preventable a. 예방할 수 있는

psychological
[sàikəládʒikəl]

a. 심리적인

Most of the questions in the survey were related to our psychological condition.
설문지의 질문들은 대체로 우리의 심리적인 상황과 관련된 거야.

• psychology n. 심리

consult
[kənsΛlt]

v. 상의하다, 의견을 묻다

If you have problems, who is the first person you consult?
만일 문제가 있으면 당신은 누구에게 가장 처음으로 의논을 합니까?

• consultation n. 상의, 상담

attempt
[ətémpt]

v. 시도하다 n. 시도

Have you ever attempted suicide?
자살을 시도해 본 적이 있습니까?

method
[méθəd]

n. 방법

What is the best method for preventing suicide among teens?
십대의 자살을 예방하기 위한 최선의 방법은 무엇입니까?

• methodology n. 방법론 • methodical a. 방법론적인

campaign
[kæmpéin]

n. 캠페인
v. 캠페인을 벌이다

Do you think anti-suicide campaigns are effective?
자살 반대 캠페인이 효과가 있다고 생각합니까?

Check Again!

A Translate each word into Korean.

1. derive ....   2. conduct ....

3. method ....   4. tough ....

5. anguish ....   6. committee ....

7. psychological ....   8. aim ....

9. attempt ....   10. astonish ....

B Translate each word into English.

1. 토론 ....

2. 억누르다 ....

3. 사라지다 ....

4. 비극적인 ....

5. 예방하다 ....

C Fill in the blank with the appropriate word. Refer to the Korean.

1. There is a close c   between smoking and lung cancer.

   흡연과 폐암은 긴밀하게 연관되어 있다.

2. Why did he c   suicide without leaving a suicide note?

   왜 그는 유서도 남기지 않고 자살을 한 것일까?

3. Are you still looking for someone you c   ?

   아직도 상담을 할 사람을 찾고 있니?

4. How come you said you'd do one thing, and then did the

   o   ?

   너는 어떻게 하겠다고 말한 것과 정반대로 할 수가 있니?

5. The bride looks so e   . I like her wedding dress.

   신부가 너무 우아해 보여요. 난 신부가 입은 웨딩드레스가 마음에 들어요.

Chapter 9
Politics and Social Issues

Unit 27. The recent food scandal is horrible.

ask to **have a bite of** a cookie

be focused on the food scandal

rid the shelves **of** something

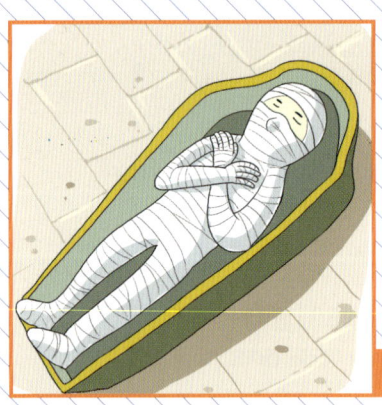

be mummified

Episode

For a whole week every news channel has been **focused** on the melamine **scandal**.

Hoony: Can I just have one **bite** of this cookie? ● Is melamine as harmful as **preservatives** or **artificial flavors**?
Mom: We don't know but the ingredients could be **deadly** to kids.
Hoony: Why would **adults** put harmful ingredients into snacks? ● It's **ridiculous** that they would do something like that. ● They are really **wicked**. ● How could they do that on **purpose**?
Mom: Maybe their brains don't **readily** react to anything but money. ● They should be **expelled** from society and put in **jail** for ever.

Mom became very **resentful** towards those manufacturers when she read about them in the paper. ● She said all the supermarkets should **rid** their shelves of those kinds of snacks. ● Some of the people **in charge** of this matter appeared on TV. ● They **swore** to **uproot** these problems before they start in the future. ● Some **representatives** of the companies that were involved in the scandal made **formal** apologies. ● Food scandals seem to **continually** occur. ● We're **used to** hearing Mom say, "Homemade food is best." ● She even makes jokes that our bodies could be **mummified**. ● She says that they'll never **decay** because of all the preservatives in store-bought food.

일주일 내내 모든 뉴스가 멜라민 파동에 집중되었다.
후니: 이 과자 한 입만 먹어도 돼요? 멜라민이 방부제나 인공 감미료처럼 해로워요?
엄마: 확실하게는 모르지만 그 성분이 아이들에게 치명적일 수 있지.
후니: 왜 어른들은 과자에 해로운 성분을 넣는 거죠? 어른들이 그런 일을 하다니 어처구니가 없어요. 그런 사람들은 정말 사악해요. 어떻게 일부러 그런 짓을 할 수 있어요?
엄마: 아마 그 사람들의 머리가 돈에만 빠르게 반응하는 것이겠지. 그 사람들은 사회에서 추방되어 영원히 감옥에서 살아야 해.

엄마는 신문을 읽으면서 제조업자들에 대해서 분개하였다. 엄마는 모든 슈퍼마켓이 진열대에서 그런 과자를 치워 버려야 한다고 말씀하셨다. 이 문제에 대해 책임이 있는 사람들이 TV에 나왔다. 그들은 앞으로 이러한 문제들을 사전에 근절하겠다고 맹세했다. 이 파동과 관련된 회사의 몇몇 대표들은 공식적인 사과를 했다. 먹거리 파동은 끊임없이 일어나는 것 같다. 우리는 엄마가, "집에서 만든 음식이 최고야."라고 말하는 것을 듣는 데 익숙하다. 엄마는 심지어 우리 몸이 미이라처럼 될 것이란 농담을 하시기도 한다. 엄마는 가게에서 사는 음식에 들어 있는 방부제 때문에 우리 몸이 절대 썩지 않을 것이라고 말씀하신다.

focus
[fóukəs]

v. 집중시키다
n. 집중

For a whole week every news channel has been focused on the melamine scandal.
일주일 내내 모든 뉴스가 멜라민 파동에 집중되었다.

• focus on ~에 집중하다

scandal
[skǽndl]

n. 추문, 비방

For a whole week every news channel has been focused on the melamine scandal.
일주일 내내 모든 뉴스가 멜라민 파동에 집중되었다.

bite
[bait]

n. 한 입   v. 깨물다

Can I just have one bite of this cookie?
이 과자 한 입만 먹어도 돼요?

• bite - bit - bitten

preservative
[prizə́ːrvətiv]

n. 방부제

Is melamine as harmful as preservatives or artificial flavors?
멜라민이 방부제나 인공 감미료처럼 해로와요?

• preserve v. 보존하다   • preservation n. 보존

artificial
[ὰːrtəfíʃəl]

a. 인공적인
n. 인공물

Is melamine as harmful as preservatives or artificial flavors?
멜라민이 방부제나 인공 감미료처럼 해로와요?

• natural a. 자연의, 천연의

flavor
[fléivər]

n. 풍미, 향미

Is melamine as harmful as preservatives or artificial flavors?
멜라민이 방부제나 인공 감미료처럼 해로와요?

deadly
[dédli]

a. 치명적인

We don't know but the ingredients could be deadly to kids.
확실하게는 모르지만 그 성분이 아이들에게 치명적일 수 있지.

adult
[ədʌ́lt]

n. 성인, 어른

Why would adults put harmful ingredients into snacks?
왜 어른들은 과자에 해로운 성분을 넣는 거죠?

• adulthood n. 성인기

ridiculous
[ridíkjuləs]

a. 터무니없는

It's ridiculous that they would do something like that.
어른들이 그런 일을 하다니 어처구니가 없어요.

wicked
[wíkid]
a. 사악한

They are really wicked.
그런 사람들은 정말 사악해요.

• wickedness n. 사악함

purpose
[pə́ːrpəs]
n. 의도

How could they do that on purpose?
어떻게 일부러 그런 짓을 할 수 있어요?

• on purpose 고의로

readily
[rédəli]
ad. 즉시, 손쉽게

Maybe their brains don't readily react to anything but money.
아마 그 사람들의 머리가 돈에만 빠르게 반응하는 것이겠지.

expel
[ikspél]
v. 추방하다

They should be expelled from society and put in jail for ever.
그 사람들은 사회에서 추방되어 영원히 감옥에서 살아야 해.

• expulsion n. 추방

jail
[dʒeil]
n. 감옥

They should be expelled from society and put in jail for ever.
그 사람들은 사회에서 추방되어 영원히 감옥에서 살아야 해.

resentful
[rizéntfəl]
a. 분개한

Mom became very resentful towards those manufacturers when she read about them in the paper.
엄마는 신문을 읽으면서 제조업자들에 대해서 분개하셨다.

• resent v. 분개하다 • resentment n. 분개

rid
[ríd]
v. 없애다

She said all the supermarkets should rid their shelves of those kinds of snacks.
엄마는 모든 슈퍼마켓이 진열대에서 그런 과자를 치워 버려야 한다고 말씀하셨다.

• rid A of B A에서 B를 없애다

in charge
[ín tʃɑːrdʒ]
책임을 맡은

Some of the people in charge of this matter appeared on TV.
이 문제에 대해 책임이 있는 사람들이 TV에 나왔다.

swear

[swɛər]

v. 맹세하다

They swore to uproot these problems before they start in the future.

그들은 앞으로 이러한 문제들을 사전에 근절하겠다고 맹세했다.

• swear - swore - sworn

uproot

[ʌprúːt]

v. 근절하다, 뿌리 뽑다

They swore to uproot these problems before they start in the future.

그들은 앞으로 이러한 문제들을 사전에 근절하겠다고 맹세했다.

representative

[rèprizéntətiv]

n. 대표

Some representatives of the companies that were involved in the scandal made formal apologies.

이 파동과 관련된 회사의 몇몇 대표들은 공식적인 사과를 했다.

• represent v. 대표하다 • representation n. 대표, 대리

formal

[fɔ́ːrməl]

a. 공식적인

Some representatives of the companies that were involved in the scandal made formal apologies.

이 파동과 관련된 회사의 몇몇 대표들은 공식적인 사과를 했다.

• formality n. 정식, 관습 • informal a. 비공식적인

continually

[kəntínjuəli]

ad. 끊임없이

Food scandals seem to continually occur.

먹거리 파동은 끊임없이 일어나는 것 같다.

• continue v. 계속하다 • continuous a. 연속적인

used to

[juːst tuː]

~에 익숙한

We're used to hearing Mom say, "Homemade food is best."

우리는 엄마가, "집에서 만든 음식이 최고야."라고 말하는 것을 듣는 데 익숙하다.

mummify

[mʌ́mifài]

v. 미라로 만들다

She even makes jokes that our bodies could be mummified.

엄마는 심지어 우리 몸이 미이라처럼 될 것이란 농담을 하시기도 한다.

• mummy n. 미라 • mummified a. 미라로 만든

decay

[dikéi]

v. 부패하다
n. 부패

She says that they'll never decay because of all the preservatives in store-bought food.

엄마는 가게에서 사는 음식에 들어있는 방부제 때문에 우리 몸이 절대 썩지 않을 것이라고 말씀하신다.

• decayed a. 부패한

Check Again!

A Translate each word into Korean.

1. artificial ....
2. readily ....
3. formal ....
4. swear ....
5. decay ....
6. representative ....
7. mummify ....
8. ridiculous ....
9. adult ....
10. flavor ....

B Translate each word into English.

1. 분개한 ....
2. 추문 ....
3. 치명적인 ....
4. 사악한 ....
5. 근절하다 ....

C Fill in the blank with the appropriate word. Refer to the Korean.

1. He lied to his girlfriend several times on p   .

   그는 고의로 여자친구에게 몇 차례 거짓말을 했다.

2. Chuck is in c   of the marketing department.

   척이 마케팅 부서의 책임자이다.

3. James is u   to walking his dog after dinner.

   제임스는 저녁을 먹고 난 후 개를 산책시키는 것에 익숙하다.

4. When are you going to r   the drawer of your old clothes?

   언제 옷장에서 오래된 옷을 없앨 거죠?

5. This book is f   on how to stay healthy.

   이 책은 건강을 유지하는 법에 초점이 맞추어져 있어요.

✦ 혼동하기 쉬운 말

일부 단어는 철자가 비슷하거나 발음이 비슷해서 혼동하는 경우가 많다. 또한 어떤 단어는 여러 가지 의미로 쓰이므로 문맥에 따라 의미를 파악해야 한다.

철자·발음이 비슷한 말

adapt 적응시키다

adopt 채택하다, 입양하다

ex) Laura was adopted by a new family.
   She needs to adapt herself to a new setting.
   로라는 새로운 가정에 입양되었다.
   그 아이는 새로운 환경에 적응할 필요가 있다.

- **affect** 영향을 주다   **effect** 영향, 효과
- **follow** 따라가다   **fellow** 동료
- **wander** 방황하다   **wonder** 놀라다, 의아하게 생각하다
- **personal** 개인적인   **personnel** 직원, 인사부
- **high** 높은, 비싼   **highly** 매우
- **sow** 씨를 뿌리다   **sew** 바느질을 하다
- **thorough** 완전한, 철저한   **through** ~을 통하여
- **zealous** 열심인   **jealous** 시샘하는

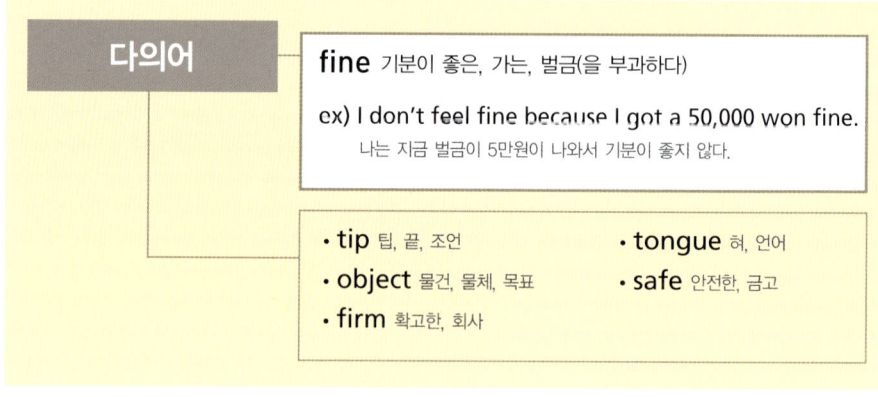

다의어

fine 기분이 좋은, 가는, 벌금(을 부과하다)

ex) I don't feel fine because I got a 50,000 won fine.
   나는 지금 벌금이 5만원이 나와서 기분이 좋지 않다.

- **tip** 팁, 끝, 조언   • **tongue** 혀, 언어
- **object** 물건, 물체, 목표   • **safe** 안전한, 금고
- **firm** 확고한, 회사

Expressing Opinions

- nod one s head 고개를 끄덕이다
  shake one s head 고개를 가로젓다

- accept 수락하다
  refuse 거절하다

- demand 주장하다
  excuse 변명하다

- be for~ ~에 찬성하다
  be against ~에 반대하다

- agree with someone ~의 의견에 동의하다
  disagree with someone ~의 의견에 반대하다

Culture Plus

Politics 정치

+ president 대통령
+ vice-president 부통령
+ Cabinet 내각
+ national assembly 국회
+ congressman 국회의원
+ party 정당

+ ruling party 여당
+ opposition party 야당

VOCA
EDGE
BLUE

Chapter 10. Economy

Unit 28. Dad is interested in art investment.

Unit 29. Seri has skin trouble.

Unit 30. Mom has become a regular customer of ABC Mart.

Chapter 10
Economy

Unit 28. Dad is interested in art investment.

bring a piece of **pottery**

tear something **open**

be doubtful

Episode

Dear Diary,

Dad brought a piece of **pottery** home. ● He bought it from a store selling **antique** furniture. ● Dad says it will be a good **investment**, expecting a good return. ● Mom complains that it's like **gambling**. ● She was **irritated** by the pottery. ● She said that it was far beyond the **budget** he was supposed to spend. ● Since Dad watched a TV program **evaluating** art, he has sometimes bought art. ● Mom worries that he might buy some items with no economic **value**. ● She is not **optimistic** about its **current** value, either. ● She worries that Dad spends money on **junk**. ● Mom says Dad has to choose investment **items** under an expert's **guidance**. ● She suggests Dad buy some foreign **currencies** as an investment. ● She says Dad needs to save money in preparation for his **retirement**. ● Although Dad says he has a **pension fund**, Mom thinks the pension fund is not enough.

Hoony says his piggy bank is **leaking** as if it had a hole. ● I know that his piggy bank has already been **torn** open. ● Once he collects a certain **amount** of money, he spends it on cards or wooden models.

Seri showed me a draft of her jewelry box and an ad for a design contest. ● She is thinking about **carving** her name on the **surface** of the box. ● Maybe she thinks she needs her own **autograph** like famous stars. ● It's **doubtful** if her autograph will raise the value of the box. ● But I hope Seri's jewelry box will win the contest.

다이어리에게,
아빠가 도자기 한 점을 집에 가지고 오셨어. 아빠는 그것을 고가구점에서 사셨지. 아빠는 그것이 수익이 괜찮을 것이라고 예상하시면서 괜찮은 투자가 될 것이라고 말씀하셔. 엄마는 그것이 도박이나 다름없다고 불평하시고, 도자기 때문에 짜증이 나셨지. 엄마는 도자기를 사는 일이 아버지가 지출해야 할 예산을 훨씬 초과했다고 말씀하셨어. 아빠는 예술 작품들을 평가하는 텔레비전 프로그램을 시청하신 후로 가끔씩 예술 작품들을 구입해 왔어. 엄마는 아빠가 경제적인 가치도 없는 작품들을 구입하실까 봐 근심하셔. 엄마는 그것의 현재 가치에 대해서도 낙관적이지 않으셔. 엄마는 아빠가 쓸모없는 작품들에 돈을 쓰신다고 걱정하셔. 엄마는 아빠가 전문가의 지도를 받고 투자해야 할 항목을 선택해야 한다고 말씀하시지. 엄마는 아빠에게 외화에 투자하라고 제안하셔. 엄마는 아빠가 은퇴에 대비해서 돈을 저축해 두어야 한다고 말씀하셔. 아빠는 연금이 있다고 말하시지만 엄마는 연금만으로는 충분하지 않다고 생각하셔.

후니는 자기 돼지 저금통에 구멍이 난 것처럼 돈이 샌다고 해. 나는 후니의 돼지 저금통이 이미 찢겨져서 열려 있다는 것을 알아. 일단 일정 금액의 돈이 모이면, 후니는 그 돈을 카드를 사거나 나무로 된 모형을 사는 데 쓰지.

세리는 나에게 보석상자 초안과 디자인 대회에 관한 광고를 보여 주었어. 세리는 그 상자 표면에 자신의 이름을 새기는 것에 관해서 생각하고 있어. 아마도 세리는 유명한 스타들처럼 자신의 서명이 필요하다고 생각하는 것 같아. 세리의 서명이 그 상자의 가치를 올려 줄지는 의심스러워. 하지만 나는 세리의 보석상자가 그 경연대회에서 우승하기를 바래.

pottery
[pátəri]
n. 도자기, 도기류

Dad brought a piece of pottery home.
아빠는 도자기 한 점을 집에 가지고 오셨어.

antique
[æntíːk]
a. 오래된, 골동의

He bought it from a store selling antique furniture.
그는 그것을 고가구점에서 사셨지.
• antiquity n. 오래됨

investment
[invéstmənt]
n. 투자

Dad says it will be a good investment, expecting a good return.
아빠는 그것이 수익이 괜찮을 것이라고 예상하시면서 괜찮은 투자가 될 것이라고 말씀하셔.
• invest v. 투자하다

gambling
[gǽmbliŋ]
n. 도박

Mom complains that it's like gambling.
엄마는 그것이 도박이나 다름없다고 불평하셔.
• gamble v. 도박하다   • gambler n. 도박꾼

irritated
[irətèitid]
a. 짜증이 난

She was irritated by the pottery.
엄마는 도자기 때문에 짜증이 나셨지.
• irritate v. 짜증나게 하다   • irritation n. 짜증

budget
[bʌ́dʒit]
n. 예산
v. 예산을 세우다

She said that it was far beyond the budget he was supposed to spend.
엄마는 도자기를 사는 일이 아버지가 지출해야 할 예산을 훨씬 초과했다고 말씀하셨어.
• beyond the budget   예산을 초과한

evaluate
[ivǽljuèit]
v. 평가하다

Since Dad watched a TV program evaluating art, he has sometimes bought art.
아빠는 예술작품들을 평가하는 텔레비전 프로그램을 시청하신 후로 가끔씩 작품들을 구입해오셨어.
• evaluation n. 평가

value
[vǽljuː]
n. 가치, 값어치
v. 값을 매기다,
   높이 평가하다

Mom worries that he might buy some items with no economic value.
엄마는 아빠가 경제적인 가치도 없는 작품들을 구입하실까 봐 근심하셔.
• valuation n. 평가, 사정

optimistic
[ὰptəmístik]
a. 낙관적인

She is not optimistic about its current value, either.
엄마는 그것의 현재 가치에 대해서도 낙관적이지 않으셔.

- optimism n. 낙관주의   • pessimistic a. 비관적인

current
[kə́:rənt]
a. 현재의

She is not optimistic about its current value, either.
엄마는 그것의 현재 가치에 대해서도 낙관적이지 않으셔.

- currently ad. 현재, 일반적으로

junk
[dʒʌŋk]
n. 잡동사니, 쓰레기

She worries that Dad spends money on junk.
엄마는 아빠가 쓸모없는 작품들에 돈을 쓰신다고 걱정하셔.

item
[áitəm]
n. 항목, 아이템

Mom says Dad has to choose investment items under an expert's guidance.
엄마는 아빠가 전문가의 지도를 받고 투자할 항목을 선택해야 한다고 말씀하셔.

- itemize v. 항목별로 쓰다

guidance
[gáidns]
n. 지도, 안내

Mom says Dad has to choose investment items under an expert's guidance.
엄마는 아빠가 전문가의 지도를 받고 투자할 항목을 선택해야 한다고 말씀하셔.

- guide v. 지도하다

currency
[kə́:rənsi]
n. 통용되는 화폐

She suggests Dad buy some foreign currencies as an investment.
엄마는 아빠에게 외화에 투자하라고 제안하셔.

retirement
[ritáiərmənt]
n. 퇴직, 은퇴

She says Dad needs to save money in preparation for his retirement.
엄마는 아빠가 은퇴에 대비해서 돈을 저축해 두어야 한다고 말씀하셔.

- retire v. 퇴직하다, 은퇴하다   • retiree n. 퇴직자

pension fund
[pénʃən fʌnd]
n. 연금

Although Dad says he has a pension fund, Mom thinks the pension fund is not enough.
아빠는 연금이 있다고 말하시지만 엄마는 연금만으로는 충분하지 않다고 생각하셔.

leak
[li:k]
v. 새다

Hoony says his piggy bank is leaking as if it had a hole. 후니는 자기 돼지 저금통에 구멍이 난 것처럼 돈이 샌다고 해.
- leakage n. 누출

tear
[tɛə(r)]
v. 찢다

I know that his piggy bank has already been torn open. 나는 후니의 돼지 저금통이 이미 찢겨져서 열려 있다는 것을 알아.
- tear - tore - torn

amount
[əmàunt]
n. 양, 액수

Once he collects a certain amount of money, he spends it on cards or wooden models. 일단 일정 금액의 돈이 모이면, 후니는 그 돈을 카드를 사거나 나무로 된 모형을 사는 데 쓰지.

carve
[kɑːrv]
v. 새기다

She is thinking about carving her name on the surface of the box. 세리는 그 상자 표면에 자신의 이름을 새기는 것에 관해서 생각하고 있어.
- carving n. 조각, 조각술

surface
[sə́ːrfis]
n. 표면

She is thinking about carving her name on the surface of the box. 세리는 그 상자 표면에 자신의 이름을 새기는 것에 관해서 생각하고 있어.

autograph
[ɔ́ːtəgræf]
n. 서명
v. 서명하다

Maybe she thinks she needs her own autograph like famous stars. 아마도 세리는 유명한 스타들처럼 자신의 서명이 필요하다고 생각하는 것 같아.

doubtful
[dáutfəl]
a. 의심스러운

It's doubtful if her autograph will raise the value of the box. 세리의 서명이 그 상자의 가치를 올려 줄지는 의심스러워.
- doubt v. 의심하다

Check Again!

A Translate each word into Korean.

1. currency ....
2. evaluate ....
3. amount ....
4. current ....
5. value ....
6. item ....
7. leak ....
8. irritated ....
9. junk ....
10. draft ....

B Translate each word into English.

1. 투자 ....
2. 낙관적인 ....
3. 퇴직 ....
4. 서명 ....
5. 새기다 ....

C Fill in the blank with the appropriate word. Refer to the Korean.

1. My hobby is collecting a   furniture.
   제 취미는 고가구 수집입니다.

2. Jerry is still d   about her comments.
   제리는 여전히 그녀가 한 말에 대해 의심을 한다.

3. Kate is in charge of public p   fund management.
   케이트는 공공 연금 관리를 맡고 있다.

4. In some places g   is legal.
   어떤 지역에서는 도박이 합법이다.

5. Make sure you don't spend more than your b   .
   예산을 초과해서 지출을 하지 않도록 해야 한다.

Chapter 10
Economy

Unit 29. Seri has skin trouble.

be harmful to one's skin

buy something **at a real bargain**

become swollen

Episode

Seri: Bomi, we need sun block.
Bomi: Why are you overreacting? • It's winter.
Seri: Don't you know how harmful ultraviolet rays are to our skin?
       • The ozone layer is depleting. • Look there is a clearance
       sale. • We can buy some cosmetic products at a real bargain.
       • They are offering a 50% discount.

Seri and I bought sun block and cleansing foam. • Seri told Mom
that we bought them at a wholesale rate. • We found that other
retailers sold them at much higher rates. • A week after, Seri's
face became swollen. • Fortunately I didn't apply the products to
my skin.

Mom: What's wrong with them? • They must be stale. • They
     smell so bad.
Seri: Can I get a refund for them?
Mom: Do you have a receipt?
Seri: I don't think so.

Seri said we should call a consumer group. • She said the sellers
should be punished. • I regretted buying them on impulse. • We
should have thought about the fundamental principles of how
prices are fixed. • According to our economics teacher, supply and
demand fix the price. • I learned the lesson that generally lower
prices mean lower quality.

세리: 보미 언니, 우리 자외선 차단제가 필요해.
보미: 웬 과잉 반응이야? 지금은 겨울이잖아.
세리: 자외선이 우리 피부에 얼마나 해로운지 몰라? 오존층이 얇아지고 있어. 저기 봐, 저기서 창고 정리 세일을 하고
     있어. 우리 정말 싸게 화장품을 살 수 있겠다. 50퍼센트 세일을 해 주고 있어.

세리와 나는 썬크림과 폼클렌저를 샀다. 세리는 엄마에게 도매 가격으로 샀다고 말씀 드렸다. 우리는 다른 소매상들은 더
높은 가격에 판다는 것을 발견했다. 일주일 후, 세리의 얼굴은 부풀었다. 다행히 나는 그 제품들을 피부에 바르지 않았다.

엄마: 이 제품에 무슨 문제가 있는 거지? 상한 게 분명해. 너무 이상한 냄새가 나.
세리: 이거 환불받을 수 있을까요?
엄마: 영수증 있니?
세리: 없는 것 같아요.

세리는 우리가 소비자 단체에 전화해야 한다고 했다. 세리는 판매자들이 처벌을 받아야 한다고 했다. 나는 그것들을 충
동적으로 구매한 것을 후회했다. 우리는 가격 결정의 기본적인 원칙들을 생각했어야 했다. 우리 경제학 선생님 말씀에
의하면, 수요와 공급이 가격을 결정한다고 한다. 나는 일반적으로 낮은 가격은 낮은 품질을 의미한다는 교훈을 얻었다.

block
[blɑk]

n. 막는 것 v. 막다

Bomi, we need sun block.
보미 언니, 우리 자외선 차단제가 필요해.

• sun block 자외선 차단제

overreact
[òuvəriǽkt]

v. 과잉 반응하다

Why are you overreacting? It's winter.
웬 과잉 반응이야? 지금은 겨울이잖아.

• overreaction n. 과잉 반응

ultraviolet
[ʌ́ltrəváiəlit]

a. 자외선의
n. 자외선

Don't you know how harmful ultraviolet rays are to our skin?
자외선이 우리 피부에 얼마나 해로운지 몰라?

ozone
[óuzoun]

n. 오존

The ozone layer is depleting.
오존층이 얇아지고 있어.

• ozone layer 오존층

deplete
[diplí:t]

v. 격감시키다, 고갈시키다

The ozone layer is depleting.
오존층이 얇아지고 있어.

• depletion n. 고갈, 소모 • depleted a. 고갈된

clearance
[klíərəns]

n. 정리

Look there is a clearance sale.
저기 봐, 저기서 창고 정리 세일을 하고 있어.

• clear v. 치우다, 제거하다
• clearance sale 창고 정리 세일, 염가 세일

cosmetic
[kɑzmétik]

a. 화장용의

We can buy some cosmetic products at a real bargain.
우리 정말 싸게 화장품을 살 수 있겠다.

• cosmetics n. 화장품

bargain
[bá:rgən]

n. 거래 v. 흥정하다

We can buy some cosmetic products at a real bargain.
우리 정말 싸게 화장품을 살.수 있겠다.

• at a bargain 싼 가격에

offer
[ɔ́(:)fər]

v. 제공하다, 제의하다
n. 제공, 제의

They are offering a 50% discount.
저기서 50퍼센트 세일을 해 주고 있어.

• offer a discount 할인을 해 주다

discount
[dískaunt]
n. 할인 v. 할인하다

They are offering a 50% discount.
저기서 50퍼센트 세일을 해 주고 있어.

wholesale
[hóulsèil]
n. 도매
a. 도매의

Seri told Mom that we bought them at a wholesale rate.
세리는 엄마에게 도매 가격으로 샀다고 말씀 드렸다.

• wholesaler n. 도매업자 • at a wholesale rate 도매로

retailer
[rí:teilər]
n. 소매업자

We found that other retailers sold them at much higher rates.
우리는 다른 소매상들은 더 높은 가격에 판다는 것을 발견했다.

• retail v. 소매하다 n. 소매 a. 소매로

swell
[swél]
v. 팽창하다, 부풀다

A week after, Seri's face became swollen.
일주일 후, 세리의 얼굴은 부풀었다.

• swell - swelled - swollen

apply
[əplái]
v. (피부에) 바르다

Fortunately I didn't apply the products to my skin.
다행히 나는 그 제품들을 피부에 바르지 않았다.

• application n. 바름, 붙임, 바르는 약

stale
[steil]
a. 상한

They must be stale. They smell so bad.
상한 게 분명해. 너무 이상한 냄새가 나.

refund
[rí:fʌnd]
n. 환불 v. 환불하다

Can I get a refund for them?
이서 환불받을 수 있을까요?

• get a refund 환불을 받다

receipt
[risí:t]
n. 영수증
v. 영수증을 발행하다

Do you have a receipt?
영수증 있니?

consumer
[kənsúːmər]
n. 소비자

Seri said we should call a consumer group.
세리는 우리가 소비자 단체에 전화해야 한다고 했다.

• consume v. 소비하다 • producer n. 생산자

punish
[pʌ́niʃ]
v. 처벌하다

She said the sellers should be punished.
세리는 판매자들이 처벌을 받아야 한다고 했다.

• punishment n. 처벌

regret
[rigrét]
v. 후회하다 n. 후회

I regretted buying them on impulse.
나는 그것들을 충동적으로 구매한 것을 후회했다.

• regretful a. 뉘우치는, 서운해하는 • regrettable a. 유감스러운

impulse
[ímpʌls]
n. 충동, 충격

I regretted buying them on impulse.
나는 그것들을 충동적으로 구매한 것을 후회했다.

• impulsive a. 충동적인 • on impulse 충동적으로

fundamental
[fʌ̀ndəméntl]
a. 기본적인, 근본적인

We should have thought about the fundamental principles of how prices are fixed.
우리는 가격 결정의 기본적인 원칙들을 생각했어야 했다.

• fundamentally ad. 근본적으로

supply
[səplái]
n. 공급
v. 공급하다

According to our economics teacher, supply and demand fix the price.
우리 경제학 선생님 말씀에 의하면, 수요와 공급이 가격을 결정한다고 한다.

• supplier n. 공급업자

demand
[diménd]
n. 수요
v. 요구하다

According to our economics teacher, supply and demand fix the price.
우리 경제 선생님 말씀에 의하면, 수요와 공급이 가격을 결정한다고 한다.

generally
[dʒénərəli]
ad. 일반적으로

I learned the lesson that generally lower prices mean lower quality.
나는 일반적으로 낮은 가격은 낮은 품질을 의미한다는 교훈을 얻었다.

• generalize v. 개괄하다, 일반적으로 말하다

Check Again!

A Translate each word into Korean.

1. ultraviolet ....
2. ozone ....
3. consumer ....
4. stale ....
5. deplete ....
6. clearance ....
7. cosmetic ....
8. supply ....
9. retailer ....
10. punish ....

B Translate each word into English.

1. 영수증 ....
2. 기본적인 ....
3. 수요 ....
4. (피부에) 바르다 ....
5. 도매의 ....

C Fill in the blank with the appropriate word. Refer to the Korean.

1. This car is a real b_____. It costs as much as a used one.

   이 차는 정말 싸. 중고 차 정도의 가격이야.

2. My brother's finger was s_____ after playing basketball.

   내 남동생의 손가락은 농구를 한 후에 부풀어 올랐다.

3. Sara bought a skirt and a jacket on i_____.

   사라는 셔츠와 재킷을 충동 구매했다.

4. Danny is sensitive. He always o_____ to criticism.

   데니는 민감해. 그 아이는 비판에 과도하게 반응해.

5. The customer is still asking for a r_____ for a skirt with a stain on it.

   손님이 여전히 얼룩이 묻은 스커트에 대해서 환불을 요구하고 있다.

Chapter 10
Economy

Unit 30. Mom has become a regular customer of ABC Mart.

attract someone **to** something

be startled to see someone

Episode

Dear Diary,

Lately, Mom goes to ABC Mart for groceries. • Formerly, ABC Mart dealt with household appliances. • She used to be a regular customer of G-Mart for groceries. • She went to G-Mart because parking was easy for her.

Then what attracted her to ABC Mart? • ABC Mart seems to have their own management style. • In terms of quantity, G-Mart is better since it is much bigger. • However, Mom really likes the staff of ABC Mart. • She says they are nice and considerate. • Grandma also says they are courteous when talking to senior citizens. • More than anything else, she likes their quick delivery service.

Yesterday I ran on an errand to ABC Mart. • I was startled to see my previous classmate. • He was working part-time there. • He was packing parcels to be delivered. • "Should I pause and say hello to him?" I wondered. • But he smiled and talked to me. • He said he's temporarily out of school because of his family's financial problems. • Actually there has been widespread rumors about him. • Some said he was suspended and some said he dropped out of school. • Some even said he was caught robbing students of money. • Finally I uncovered the mysteries surrounding him. • Now I can say to my classmates that he is doing good.

다이어리에게,

최근에 엄마는 식료품을 사러 ABC 마트로 가셔. 예전에는 ABC 마트가 가전제품을 취급했었어. 엄마는 전에 G마트에서 식료품을 구입하는 단골 고객이셨어. 엄마는 주차하기가 편리해서 G마트에 가셨던 거야.

그러면 무엇이 엄마를 ABC마트로 가게 만들었을까? ABC 마트는 그들만의 경영 스타일이 있는 듯해. 규모는 G마트가 훨씬 크기 때문에 양적인 면에서는 더 낫지. 엄마는 ABC 마트의 직원들을 무척 좋아하셔. 엄마는 ABC 마트 직원들이 친절하고 사려 깊다고 하셔. 할머니 또한 직원들이 나이 드신 어른들에게 말할 때 예의가 바르다고 하시지. 무엇보다도 할머니는 그들의 빠른 배달서비스를 좋아하셔.

어제 나는 심부름으로 ABC 마트에 갔었어. 나는 예전 학급 친구를 보고는 놀랐어. 그 아이는 거기서 시간제로 일하고 있었어. 그는 거기서 배달할 꾸러미들을 포장하고 있었어. "잠깐 멈춰서 그 아이에게 인사를 해야 하는 걸까?"라고 나는 생각했어. 하지만 그는 미소를 지으며 나에게 말을 걸었어. 그는 집안 경제 사정이 안 좋아서 잠시 학교를 그만두었다고 말했어. 사실 그에 대한 소문들이 여기저기 퍼져 있었어. 어떤 아이들은 그 아이가 정학을 받았다고 했고 어떤 아이들은 그 애가 자퇴를 했다고 했어. 심지어는 그가 다른 학생의 돈을 빼앗다가 걸렸다고도 했지. 드디어 나는 그 아이를 둘러싼 의혹을 밝히게 되었어. 이제 나는 우리반 아이들에게 그가 잘 지내고 있다고 말할 수 있을 것 같아.

lately
[léitli]
ad. 최근에

Lately, Mom goes to ABC Mart for groceries.
최근에 엄마는 식료품을 사러 ABC 마트로 가셔.

• latest a. 가장 최신의

grocery
[gróusəri]
n. 식료품

Lately, Mom goes to ABC Mart for groceries.
최근에 엄마는 식료품을 사러 ABC 마트로 가셔.

formerly
[fɔ́ːrmərli]
ad. 예전에

Formerly, ABC Mart dealt with household appliances.
예전에는 ABC 마트가 가전제품을 취급했었어.

• former a. 이전의

household appliance
[háushòuld əpláiəns]
n. 가전제품

Formerly, ABC Mart dealt with household appliances.
예전에는 ABC 마트가 가전제품을 취급했었어.

customer
[kʌ́stəmər]
n. 고객

She used to be a regular customer of G-Mart for groceries.
엄마는 전에 G마트에서 식료품을 구입하는 단골 고객이셨어.

parking
[páːrkiŋ]
n. 주차

She went to G-Mart because parking was easy for her.
엄마는 주차하기가 편리해서 G마트에 가셨던 거야.

• park v. 주차하다

attract
[ətrǽkt]
v. 이끌다

Then what attracted her to ABC Mart?
그러면 무엇이 엄마를 ABC 마트로 가게 만들었을까?

• attraction n. 유인, 끌어당김 • attractive a. 매력적인

management
[mǽnidʒmənt]
n. 관리

ABC Mart seems to have their own management style.
ABC 마트는 그들만의 경영 스타일이 있는 듯해.

• manage v. 관리하다 • manager n. 관리자

quantity
[kwántəti]

n. 양

In terms of quantity, G-Mart is better since it is much bigger.
규모는 G마트가 훨씬 크기 때문에 양적인 면에서는 더 낫지.

• quality n. 질

staff
[stæf]

n. 직원

However, Mom really likes the staff of ABC Mart.
하지만 엄마는 ABC 마트의 직원들을 무척 좋아하셔.

considerate
[kənsídərit]

a. 사려 깊은, 세심한

She says they are nice and considerate.
엄마는 ABC 마트 직원들이 친절하고 사려 깊다고 하셔.

• consideration n. 고려   • considerately ad. 사려 깊게

courteous
[kə́ːrtiəs]

a. 예의 바른, 공손한

Grandma also says they are courteous when talking to senior citizens.
할머니 또한 직원들이 나이 드신 어른들에게 말할 때 예의가 바르다고 하셔.

• courtesy n. 예의 바름, 공손   • courteously ad. 공손하게

delivery
[dilívəri]

n. 배달

More than anything else, she likes their quick delivery service.
무엇보다도 할머니는 그들의 빠른 배달서비스를 좋아하셔.

• deliver v. 배달하다

errand
[érənd]

n. 심부름

Yesterday I ran (on) an errand to ABC Mart.
어제 나는 심부름으로 ABC 마트에 갔었어.

• run (on) an errand 심부름을 가다

startle
[stáːrtl]

v. 놀라게 하다

I was startled to see my previous classmate.
나는 예전 학급 친구를 보고는 놀랐어.

• startled ad. 놀란

part-time
[pɑːrt-taim]

파트 타임

He was working part-time there.
그 아이는 거기서 시간제로 일하고 있었어.

• work part-time 시간제로 일하다

parcel
[pá:rsəl]
n. 꾸러미

He was packing parcels to be delivered.
그 아이는 거기서 배달할 꾸러미들을 포장하고 있었어.

pause
[pɔːz]
v. 잠시 멈추다
n. 정지

"Should I pause and say hello to him?" I wondered.
"잠깐 멈춰서 그 아이에게 인사를 해야 하는 걸까?"라고 나는 생각했어.

financial
[finǽnʃəl]
a. 재정적인

He said he's temporarily out of school because of his family's financial problems.
그는 집안 경제 사정이 안 좋아서 잠시 학교를 그만두었다고 말했어.

• finance n. 재정 • financially ad. 재정적으로

widespread
[wáidspréd]
a. 널리 퍼진

Actually there has been widespread rumors about him.
사실 그에 대한 소문들이 여기저기 퍼져 있었어.

suspend
[səspénd]
v. 정학시키다,
  일시 정지하다

Some said he was suspended and some said he dropped out of school.
어떤 아이들은 그가 정학을 당했다고 했고 어떤 아이들은 그가 자퇴를 했다고 했어.

• suspension n. 정학, 정직 • suspended a. 정학된

rob
[rɑb]
v. 강탈하다

Some even said he was caught robbing students of money.
심지어는 그가 다른 학생의 돈을 빼앗다가 걸렸다고도 했어.

• robber n. 강도 • rob A of B A 에게서 B를 빼앗다

uncover
[ʌnkʌ́vər]
v. 진실을 밝히다, 드러내다

Finally I uncovered the mysteries surrounding him.
드디어 나는 그 아이를 둘러싼 의혹을 밝히게 되었어.

• cover v. 감추다

Check Again!

A Translate each word into Korean.

1. quantity ....
2. widespread ....
3. formerly ....
4. courteous ....
5. management ....
6. staff ....
7. grocery ....
8. parcel ....
9. pause ....
10. startle ....

B Translate each word into English.

1. 재정적인 ....
2. 사려 깊은 ....
3. 배달 ....
4. 진실을 밝히다 ....
5. 가전제품 ....

C Fill in the blank with the appropriate word. Refer to the Korean.

1. I ran (on) an e   to the supermarket for Grandma.

   나는 할머니 심부름으로 슈퍼마켓에 갔다.

2. Is it true that Tommy will be s   for a month?

   토미가 한 달 동안 정학당할 것이라는 것이 정말이니?

3. The little boy was crying because he was r   of some money.

   그 어린 소년은 돈을 빼앗겨서 울고 있었다.

4. L   , consumer prices have been rising sharply.

   최근에 소비자 물가가 빠르게 오르고 있다.

5. I'm working p   because I need to save money for tuition.

   나는 수업료를 모아야 하기 때문에 시간제로 일을 하고 있다.

✤ 반대의 의미를 만들어 주는 말 1

동사, 형용사 혹은 명사 앞에 있는 un-, im-, in- 등은 의미를 반대로 만들어 주는
역할을 한다.

un- + 동사 형용사

tie 끈을 매다
untie 끈을 풀다

ex) Sandy is untying her shoelaces.
샌디는 신발 끈을 풀고 있다.

- **pack** 포장하다   **unpack** 짐을 풀다
- **load** 짐을 싣다   **unload** 짐을 내리다
- **zip** 지퍼를 닫다   **unzip** 지퍼를 열다
- **fair** 공정한   **unfair** 불공정한
- **fortunate** 운이 좋은   **unfortunate** 운이 없는

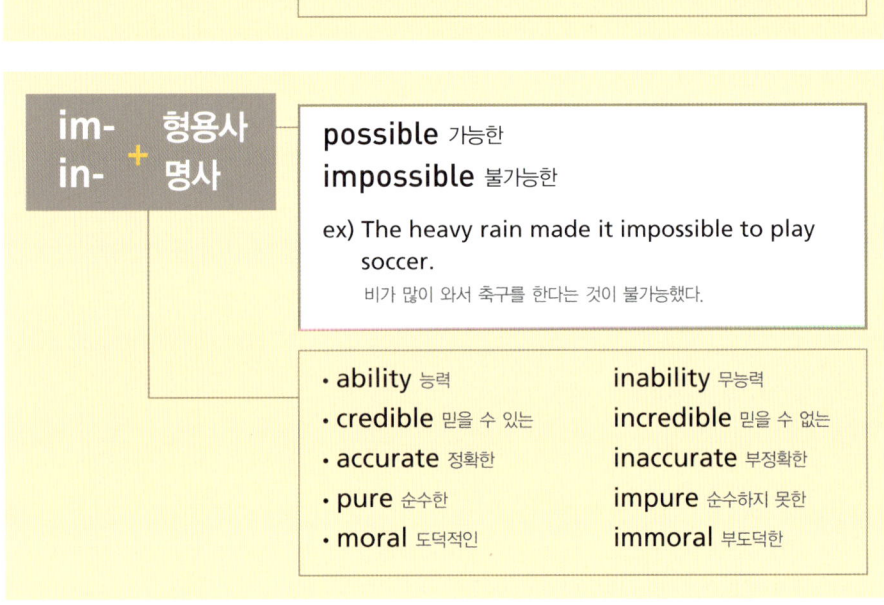

im- in- + 형용사 명사

possible 가능한
impossible 불가능한

ex) The heavy rain made it impossible to play
soccer.
비가 많이 와서 축구를 한다는 것이 불가능했다.

- **ability** 능력   **inability** 무능력
- **credible** 믿을 수 있는   **incredible** 믿을 수 없는
- **accurate** 정확한   **inaccurate** 부정확한
- **pure** 순수한   **impure** 순수하지 못한
- **moral** 도덕적인   **immoral** 부도덕한

Words Related to Money

- fee 수수료, 사례금
- rent 집세
- wage 임금
- fine 벌금
- tax 세금
- commission 수수료
- subsidy 보조금

At a supermarket 수퍼마켓

+ dairy product 유제품
+ scale 저울
+ canned food 통조림
+ meat 육류
+ bakcry 제과, 제빵
+ detergent 세제
+ frozen food 냉동 식품

+ produce 농산물
+ beverage 음료

VOCA EDGE

BLUE

Chapter 11. Technology

Chapter 11
Technology

Unit 31. Mom is impressed by home intelligence systems.

make a phone call home

go to a housing **fair**

heated by solar energy

be controlled from outside the home

Episode

Yesterday Mom attended a school reunion. ● She made a phone call home and hastily said, "Please check if the iron is unplugged." ● Today Mom went to a housing fair. ● She saw a lot of building models on display. ● Among them, in particular, a home intelligence system impressed her.

Mom: A home intelligence system will enhance our quality of life. ● For example, we won't have to carry house keys or memorize our door lock combination. ● Sensors in the door lock systems detect the owners automatically. ● The gas stove can be controlled from outside the home.

Bomi: How nice! ● Do you remember calling home and saying in an urgent voice, "Bomi, turn off the stove."? ● Is it true that doors can identify their owners by reading their fingerprints?

Mom: Yeah, they just open automatically by identifying the owners. ● Technology contributes a lot to our lives.

Bomi: Mom, why don't we move to a house furnished with a home intelligence system? ● Or we can live in a house heated by solar energy. ● Solar energy is not only eco-friendly but it is economical.

Mom: Right. ● It can reduce our heating bills.

Bomi: Furthermore, solar energy doesn't run out. ● There is a shortage of natural resources, so using solar energy can help solve this problem.

A home intelligence system will be good for forgetful people like my mom. ● It will definitely improve our work efficiency since people can concentrate more on their jobs.

어제 엄마는 동창회에 참석하셨다. 엄마는 집에 전화를 걸어서는 급하게 "다리미 코드가 빠져 있는지 좀 봐 줘."라고 말씀하셨다. 오늘 엄마는 주택 박람회에 가셨다. 엄마는 여러 건축모형들이 진열되어 있는 것을 보셨다. 그것들 중에서 주택지능시스템이 특히 엄마에게 깊은 인상을 주었다.

엄마: 주택지능시스템은 삶의 질을 향상시켜 줄 거야. 예를 들어 우리는 집 열쇠를 가지고 다니지 않아도 될 테고 비밀번호를 기억하지 않아도 될 거야. 잠금 장치에 달려 있는 센서가 주인을 자동으로 인식해. 가스장치는 집 밖에서도 조종할 수 있어.

보미: 어머 멋져라! 엄마 저번에 다급한 목소리로 전화해서, "보미야, 가스렌지 좀 꺼주렴."이라고 했던 거 기억나세요? 문이 지문을 인식해서 주인을 알아볼 수 있다는 것이 사실이에요?

엄마: 응, 자동으로 주인을 인식해서 문을 열어 준단다. 과학 기술은 우리 삶에 크게 기여하지.

보미: 엄마, 우리 주택지능시스템이 갖추어진 집으로 이사 가는 것이 어때요? 아니면 태양열로 난방이 되는 집에서 살 수도 있고요. 태양열은 친환경적일 뿐만 아니라 경제적이잖아요.

엄마 : 맞아. 난방비용을 줄일 수 있지.

보미: 더욱이 태양열은 고갈되지 않잖아요. 천연자원이 부족하니까 태양열을 이용하면 이 문제를 해결할 수 있을 거에요.

주택 지능 시스템은 우리 엄마처럼 건망증이 있는 사람들에게 제격일 것이다. 사람들이 더욱 자신의 일에 집중할 수 있기 때문에 당연히 일의 효율을 향상시킬 것이다.

reunion
[riːjúːniən]

n. 동창회, 재결합

Yesterday Mom attended a school reunion.
어제 엄마는 동창회에 참석하셨다.

---

hastily
[héistili]

ad. 급하게, 서둘러서

She made a phone call home and hastily said,
"Please check if the iron is unplugged."
엄마는 집에 전화를 걸어서는 급하게 "다리미 코드가 빠져 있는지 좀 봐 줘."라고 말씀하셨다.

• haste v. 서두르다   • hasty a. 서두르는

---

unplug
[ʌnplʌ́g]

v, 플러그를 뽑다

She made a phone call home and hastily said,
"Please check if the iron is unplugged."
엄마는 집에 전화를 걸어서는 급하게 "다리미 코드가 빠져 있는지 좀 봐 줘."라고 말씀하셨다.

• plug v. 플러그를 꽂다

---

fair
[fɛər]

n. 박람회

Today Mom went to a housing fair.
오늘 엄마는 주택 박람회에 가셨다.

---

display
[displéi]

n. 진열
v. 진열하다

She saw a lot of building models on display.
엄마는 여러 건축 모형들이 진열되어 있는 것을 보셨다.

• on display 진열된

---

home intelligence system
[houm intélədʒəns sístəm]

주택 지능 시스템

Among them, in particular, a home intelligence system impressed her.
그것들 중에서 주택지능시스템이 특히 엄마에게 깊은 인상을 주었다.

---

enhance
[enhǽns]

v. 향상시키다

A home intelligence system will enhance our quality of life.
주택지능시스템은 삶의 질을 향상시켜 줄 거야.

• enhancement n. 향상

---

lock
[lɑk]

n. 잠금 장치
v. 잠그다

For example, we won't have to carry house keys or memorize our door lock combination.
예를 들어 우리는 집 열쇠를 가지고 다니지 않아도 될 테고 비밀번호를 기억하지 않아도 될 거야.

detect
[ditékt]

v. 탐지하다, 발견하다

Sensors in the door lock systems detect the owners automatically.

잠금 장치에 달려 있는 센서가 주인을 자동으로 인식해.

• detection n. 감지, 탐지 • detector n. 탐지기

outside
[àutsáid]

prep. ~의 바깥쪽
a. 밖의

The gas stove can be controlled from outside the home.

가스장치는 집 밖에서도 조종할 수 있어.

urgent
[ə́:rdʒənt]

a. 긴급한

Do you remember calling home and saying in an urgent voice, "Bomi, turn off the stove."?

엄마 저번에 다급한 목소리로 전화해서, "보미야, 가스렌지 좀 꺼주렴."이라고 했던 거 기억나세요?

• urgency n. 긴급 • urgently ad. 긴급하게

fingerprint
[fíŋgərprìnt]

n. 지문

Is it true that doors can identify their owners by reading their fingerprints?

문이 지문을 인식해서 주인을 알아볼 수 있다는 것이 사실이에요?

automatically
[ɔ́:təmǽtikəli]

ad. 자동으로

Yeah, they just open automatically by identifying the owners.

응, 자동으로 주인을 인식해서 문을 열어 준단다.

• automation n. 자동화 • automatic a. 자동의

contribute
[kəntríbjut]

v. 기여하다, 공헌하다

Technology contributes a lot to our lives.

과학 기술은 우리 삶에 크게 기여하지.

• contribution n. 공헌, 기여 • contributive a. 공헌하는, 기여하는
• contribute to ~에 기여하다

furnish
[fə́:rniʃ]

v. 제공하다, 갖추다

Mom, why don't we move to a house furnished with a home intelligence system?

엄마, 우리 주택지능시스템이 갖추어진 집으로 이사 가는 것이 어때요?

• furnishing n. 가구, 비품

solar
[sóulər]

a. 태양의

Or we can live in a house heated by solar energy.

아니면 태양열로 난방이 되는 집에서 살 수도 있고요.

• lunar a. 달의

eco-friendly
[èkoufréndli]
a. 친환경적인

Solar energy is not only eco-friendly but it is economical.

태양열은 친환경적일 뿐만 아니라 경제적이잖아요.

economical
[ìːkənámikəl]
a. 경제적인

Solar energy is not only eco-friendly but it is economical. 태양열은 친환경적일 뿐만 아니라 경제적이잖아요.

• economy n. 경제 • economics n. 경제학
• economically ad. 경제적으로

reduce
[ridʒúːs]
v. 줄이다

Right. It can reduce our heating bills.
맞아. 난방비용을 줄일 수 있지.

• reduction n. 감소, 축소

furthermore
[fáːrðərmɔ̀ːr]
ad. 더욱이

Furthermore, solar energy doesn't run out.
더욱이 태양열은 고갈되지 않잖아요.

shortage
[ʃɔ́ːrtidʒ]
n. 부족, 결핍

There is a shortage of natural resources, so using solar energy can help solve this problem.
천연자원이 부족하니까 태양열을 이용하면 이 문제를 해결할 수 있을 거예요.

• short a. 불충분한

resource
[risɔ́ːrs]
n. 자원, 수단, 재원

There is a shortage of natural resources, so using solar energy can help solve this problem.
천연자원이 부족하니까 태양열을 이용하면 이 문제를 해결 할 수 있을 거에요.

• natural resources 천연자원 • resourceful a. 자원이 풍부한

forgetful
[fərgétfəl]
a. 잊기 쉬운,
   잘 잊어버리는

A home intelligence system will be good for forgetful people like my mom.
주택 지능 시스템은 우리 엄마처럼 건망증이 있는 사람들에게 제격일 것이다.

• forgetfulness n. 건망증

efficiency
[ifíʃ ənsi]
n. 능률

It will definitely improve our work efficiency since people can concentrate more on their jobs.
사람들이 더욱 자신의 일에 집중할 수 있기 때문에 당연히 일의 효율을 향상시킬 것이다.

• efficient a. 능률적인 • efficiently ad. 능률적으로

Check Again!

A Translate each word into Korean.

1. reunion ....
2. efficiency ....
3. fair ....
4. enhance ....
5. furthermore ....
6. urgent ....
7. shortage ....
8. outside ....
9. economical ....
10. fingerprint ....

B Translate each word into English.

1. 자동으로 ....
2. 잠금 장치 ....
3. 친환경적인 ....
4. 탐지하다 ....
5. 태양의 ....

C Fill in the blank with the appropriate word. Refer to the Korean.

1. He h_____ wrote an email and sent it to her.

   그 남자는 급하게 이메일을 써서 그녀에게 보냈다.

2. As Christmas draws nearer, more people c_____ money to charities.

   크리스마스가 가까워지면서 더 많은 사람들이 자선단체에 돈을 기부한다.

3. I like this house. It is fully f_____ .

   나는 이 집이 마음에 들어. 가구가 다 비치되어 있어.

4. Judy is very f_____ . She has a poor memory.

   주디는 건망증이 심해. 그 아이는 기억력이 형편없어.

5. We have to do something to r_____ teenage smoking.

   십대 흡연을 줄이기 위해 우리는 뭔가 해야 한다.

Chapter 11
Technology

Unit 32. Cloning can be good and bad.

give rise to a new notion

use one's **clone** during an exam

Episode

Dear Diary,

Cloning has been a hot issue for some time. • People say it gives rise to a new notion of what life is. • Sincere Christians strongly disagree with the idea. • They contend that cloning is an attack on divine power. • They seem to show hatred towards the idea of cloning. • But not everyone shares this idea. • On the contrary, some people agree with cloning. • They contend that cloning can bring new hope to people. • They believe that cloning can be used to eradicate fatal diseases. • Patients suffering from fatal diseases have been awaiting this news. • They think cloning will be commercially available soon.

Sara: Bomi, do you believe humans can be created from tiny cells? • Creating life seems to be within our realm of possibility.

Bomi: It's awful to think of someone who is exactly like me. • If I'm reproduced into countless clones of myself, who will be the real me?

Sara: But it's fun to think of a life form which can inherit all my characteristics.

Bomi: It will be good if my clone can replace me during an exam. • But I have to be alert since one of my clones might cause mischief for others.

Sara: Hmm, we can't be sure that scientific development is always good. • Anyway, using my clone during an exam is one merit.

Bomi: That may be the biggest advantage.

다이어리에게,
얼마 전부터 복제가 사람들 사이에서 크게 화제가 되어 왔어. 사람들은 복제가 생명이 무엇인지에 관해 새로운 개념을 제시한다고 말하지. 독실한 기독교인들은 이러한 생각에 대해 동의하지 않아. 그들은 복제가 신의 권능에 대한 침해라고 주장해. 그들은 복제에 대해서 증오를 나타내는 것 같아. 하지만 모두가 이 생각을 갖고 있는 것은 아니야. 오히려 어떤 사람들은 복제에 동의해. 그들은 복제가 사람들에게 새로운 희망을 가져다 줄 수 있다고 주장하지. 그들은 복제가 치명석인 병을 근절하는 데 도움을 줄 수 있다고 생각해. 치명적인 병으로 고생하는 환자들은 이 소식만을 기다려 왔어. 그들은 복제가 곧 상업적으로 이용될 수 있을 거라고 생각해.

사라 : 보미야, 너는 사람들이 아주 작은 세포에서 창조될 수 있다는 것을 믿니? 생명체를 창조하는 건 가능해진 것 같아.
보미 : 나랑 완전히 똑같은 사람이 있다는 것을 생각만 해도 끔찍해. 만약에 나를 복제한 인간이 엄청나게 많이 있다면, 도대체 진짜 나는 누구야?
사라 : 하지만 내 특성을 모두 물려받은 생명체가 있다는 것을 생각해 보면 재미있잖아.
보미 : 내 복제 인간이 내 대신 시험을 봐 줄 수 있으면 좋을 거 같아. 하지만 내 복제 인간들이 다른 사람들을 괴롭힐 수 있으니까 방심할 수 없잖아.
사라 : 흠, 과학의 발전이 언제나 좋다고는 확신할 수 없네. 어쨌든 시험 기간에 내 복제 인간을 쓸 수 있다는 건 하나의 장점이지.
보미 : 그것이 제일 큰 장점일 것 같네.

cloning
[klóuniŋ]
n. 복제

Cloning has been a hot issue for some time.
얼마 전부터 복제가 사람들 사이에서 크게 화제가 되어왔어.
• clone v. 복제하다

notion
[nóuʃən]
n. 생각, 개념

People say it gives rise to a new notion of what life is.
사람들은 복제가 생명이 무엇인지에 관해 새로운 개념을 제시한다고 말하지.

sincere
[sinsíər]
a. 독실한, 진지한

Sincere Christians strongly disagree with the idea.
독실한 기독교인들은 이러한 생각에 대해 동의하지 않아.
• sincerity n. 성실함, 진실함 • sincerely ad. 진정으로, 진실로

divine
[diváin]
a. 신의, 신성한

They contend that cloning is an attack on divine power.
그들은 복제가 신의 권능에 대한 침해라고 주장해.
• divinity n. 신성 • divinely ad. 거룩하게

hatred
[héitrid]
n. 증오

They seem to show hatred towards the idea of cloning.
그들은 복제에 대해서 증오를 나타내는 것 같아.
• hate v. 증오하다 • hateful a. 가증스러운, 증오에 찬

contrary
[kántreri]
n. 반대
a. 반대의

On the contrary, some people agree with cloning.
오히려 어떤 사람들은 복제에 동의해.
• on the contrary 그와는 정반대로, 그러기는 커녕, 오히려

contend
[kənténd]
v. 주장하다, 다투다

They contend that cloning can bring new hope to people.
그들은 복제가 사람들에게 새로운 희망을 가져다 줄 수 있다고 주장하지.
• contention n. 주장, 논쟁

eradicate
[irǽdəkèit]
v. 뿌리 뽑다, 근절하다

They believe that cloning can be used to eradicate fatal diseases.
그들은 복제가 치명적인 병을 근절하는 데 도움을 줄 수 있다고 생각해.
• eradication n. 근절

fatal
[féitl]
a. 치명적인

Patients suffering from fatal diseases have been awaiting this news.
치명적인 병으로 고생하는 환자들은 이 소식만을 기다려 왔어.

- fatality n. 재난, 불행, 죽음

await
[əwéit]
v. ~을 기다리다

Patients suffering from fatal diseases have been awaiting this news.
치명적인 병으로 고생하는 환자들은 이 소식만을 기다려 왔어.

commercially
[kəmə́:rʃəli]
ad. 상업적으로

They think cloning will be commercially available soon.
그들은 복제가 곧 상업적으로 이용될 수 있을 거라고 생각해.

- commercialism n. 상업주의 • commercial a. 상업적인

available
[əvéiləbl]
a. 이용 가능한

They think cloning will be commercially available soon.
그들은 복제가 곧 상업적으로 이용될 수 있을 거라고 생각해.

- avail v. 이용하다

cell
[sel]
n. 세포

Bomi, do you believe humans can be created from tiny cells?
보미야, 너는 사람들이 아주 작은 세포에서 창조될 수 있다는 것을 믿니?

realm
[relm]
n. 영역, 왕국

Creating life seems to be within our realm of possibility.
생명체를 창조하는 건 가능해진 것 같아.

reproduce
[rì:prədjú:s]
v. 복제하다, 재생하다

If I'm reproduced into countless clones of myself, who will be the real me?
만약에 나를 복제한 인간이 엄청나게 많이 있다면, 도대체 진짜 나는 누구야?

- reproduction n. 복제, 재생

countless
[káuntlis]
a. 셀 수 없는, 무수한

If I'm reproduced into countless clones of myself, who will be the real me?
만약에 나를 복제한 인간이 엄청나게 많이 있다면, 도대체 진짜 나는 누구야?

- count v. 세다 • countable a. 셀 수 있는

inherit

[inhérit]

v. 물려받다, 상속하다

But it's fun to think of a life form which can inherit all my characteristics.

하지만 내 특성을 모두 물려받은 생명체가 있다는 것을 생각해 보면 재미있잖아.

• inheritance n. 상속, 유산

characteristic

[kæriktərístik]

n. 특성, a. 독특한

But it's fun to think of a life form which can inherit all my characteristics.

하지만 내 특성을 완전히 똑같이 물려받은 생명체가 있다는 것을 생각해 보면 재미있잖아.

replace

[ripléis]

v. 대신하다, 바꾸다

It will be good if my clone can replace me during an exam. 내 복제 인간이 내 대신 시험을 봐 줄 수 있으면 좋을 것 같아.

• replacement n. 교체, 대체

alert

[ələ́:rt]

a. 방심하지 않는
n. 경보, 경계

But I have to be alert since one of my clones might cause mischief for others.

하지만 내 복제 인간들이 다른 사람들을 괴롭힐 수 있으니까 방심할 수 없잖아.

mischief

[místʃif]

n. 장난, 손해

But I have to be alert since one of my clones might cause mischief for others.

하지만 내 복제 인간들이 다른 사람들을 괴롭힐 수 있으니까 방심할 수 없잖아.

• mischievous a. 장난이 심한, 해를 끼치는

scientific

[sàiəntífik]

a. 과학적인

Hmm, we can't be sure that scientific development is always good. 흠, 과학의 발전이 언제나 좋다고는 확신할 수 없네.

• scientifically ad. 과학적으로

merit

[mérit]

n. 장점

Anyway, using my clone during an exam is one merit.

어쨌든 시험 기간에 내 복제 인간을 쓸 수 있다는 건 하나의 장점이지.

advantage

[ədvǽntidʒ]

n. 유리한 점, 이로운 점

That may be the biggest advantage.

그것이 제일 큰 장점일 것 같네.

• advantageous a. 유리한, 이로운   • disadvantage n. 해로운 점

Check Again!

A Translate each word into Korean.

1. sincere ....
2. cell ....
3. hatred ....
4. realm ....
5. contend ....
6. fatal ....
7. awful ....
8. commercially ....
9. countless ....
10. await ....

B Translate each word into English.

1. 신의, 신성한 ....
2. 복제 ....
3. 복제하다, 재생하다 ....
4. 뿌리뽑다, 근절하다 ....
5. 방심하지 않는 ....

C Fill in the blank with the appropriate word. Refer to the Korean.

1. The computers are not cheap. On the c_____, they are much more expensive.

   그 컴퓨터는 싸지 않다. 그와는 정반대로 훨씬 더 비싸다.

2. The new invention can't r_____ people.

   그 새로운 발명품이 사람을 대신할 수는 없다.

3. Did Jane i_____ the mansion from her uncle?

   제인이 삼촌에게서 그 고급 주택을 상속받은 거예요?

4. The kids were running around the restaurant, causing m_____.

   그 아이들은 식당에서 뛰어 다니면서 말썽을 피우고 있었다.

5. Learning foreign languages can be an a_____.

   외국어를 공부하는 것은 장점이 될 수 있다.

Chapter 11
Technology

Unit 33. Plants can grow without sunlight.

grow plants in a **factory**

take a **blood test**

provide **clues** to predict one's health

Episode

Sara and I were preparing for our team **presentation** on the **effects** of scientific development. ● We discussed what subject would be **suitable**. ● After we **searched** on the Internet, we talked about some interesting articles.

Sara: It's incredible. ● **Normally**, plants require sunlight and **carbon dioxide** to grow. ● Sunlight is known to be **vital** for plants to grow. ● How come **light bulbs** can replace sunlight? ● Sounds like growing plants in a **factory**.

Bomi: You're right. ● At first, I thought the researchers were **daydreaming**. ● But the plants survived indoors in a **damp** environment. ● Isn't it amazing that farmers don't have to **sow** seeds in the soil? ● Researchers **discovered** that plants can grow in the air. ● They just spray nutrients on the plants and the leaves of plants absorb **dissolved** nutrients.

Sara: If our **ancestors** came back to life, they would be surprised. ● They need to listen to a **lecture** about how their descendants are growing plants. ● Science has surely made major **progress**.

Bomi: You're right. ● Our blood can even provide **clues** to predict our health. ● After a blood test, my dad heard that he should eat more food that is high in **fiber**. ● He has a high risk of having a **stroke** in the future.

Sara: Blood tests are also used for **sensitive** issues like using DNA to detect criminals.

Bomi: Right. ● The test results are really important in **convicting** criminals.

Sara: Hey, what about this article? ● It explains how **icebergs** can be used to help **mankind**.

Bomi: I think this article is too **subjective**.

Sara and I decided to make a presentation on plants growing without sunlight. ● I hope our classmates are interested in the topic.

사라와 나는 과학 발달의 효과에 관한 팀 프레젠테이션을 준비하고 있었다. 우리는 어떤 주제가 적당할지 토의했다. 인터넷으로 검색을 한 후에 우리는 흥미로운 기사에 관해 이야기했다.

사라: 정말 믿을 수 없어. 일반적으로 식물이 자라려면 햇빛과 이산화탄소가 필요하잖아. 햇빛이 식물들이 자라는 데 필수 적이라고 알려져 있잖아. 어떻게 전구가 햇빛을 대신할 수 있지? 마치 공킹에서 식물을 길러내는 것처럼 늘리는데.

보미: 그래. 저음에 나는 연구자들이 공상에 잠겨 있는 것이라고 생각했어. 하지만 식물들은 실내의 축축한 환경에서도 살아남았잖아. 농부들이 땅에다가 씨를 심지 않아도 된다는 것이 신기하지 않아? 연구자들이 식물들이 공기 중에 서도 자랄 수 있다는 걸 발견한 것이지. 그들이 영양분을 식물에 뿌려주기만 하면 식물의 잎사귀가 용해된 영양분 을 흡수하는 것이지.

사라: 만약 우리 조상들이 다시 살아 돌아온다면 굉장히 놀라실 거야. 조상님들은 후손들이 식물을 어떻게 키우는지에 관한 강의를 들어야 할 걸. 과학은 정말 커다란 진보를 했어.

보미: 네 말이 맞아. 우리 피는 우리 건강을 예측할 수 있는 단서를 제공하잖아. 우리 아빠는 혈액 검사 후 섬유소가 풍 부한 음식을 먹어야 한다는 말을 들으셨어. 아빠는 앞으로 뇌졸중에 걸릴 위험이 크시대.

사라: 혈액 검사는 또한 범인을 가려내기 위해서 DNA를 사용하는 것과 같은 민감한 사안에도 쓰여.

보미: 맞아. 검사 결과가 범인들을 유죄 판결하는 데 매우 중요하지.

사라: 야, 이 기사는 어때? 여기서는 빙산이 사람들에게 어떻게 이용될 수 있는지 설명하고 있어.

보미: 내 생각에 이 기사는 너무 주관적인 거 같아.

사라와 나는 어떻게 식물이 햇빛 없이 자라는지에 대해 프레젠테이션을 준비하기로 했다. 우리 반 친구들이 이 주제에 대해서 흥미를 가지기를 바란다.

presentation
[prèzəntéiʃən]

n. 프레젠테이션, 발표

Sara and I were preparing for our team presentation on the effects of scientific development.
사라와 나는 과학 발달의 효과에 관한 팀 프레젠테이션을 준비하고 있었다.

• present   v. 제출하다, 나타내다

effect
[ifékt]

n. 효과, 영향

Sara and I were preparing for our team presentation on the effects of scientific development.
사라와 나는 과학 발달의 효과에 관한 팀 프레젠테이션을 준비하고 있었다.

• effective   a. 효과적인

suitable
[súːtəbl]

a. 적절한, 어울리는

We discussed what subject would be suitable.
우리는 어떤 주제가 적당할지 토의했다.

• suitability   n. 적절함, 어울림

search
[səːrtʃ]

v. 탐색하다, 조사하다
n. 탐색, 조사

After we searched on the Internet, we talked about some interesting articles.
인터넷으로 검색을 한 후에 우리는 흥미로운 기사에 관해 이야기했다.

normally
[nɔ́ːrməli]

ad. 보통, 정상적으로

It's incredible. Normally, plants require sunlight and carbon dioxide to grow.
정말 믿을 수 없어. 일반적으로 식물이 자라라면 햇빛과 이산화탄소가 필요하잖아.

• normal   a. 표준의, 보통의   n. 표준, 규격

carbon dioxide
[káːrbən daiáksaid]

n. 이산화탄소

It's incredible. Normally, plants require sunlight and carbon dioxide to grow.
정말 믿을 수 없어. 일반적으로 식물이 자라려면 햇빛과 이산화탄소가 필요하잖아.

vital
[váitl]

a. 생명의, 극히 중대한

Sunlight is known to be vital for plants to grow.
햇빛이 식물들이 자라는 데 필수적이라고 알려져 있잖아.

• vitality   n. 생명력, 활기   • vitally   ad. 극히 중요하게

light bulb
[lait bʌlb]

n. 전구

How come light bulbs can replace sunlight?
어떻게 전구가 햇빛을 대신할 수 있지?

factory
[fǽktəri]

n. 공장

Sounds like growing plants in a factory.
마치 공장에서 식물을 길러내는 것처럼 들리는데.

daydream
[déidrìːm]

v. 공상에 잠기다

At first, I thought the researchers were daydreaming.
처음에 나는 연구자들이 공상에 잠겨 있는 것이라고 생각했어.

• daydreamer n. 공상가

damp
[dæmp]

a. 습기찬, 축축한

But the plants survived indoors in a damp environment. 하지만 식물들은 실내의 축축한 환경에서도 살아남았잖아.

• dampen v. 축축하게 하다 • dampness n. 축축함

sow
[sou]

v. 씨를 뿌리다

Isn't it amazing that farmers don't have to sow seeds in the soil?
농부들이 땅에다가 씨를 심지 않아도 된다는 것이 신기하지 않아?

discover
[diskʌ́vər]

v. 발견하다

Researchers discovered that plants can grow in the air. 연구자들은 식물들이 공기 중에서도 자랄 수 있다는 걸 발견한 것이지.

• discovery n. 발견

dissolve
[dizálv]

v. 녹이다, 풀다

They just spray nutrients on the plants and the leaves of plants absorb dissolved nutrients.
그들이 영양분을 식물에 뿌려주기만 하면 식물의 잎사귀가 용해된 영양분을 흡수하는 것이지.

• dissolvent n. 용해제, 용해 a. 용해력이 있는 • dissolved a. 용해된

ancestor
[ǽnsestər]

n. 조상

If our ancestors came back to life, they would be surprised.
만약 우리 조상들이 다시 살아 돌아온다면 굉장히 놀라실 거야.

• descendant n. 후손

lecture
[léktʃər]

n. 강의 v. 강의하다

They need to listen to a lecture about how their descendants are growing plants.
조상님들은 후손들이 식물을 어떻게 키우는지에 관한 강의를 들어야 할 걸.

progress
[prɑ́grəs]

n. 진보, 발전
v. 전진하다

Science has surely made major progress.
과학은 정말 커다란 진보를 했어.

• progressive a. 진보적인 • make progress 진보하다

clue
[klu:]

n. 단서, 실마리
v. 실마리를 주다

Our blood can even provide clues to predict our health.
우리 피는 우리 건강을 예측할 수 있는 단서를 제공하잖아.

• clueless a. 단서가 없는

fiber
[fáibər]

n. 섬유질

After a blood test, my dad heard that he should eat more food that is high in fiber.
우리 아빠는 혈액 검사 후에 섬유소가 풍부한 음식을 먹어야 한다는 말을 들으셨어.

stroke
[strouk]

n. 뇌졸중

He has a high risk of having a stroke in the future.
아빠는 앞으로 뇌졸중에 걸릴 위험이 크시대.

sensitive
[sénsətiv]

a. 민감함, 예민한

Blood tests are also used for sensitive issues like using DNA to detect criminals.
혈액 검사는 또한 범인을 가려내기 위해서 DNA를 사용하는 것과 같은 민감한 사안에도 쓰여.

• sensitivity n. 민감도, 감수성

convict
[kənvíkt]

v. 유죄 판결하다

The test results are really important in convicting criminals.
검사 결과가 범인들을 유죄 판결하는 데 매우 중요하지.

• conviction n. 유죄 판결

iceberg
[áisbə:rg]

n. 빙산

It explains how icebergs can be used to help mankind.
여기서는 빙산이 사람들에게 어떻게 이용될 수 있는지 설명하고 있어.

mankind
[mænkáind]

n. 인류

It explains how icebergs can be used to help mankind.
여기서는 빙산이 사람들에게 어떻게 이용될 수 있는지 설명하고 있어.

subjective
[səbdʒéktiv]

a. 주관적인

I think this article is too subjective.
내 생각에 이 기사는 너무 주관적인 거 같아.

• objective a. 객관적인 • subjectively ad. 주관적으로

Check Again!

A Translate each word into Korean.

1. presentation ....   2. suitable ....

3. ancestor ....   4. factory ....

5. clue ....   6. fiber ....

7. lecture ....   8. sensitive ....

9. normally ....   10. carbon dioxide ....

B Translate each word into English.

1. 축축한 ....

2. 유죄 판결하다 ....

3. 씨를 뿌리다 ....

4. 뇌졸중 ....

5. 생명의 ....

C Fill in the blank with the appropriate word. Refer to the Korean.

1. What are you doing? Are you d   ?

   뭘 하고 있는 거예요? 몽상에 잠겨 있는 거예요?

2. This article shows the writer's s   view strongly.

   이 기사는 필자의 주관적인 견해를 강하게 드러내 준다.

3. The mixture is d   in warm water.

   그 혼합물은 따뜻한 물에 용해되어 있다.

4. The use of fire was revolutionary in the history of m   .

   인류 역사에 있어서 불의 사용은 혁명적이었다.

5. Our country has made great economic p   within 10 years.

   우리나라는 10년 안에 경제적으로 대단한 발전을 했다.

✚ 반대의 의미를 만들어 주는 말 2

동사, 형용사 혹은 명사 앞에 있는 dis- 혹은 il- / ir- 등은 의미를 반대로 만들어 주는
역할을 하기도 한다.

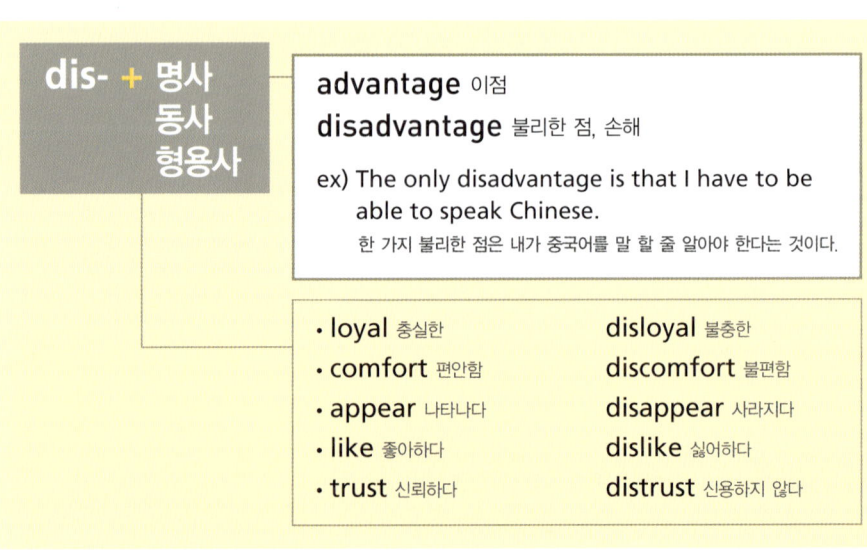

dis- + 명사
동사
형용사

advantage 이점
disadvantage 불리한 점, 손해

ex) The only disadvantage is that I have to be
able to speak Chinese.
한 가지 불리한 점은 내가 중국어를 말 할 줄 알아야 한다는 것이다.

- **loyal** 충실한   **disloyal** 불충한
- **comfort** 편안함   **discomfort** 불편함
- **appear** 나타나다   **disappear** 사라지다
- **like** 좋아하다   **dislike** 싫어하다
- **trust** 신뢰하다   **distrust** 신용하지 않다

il-
im- + 형용사
ir-

responsible 책임감 있는
irresponsible 책임감이 없는

ex) You're irresponsible. You didn't finish
your job.
당신은 참 책임감이 없으시군요. 당신이 맡은 일을 끝내지 않았네요.

- **logical** 논리적인   **illogical** 논리적인지 않은
- **literate** 읽고 쓸 줄 아는   **illiterate** 문맹의
- **perfect** 완벽한   **imperfect** 완벽하지 않은
- **practical** 실용적인   **impractical** 실용적이지 않은
- **regular** 규칙적인   **irregular** 불규칙적인

Relationships

- teacher 교사
  pupil 제자

- employer 고용주
  employee 고용인

- interviewer 인터뷰 하는 사람
  interviewee 인터뷰를 받는 사람

- landlord/ landlady 집주인
  tenant 세입자

- driver 운전자   - male 남성(의)
  passenger 승객   female 여성(의)

Technology 기술

+ e-commerce 전자 상거래   + e-pal 이메일을 주고 받는 친구
+ Internet banking 인터넷 뱅킹
+ online shopping 온라인 쇼핑
+ cybercafe 인터넷을 사용 할 수 있는 카페
+ video conference 화상 회의
+ mouse potato 컴퓨터를 너무 많이 하는 사람
  cf) couch potato 소파에 앉아 TV만 보는 사람

VOCA EDGE
BLUE

love you, Kite We moved today. I want to join the drama club. We have a team projec

the send button. Kite will attend the wonder dog championship. Relationships count most

e! We made homemade pancakes. Hoony is taking taekwondo lessons. My dad's car is ir

it an interesting festival! Sara's brother is running for president. Our school is doing an anti-

as skin trouble. Mom has become a regular customer of ABC Mart. Mom is impressed by

hy do floods and droughts alternate? Astronauts need to know special drills. Two whale

it facilities. We love you, Kite We moved today. I want to join the drama club. We have c

safari tour. I pressed the send button. Kite will attend the wonder dog championship

c. Mud cookies are terrible! We made homemade pancakes. Hoony is taking taekwonde

d music for Brownie. What an interesting festival! Sara's brother is running for president. Ou

n art investment. Seri has skin trouble. Mom has become a regular customer of ABC Mart

without sunlight. Why do floods and droughts alternate? Astronauts need to know specia

d boys use different facilities. We love you, Kite We moved today. I want to join the drama

We went on a safari tour. I pressed the send button. Kite will attend the wonder dog

to a growth clinic. Mud cookies are terrible! We made homemade pancakes. Hoony is

Chapter 12. Nature and Space

emorial. Sara composed music for Brownie. What an interesting festival! Sara's brothe

Unit 34. Why do floods and droughts alternate?

is horrible. Dad is interested in art investment. Seri has skin trouble. Mom has become

Unit 35. Astronauts need to know special drills.

good and bad. Plants can grow without sunlight. Why do floods and droughts alterna

Unit 36. Two whales drifted ashore!

's puberty? Visit my blog Girls and boys use different facilities. We love you, Kite We movec

. There will be a talent show. We went on a safari tour. I pressed the send button. Kite wil

n the same boat. I go to a growth clinic. Mud cookies are terrible! We made homemade

trip to the War Memorial. Sara composed music for Brownie. What an interesting festival

Chapter 12
Nature and Space

Unit 34. Why do floods and droughts alternate?

be asked to **extinguish** one's cigarettes

yearn for rainfall

sweep through everything

Episode

Dear Diary,

Several **forest fires** have broken out. ● People have been asked to **extinguish** their cigarettes before climbing mountains. ● For nearly three months, we've had a dry **spell**. ● In the bathroom, Hoony made a big splash and Seri and I got **soaked**. ● "What a **disaster**!" Seri screamed. ● But we don't seem to know what a real disaster is. The news says that the water **levels** in some **reservoirs** are down to less than 40%. ● Farmers are **yearning** for **rainfall**. ● They worry that their **crops** may not grow well because of the **drought**. ● I saw a farmer **commenting** on the drought by **quoting** a popular saying. ● He said, "You **reap** what you sow." ● He **cursed** himself, saying he shouldn't have accepted farming as his **vocation**. ● Are they going to be offered **grants** by the government?

Seri: Wow, the water **swept** through everything. ● It left some buildings with nothing but their **frameworks**. ● People living there had to **escape** their homes.

Bomi: Do we have to help them **restore** their houses?

It's really **odd** that floods and droughts alternate. ● Seri and I remembered the **flood** we had last year. ● At that time, the amount of water in the region almost **tripled**. ● Nature is said to be a mother god. ● But at times it leaves us with a **scar**.

다이어리에게,
여러 산불이 발생했어. 사람들은 산을 오르기 전에 담뱃불을 끄라는 요청을 받고 있어. 약 세 달째 기후가 건조하거든. 욕실에서 후니가 물을 크게 튀겨서 세리와 내가 흠뻑 젖었지. "이게 무슨 난리야!" 세리가 소리질렀어. 하지만 우리는 진짜 난리가 뭔지 모르는 듯해.
뉴스에 의하면 몇몇 저수지 수위가 40%도 안 된다고 해. 농부들은 비가 오기를 바라고 있어. 농부들은 가뭄 때문에 자신의 작물들이 잘 자라지 못할까 봐 근심해. 나는 한 농부가 유명한 속담을 인용해서 가뭄에 대해 말하는 것을 봤어. 그는 "뿌린대로 거둔다." 라고 했지. 그는 농사를 천직으로 삼지 말았어야 했다고 자신을 한탄했어. 그들은 정부에서 보조금을 받게 될까?

세리: 우와, 물이 다 휩쓸고 지나갔네. 건물 뼈대만 남겼잖아. 거기 사는 주민들이 집에서 대피해야만 했대.
보미 : 우리가 그들의 집을 복구할 수 있게 도와줘야 할까?

홍수와 가뭄이 번갈아 일어나는 건 매우 이상해. 세리와 나는 작년에 홍수가 났던 것을 기억했어. 그때에는 그 지역의 수량이 거의 세 배가 되었지. 자연은 어머니 신이라고 하잖아. 하지만 가끔은 우리에게 상처를 남기기도 해.

forest fire
[fɔ́(:)rist faiər]

n. 산불

Several forest fires have broken out.
여러 산불이 발생했어.

extinguish
[ikstíŋgwiʃ]

v. 불을 끄다

People have been asked to extinguish their cigarettes before climbing mountains.
사람들은 산을 오르기 전에 담뱃불을 끄라는 요청을 받고 있어.

- extinguisher n. 불 끄는 사람, 소화기
- extinguished a. 불이 꺼진

spell
[spel]

n. (날씨 등이 계속되는) 기간

For nearly three months, we've had a dry spell.
약 세 달째 기후가 건조거든.

- dry spell 건조기, 가뭄

soak
[souk]

v. 적시다, 젖다

In the bathroom, Hoony made a big splash and Seri and I got soaked.
욕실에서 후니가 물을 크게 튀겨서 세리와 내가 흠뻑 젖었지.

- soaked a. 젖은

disaster
[dizǽstər]

n. 재앙, 재난, 난리

"What a disaster!" Seri screamed.
"이게 무슨 난리야!" 세리가 소리질렀어.

- disastrous a. 피해가 막심한, 재난의

level
[lévəl]

n. 높이, 수준
v. 같은 높이로 하다

The news says that the water levels in some reservoirs are down to less than 40%.
뉴스에 의하면 몇몇 저수지 수위가 40%도 안 된다고 해.

reservoir
[rézərvwɑ̀:r]

n. 저수지

The news says that the water levels in some reservoirs are down to less than 40%.
뉴스에 의하면 몇몇 저수지 수위가 40%도 안 된다고 해.

- reserve v. 따로 떼어놓다, 남겨두다

yearn
[jə:rn]

v. 갈망하다, 열망하다

Farmers are yearning for rainfall.
농부들은 비가 오기를 바라고 있어.

- yearn for ~을 갈망하다

rainfall
[réinfɔːl]
n. 강우량

Farmers are yearning for rainfall.
농부들은 비가 오기를 바라고 있어.

crop
[krɑp]
n. 농작물 v. 수확하다

They worry that their crops may not grow well because of the drought.
농부들은 가뭄 때문에 자신의 작물들이 잘 자라지 못할까 봐 근심해.

drought
[draut]
n. 가뭄

They worry that their crops may not grow well because of the drought.
농부들은 가뭄 때문에 자신의 작물들이 잘 자라지 못할까 봐 근심해.

comment
[kámənt]
v. 언급하다 n. 언급

I saw a farmer commenting on the drought by quoting a popular saying.
나는 한 농부가 유명한 속담을 인용해서 가뭄에 대해 말하는 것을 봤어.

• commentator n. 논평자

quote
[kwout]
v. 인용하다 n. 인용

I saw a farmer commenting on the drought by quoting a popular saying.
나는 한 농부가 유명한 속담을 인용해서 가뭄에 대해 말하는 것을 봤어.

reap
[riːp]
v. 수확하다, 거둬들이다

He said, "You reap what you sow."
그는 "뿌린대로 거둔다."라고 했어.

• reaper n. 수확자, 수확기

curse
[kəːrs]
v. 저주하다, 욕하다
n. 저주, 악담

He cursed himself, saying he shouldn't have accepted farming as his vocation.
그는 농사를 천직으로 삼지 말았어야 했다고 자신을 한탄했어.

vocation
[voukéiʃən]
n. 직업, 천직

He cursed himself, saying he shouldn't have accepted farming as his vocation.
그는 농사를 천직으로 삼지 말았어야 했다고 자신을 한탄했어.

• vocational a. 직업상의

grant
[grænt]
n. 보조금
v. 주다, 수여하다

Are they going to be offered grants by the government?
그들은 정부에서 보조금을 받게 될까?

sweep
[swi:p]

v. 휩쓸고 가다,
휩쓸어가다

Wow, the water sweep through everything.
우와, 물이 다 휩쓸고 지나갔네.

• sweep - swept - swept

framework
[fréimwə̀:rk]

n. 구조, 틀

It left some buildings with nothing but their frameworks.
건물 뼈대만 남겼잖아.

escape
[iskéip]

v. 도망치다, 피하다
n. 도피, 탈출

People living there had to escape their homes.
거기 사는 주민들이 집에서 대피해야만 했대.

restore
[ristɔ́:r]

v. 복구하다, 회복하다

Do we have to help them restore their houses?
우리가 그들의 집을 복구할 수 있게 도와줘야 할까?

• restoration n. 회복, 복구

odd
[ɑd]

a. 이상한

It's really odd that floods and droughts alternate.
홍수와 가뭄이 번갈아 일어나는 건 매우 이상해.

• oddness n. 기묘함, 색다름

flood
[flʌd]

n. 홍수 v. 범람하다

Seri and I remembered the flood we had last year.
세리와 나는 작년에 홍수가 났던 것을 기억했어.

• flooded a. 물에 잠긴, 침수된

triple
[trípəl]

v. 3배가 되다
a. 3배의

At that time, the amount of water in the region almost tripled.
그때에는 그 지역의 수량이 거의 세 배가 되었지.

scar
[skɑ:r]

n. 상처
v. 상처를 남기다

Nature is said to be a mother god. But at times it leaves us with a scar.
자연은 어머니 신이라고 하잖아. 하지만 가끔은 우리에게 상처를 남기기도 해.

• scarred a. 흉터가 있는

Check Again!

A Translate each word into Korean.

1. spell ....
2. escape ....
3. disaster ....
4. scar ....
5. flood ....
6. vocation ....
7. curse ....
8. level ....
9. triple ....
10. soak ....

B Translate each word into English.

1. 보조금 ....
2. 가뭄 ....
3. 인용하다 ....
4. 구조, 틀 ....
5. 저수지 ....

C Fill in the blank with the appropriate word. Refer to the Korean.

1. The patient is y_____ for medicine to cure the disease.

   그 환자는 병을 고쳐 줄 약을 바라고 있다.

2. Please e_____ all the cigarettes before you get in.

   안에 들어오시기 전에 담뱃불을 모두 꺼 주세요.

3. This layered hair style is s_____ the nation among girls.

   이 층을 낸 헤어스타일이 여자 아이들 사이에서 전국적으로 휩쓸고 있다.

4. It took two days to r_____ the damaged file.

   손상된 파일을 복구하는 데 이틀이 걸렸다.

5. Isn't it o_____ that they haven't arrived at the stadium yet?

   그 사람들이 경기장에 아직 도착하지 않았다는 것이 이상하지 않나요?

Chapter 12
Nature and Space

Unit 35. Astronauts need to know special drills.

be launched into space

look like a **glowing** blue marble

float in space

Episode

Hoony: How many spaceships have been launched into space?

Bomi: We don't know for sure but there is definitely a multitude of spaceships up there.

Hoony: Probably at least a minimum of 10 spaceships have been launched, right? ● Why do nations strive to launch spaceships? ● Do they want to expand their frontiers to space?

Bomi: Well, they may want to show off how advanced their technology is. ● They may think launching a spaceship is like building a monument. ● Or they think the earth will exceed its capacity soon. ● Scientists possibly have a burden. ● They may try to solve the problem of overpopulation.

Hoony: What does the earth look like from space?

Bomi: Some people say it looks like a glowing blue marble. ● I guess it probably looks like a ball with a diameter of about 10 centimeters.

Hoony: I think astronauts must have fun, floating in space.

Bomi: Before their journey into space, astronauts go through a computer simulation for training. ● They need to know various drills to survive the extreme conditions.

Hoony: Extreme conditions? Like what?

Bomi: For example, there's hardly any oxygen in space. ● Sometimes, they may have to fix the spaceship.

Hoony: I see. ● They really need a lot of zeal to overcome such difficulties. ● They also need to simplify their lives. ● No games, no TVs. What boredom!

Bomi: I think they really have to be able to make sacrifices.

Hoony: The astronauts should start their own mining business. ● They could collect moon rocks.

Bomi: What?

Hoony: I'm just joking. ● Actually I have a tremendous amount of respect for them.

후니: 얼마나 많은 우주선들이 우주로 발사된 거지?
보미: 정확히는 모르지만 분명히 수많은 우주선들이 우주에 떠 있겠지.
후니: 아마 적어도 10개는 발사되었겠지, 맞지? 왜 나라들은 우주선을 발사하려고 애를 쓰는 거지? 우주까지 영역을 넓히고 싶은 것일까?
보미: 뭐, 아마 그들은 자신들의 기술이 얼마나 발전했는지 과시하고 싶은 것일 거야. 아마 그들은 우주선을 발사하는 것이 기념비를 세우는 것과 같은 것이라고 생각할 수도 있지. 아니면 그들은 지구가 곧 정원을 초과할 거라고 생각하는 거겠지. 과학자들은 아마 부담감을 가지고 있겠지. 그들은 인구과잉 문제를 해결하려고 노력하는 건지도 몰라.
후니: 우주에서 본 지구는 어떻게 생겼지?
보미: 어떤 사람들은 그것이 꼭 반짝이는 파란 구슬같이 생겼다고 해. 내 생각에 아마 지름이 10센티미터 정도 되는 공처럼 보일 거야.
후니: 내 생각에 우주인들은 우주를 떠다니면서 재미있을 것 같아.
보미: 우주로 여행을 가기 전에, 우주인들은 컴퓨터 시뮬레이션을 통한 훈련을 해. 그들은 극한 상황에서도 살아남기 위해 다양한 기술을 익혀야 해.
후니: 극한 상황? 예를 들면?
보미: 예를 들면 우주에는 산소가 거의 없잖아. 가끔씩 우주선을 고쳐야 할 수도 있지.
후니: 그렇구나. 그 상황을 극복하려면 많은 열정이 필요하겠구나. 또한 그들의 삶을 단순화시켜야 하지. 게임도 없고 텔레비전도 없고, 얼마나 지루할까!
보미: 내 생각에 그들은 굉장한 희생을 할 수 있어야 해.
후니: 우주인들은 광산업을 시작할 수 있겠어. 달에 있는 돌을 모을 수도 있잖아.
보미: 뭐라고?
후니: 그냥 농담으로 말한 거야. 사실 난 그들에게 굉장한 존경심을 갖고 있어.

launch
[lɔːntʃ]

v. 발사하다 n. 발사

How many spaceships have been launched into space?

얼마나 많은 우주선들이 우주로 발사된 거지?

multitude
[mʌ́ltitjùːd]

n. 다수, 수많은

We don't know for sure but there is definitely a multitude of spaceships up there.

정확히는 모르지만 분명히 수많은 우주선들이 우주에 떠 있겠지.

minimum
[mínəməm]

n. 최소 한도

Probably at least a minimum of 10 spaceships have been launched, right?

아마 적어도 10개는 발사되었겠지, 맞지?

• minimize v. 최소화하다   • minimal a. 최소의
• maximum n. 최대 한도

strive
[straiv]

v. 애쓰다, 노력하다

Why do nations strive to launch spaceships?

왜 나라들은 우주선을 발사하려고 애를 쓰는 거지?

• strife n. 투쟁, 경쟁

frontier
[frʌntíər]

n. 영역 (보통 복수형으로)

Do they want to expand their frontiers to space?

우주까지 영역을 넓히고 싶은 것일까?

advanced
[ədvǽnst]

a. 발달한, 진보한

Well, they may want to show off how advanced their technology is.

뭐, 아마 그들은 자신들의 기술이 얼마나 발전했는지 과시하고 싶은 것 일 거야.

• advance v. 발전시키다 n. 발전, 진보

monument
[mɑ́njumənt]

n. 기념비

They may think launching a spaceship is like building a monument.

아마 그들은 우주선을 발사하는 것이 기념비를 세우는 것과 같은 것이라고 생각할 수도 있지.

• monumental a. 기념이 되는

capacity
[kəpǽsəti]

n. 용량, 수용력

Or they think the earth will exceed its capacity soon.

아니면 그들은 지구가 곧 정원을 초과할 거라고 생각하는 거겠지.

• capacious a. 용량이 큰

burden
[bə́:rdn]

n. 짐, 부담
v. 짐을 지우다

Scientists possibly have a burden.
과학자들은 아마 부담감을 가기고 있겠지.

• burdener   n. 짐을 싣는 사람, 부담을 주는 사람(것)

overpopulation
[òuvərpápjuléiʃən]

n. 인구 과잉

They may try to solve the problem of overpopulation.
그들은 인구 과잉 문제를 해결하려고 노력하는 건지도 몰라.

• overpopulate   v. 과밀화시키다
• overpopulated   a. 인구 과잉의

glowing
[glóuiŋ]

a. 빛나는

Some people say it looks like a glowing blue marble.
어떤 사람들은 그것이 꼭 반짝이는 파란 구슬같이 생겼다고 해.

• glow   v. 빛을 내다   n. 작열

diameter
[daiǽmitər]

n. 직경

I guess it probably looks like a ball with a diameter
of about 10 centimeters.
내 생각에 아마 지름이 10센티미터 정도 되는 공처럼 보일 거야.

astronaut
[ǽstrənɔ̀:t]

n. 우주 비행사

I think astronauts must have fun, floating in space.
내 생각에 우주인들은 우주를 떠다니면서 재미있을 것 같아.

• astronomy   n. 천문학

journey
[dʒə́:rni]

n. 여정, 여행
v. 여행하다

Before their journey into space, astronauts go
through a computer simulation for training.
우주로 여행을 가기 전에, 우주인들은 컴퓨터 시뮬레이션을 통한 훈련을 해.

simulation
[sìmjuléiʃən]

n. 시뮬레이션,
   모의 실험

Before their journey into space, astronauts go
through a computer simulation for training.
우주토 여행을 가기 전에, 우주인들은 컴퓨터 시뮬레이션을 통한 훈련을 해.

• simulate   v. 모의 실험하다   • simulated   a. 모의 실험의

drill
[dril]

n. 훈련
v. 훈련시키다

They need to know various drills to survive the
extreme conditions.
그들은 극한 상황에서도 살아남기 위해 다양한 기술을 익혀야 해.

survive
[sərváiv]
v. 생존하다, 살아남다

They need to know various drills to survive the extreme conditions.
그들은 극한 상황에서도 살아남기 위해 다양한 기술을 익혀야 해.
• survival n. 생존

oxygen
[áksidʒən]
n. 산소

For example, there's hardly any oxygen in space.
예를 들면 우주에는 산소가 거의 없잖아.

zeal
[zi:l]
n. 열심, 열의

They really need a lot of zeal to overcome such difficulties. 그 상황을 극복하려면 많은 열정이 필요하겠구나.
• zealous a. 열정적인

simplify
[símpləfài]
v. 단순화시키다

They also need to simplify their lives.
그들은 또한 그들의 삶을 단순화시켜야 하지.
• simplification n. 단순화   • simplicity n. 단순, 간단

boredom
[bɔ́:rdəm]
n. 권태로움, 지루함

No games, no TVs. What boredom!
게임도 없고 텔레비전도 없고. 얼마나 지루할까!
• bored a. 지루한

sacrifice
[sǽkrəfàis]
n. 희생 v. 희생하다

I think they really have to be able to make sacrifices.
내 생각에 그들은 굉장한 희생을 할 수 있어야 해.
• make a sacrifice   희생하다

mining
[máiniŋ]
n. 광업

The astronauts should start their own mining business. 우주인들은 광산업을 시작할 수 있어.
• mine v. 채굴하다 n. 광산

tremendous
[triméndəs]
a. 굉장한, 거대한

Actually I have a tremendous amount of respect for them. 사실 난 그들에게 굉장한 존경심을 갖고 있어.
• tremendously ad. 무시무시하게

Check Again!

A Translate each word into Korean.

1. launch ....
2. burden ....
3. overpopulation ....
4. glowing ....
5. tremendous ....
6. oxygen ....
7. multitude ....
8. boredom ....
9. strive ....
10. drill ....

B Translate each word into English.

1. 여정, 여행 ....
2. 열의 ....
3. 살아남다 ....
4. 광업 ....
5. 직경 ....

C Fill in the blank with the appropriate word. Refer to the Korean.

1. F_____ of bioengineering have been expanded a lot.

   생체 공학의 영역은 많이 확대되어 왔다.

2. At that time people made a lot of s_____ for the independence of their country.

   그 당시에 사람들은 조국의 독립을 위해 많은 희생을 했다.

3. To concentrate on your job, you need to s_____ your life.

   너의 일에 좀 더 집중을 하려면 생활을 단순화시킬 필요가 있다.

4. This laptop has a c_____ of 500 megabytes.

   이 노트북 컴퓨터는 용량이 500메가바이트이다.

5. This m_____ is dedicated to unknown soldiers killed in the war.

   이 기념비는 전쟁에서 전사한 무명용사들을 위한 것이다.

Chapter 12
Nature and Space

Unit 36. Two whales drifted ashore!

drift ashore

have **excessive** military training

clean up some **sewage**

Episode

Dear Diary,

We seem to owe too much to nature. • Two whales drifted ashore. • Even though the rescue team kept them wet, they weren't able to save them. • What a tragedy! • What caused these mammals to die? • I know that there are limitations on the number of whales that can be hunted. • Did they die because of water pollution? • Or was there excessive military training going on near them?

Once I read a book about marine creatures. • It said that military training in the ocean could be responsible for the deaths of whales. • The author also said that the populations of a lot of other species of fish are declining sharply. • What should we do? • The author tried to convey a strong message. • Her viewpoints were quite simple. • She suggests that we endeavor to save marine creatures. • She claims that hunting for specific species should be prohibited. • If we delay, the many various species in the ocean will diminish rapidly. • I agree that illegal hunting for some species should be forbidden.

Once a month, our class cleans up our neighborhood. • Tomorrow we're going to clean up some sewage. • It's going to stink so bad. • We're just going to have to endure it. • But if we can make a difference, then it'll be worth it.

다이어리에게,

우리는 자연에 너무 많은 빚을 지는 것 같아. 두 마리의 고래가 해안으로 표류했어. 구조팀에서 고래의 몸이 마르지 않도록 적셔주었지만 그들을 살리지 못했어. 정말 비극이야! 무엇이 이 포유류를 죽게 한 것일까? 나는 사냥할 수 있는 고래의 수에 대한 규제가 있다는 것을 알고 있어. 물이 오염되어서 고래가 죽은 것일까? 아니면 그들 근처에서 과도한 군사훈련을 했던 것일까?

예전에 나는 해양생물들에 관한 책을 읽었어. 거기서는 해양 군사훈련이 고래 죽음의 원인이 될 수 있다고 적혀 있었어. 작가는 또한 다른 어류들의 수도 급속히 감소하고 있다고 했지. 우리가 무엇을 해야 할까? 작가는 우리에게 강한 메시지를 전해 주고자 했어. 그녀의 관점은 꽤나 간단해. 그녀는 우리가 해양생물을 구하기 위해 노력해야 한다고 권고하지. 그녀는 특정 어종을 사냥하는 것은 금지되어야 한다고 주장해. 만약 우리가 우물쭈물한다면 해양생물들은 급속도로 감소할 거야. 나는 어떤 종들을 불법으로 사냥하는 것은 금지되어야 한다는 것에 동의해.

한 달에 한번 우리 반은 우리 동네를 청소해. 내일 우리는 하수를 청소하러 가. 그것은 심한 악취가 날 거야. 우리는 그 악취를 견뎌야 할 거야. 하지만 우리가 변화를 만들 수 있다면, 그것은 그만한 가치가 있을 거야.

owe
[ou]
v. 빚지다

We seem to owe too much to nature.
우리는 자연에 너무 많은 빚을 지는 것 같아.

• owe A to B A를 B에 빚지다, A는 B 덕택이다.

drift
[drift]
v. 표류하다

Two whales drifted ashore.
두 마리의 고래가 해안으로 표류했어.

• drifting a. 표류하는

ashore
[əʃɔ́:r]
ad. 해안으로

Two whales drifted ashore.
두 마리의 고래가 해안으로 표류했어.

• shore n. 해안

rescue
[réskju:]
n. 구조
v. 구조하다

Even though the rescue team kept them wet, they weren't able to save them.
구조팀에서 고래의 몸이 마르지 않도록 적셔주었지만 그들을 살리지 못했어.

• rescuee n. 구출된 사람 • rescuer n. 구조자

tragedy
[trǽdʒədi]
n. 비극

What a tragedy!
정말 비극이야!

• tragic a. 비극적인

mammal
[mǽməl]
n. 포유류

What caused these mammals to die?
무엇이 이 포유류를 죽게 한 것일까?

• mammary a. 유방의, 유방 모양의

limitation
[lìmətéiʃən]
n. 제한, 제약

I know that there are limitations on the number of whales that can be hunted.
나는 사냥할 수 있는 고래의 수에 대한 규제가 있다는 것을 알고 있어.

• limit v. 제한하다 • limited a. 제한된, 한정된

excessive
[iksésiv]
a. 과도한

Or was there excessive military training going on near them?
아니면 그들 근처에서 과도한 군사훈련을 했던 것일까?

• exceed v. 초과하다 • excess n. 초과, 과도함

marine
[mərí:n]

a. 바다의, 해양의

Once I read a book about marine creatures.
예전에 나는 해양생물들에 관한 책을 읽었어.

creature
[krí:tʃər]

n. 피조물

Once I read a book about marine creatures.
예전에 나는 해양생물들에 관한 책을 읽었어.

• create v. 창조하다 • creative a. 창조적인

military
[mílitèri]

a. 군대의
n. 군대

It said that military training in the ocean could be responsible for the deaths of whales.
거기서는 해양 군사훈련이 고래 죽음의 원인이 될 수 있다고 적혀 있었어.

• militarism n. 군국주의

author
[ɔ́:θər]

n. 작가
v. 저술하다

The author also said that the populations of a lot of other species of fish are declining sharply.
작가는 또한 다른 어류들의 수도 급속히 감소하고 있다고 했지.

• authorless a. 저자 불명의, 익명의

decline
[dikláin]

v. 감소하다
n. 감소, 쇠퇴

The author also said that the populations of a lot of other species of fish are declining sharply.
작가는 또한 다른 어류들의 수도 급속히 감소하고 있다고 했지.

• declination n. 기움, 경사

convey
[kənvéi]

v. 전달하다

The author tried to convey a strong message.
작가는 우리에게 강한 메시지를 전해 주고자 했어.

• conveyor n. 전달자, 운반 장치

viewpoint
[vjú:pɔ̀int]

n. 관점

Her viewpoints were quite simple.
그녀의 관점은 꽤나 간단해.

• view n. 견해

endeavor
[endévər]

v. 애쓰다
n. 노력, 애씀

She suggests that we endeavor to save marine creatures.
그녀는 우리가 해양생물을 구하기 위해 노력해야 한다고 권고하지.

prohibit

[prouhíbit]

v. 금지하다

She claims that hunting for specific species should be prohibited.

그녀는 특정 어종을 사냥하는 것은 금지되어야 한다고 주장해.

• prohibition n. 금지 • prohibited a. 금지된

delay

[diléi]

v. 우물쭈물하다, 늦추다
n. 연기

If we delay, the many various species in the ocean will diminish rapidly.

만약 우리가 우물쭈물한다면 해양생물들은 급속도로 감소할 거야.

• delayed a. 연기된

diminish

[dimíniʃ]

v. 줄이다, 감소하다

If we delay, the many various species in the ocean will diminish rapidly.

만약 우리가 우물쭈물한다면 해양생물들은 급속도로 감소할 거야.

• diminution n. 감소

illegal

[ilí:gəl]

a. 불법의

I agree that illegal hunting for some species should be forbidden.

나는 어떤 종들을 불법으로 사냥하는 것은 금지되야 한다는 것에 동의해.

• illegalize v. 불법화시키다 • legal a. 합법적인

forbid

[fərbíd]

v. 금지시키다

I agree that illegal hunting for some species should be forbidden.

나는 어떤 종들을 불법으로 사냥하는 것은 금지되야 한다는 것에 동의해.

• forbid - forbade - forbidden

sewage

[sú:idʒ]

n. 하수, 오수

Tomorrow we're going to clean up some sewage.

내일 우리는 하수를 청소하러 가.

stink

[stíŋk]

v. 악취를 풍기다
n. 악취

It's going to stink so bad.

그것은 심한 악취가 날 거야.

• stink - stank(stunk) - stunk

endure

[endʒúər]

v. 참다, 인내하다

We're just going to have to endure it.

우리는 그 악취를 견뎌야 할 거야.

• endurance n. 인내, 지구력

Check Again!

A Translate each word into Korean.

1. drift ....
2. creature ....
3. mammal ....
4. delay ....
5. prohibit ....
6. illegal ....
7. diminish ....
8. convey ....
9. sewage ....
10. ashore ....

B Translate each word into English.

1. 슬픔 ....
2. 과도한 ....
3. 바다의, 해양의 ....
4. 군대의 ....
5. 악취를 풍기다 ....

C Fill in the blank with the appropriate word. Refer to the Korean.

1. There was a special training for the r_____ team.
   구조 대원들을 위한 특별 훈련이 있었다.

2. Because of a lot of l_____ on parking, I decided to use the subway.
   주차에 관한 여러 가지 제약 때문에 지하철을 이용하기로 결정했다.

3. I like the a_____ of this novel. His book depicts our psychology in detail.
   나는 이 소설의 작가를 좋아한다. 그의 책은 우리의 심리를 상세하게 설명해 주고 있다.

4. No one denies that the population of this species is d_____.
   누구도 이 종의 수가 감소하고 있다는 것을 부인하지 않는다.

5. From my v_____ her explanation is too ambiguous.
   내 관점에서 볼 때, 그녀의 설명의 너무 애매하다.

✚ 주의해야 할 표현

문장의 의미를 이해하기 위해서 서로 다른 두 문장을 자연스럽게 연결해 주는
연결어의 의미에 유의해 보아야 하고 우리말과 다르게 부정의 의미를 내포하고 있는
단어에도 유의해야 한다.

연결어로 쓰이는 말

unless ~가 아니라면

ex) I will attend the festival unless I have to pick up my grandma.
할머니를 모셔오는 것만 아니라면 축제에 갈 거야.

- **if** 만일 ~라면
- **whether** ~인지 아닌지
- **although** 비록 ~이지만
- **therefore** 그러므로
- **thus** 따라서

부정의 의미를 포함하는 경우

rarely 좀처럼 ~하지 않다

ex) I can't see you at home. You're rarely home.
난 너를 집에서 볼 수가 없구나. 넌 좀처럼 집에 있지를 않는구나.

- **seldom** 좀처럼 ~하지 않다
- **hardly** 거의 ~하지 않다
- **scarcely** 거의 ~하지 않다
- **barely** 좀처럼 ~하지 않다

Difference in some words

웃음과 관련된 표현

giggle 킬킬거리다
smile 미소짓다
laugh 소리내서 웃다

ex) Stop giggling. I can't concentrate on my studies.
그만 좀 킬킬거려. 공부에 집중이 안 되잖아.

쳐다보는 것과 관련된 표현

see 의식하지 않고 보다
gaze (오랫동안) 응시하다
stare 노려보다

ex) Why are you staring at me?
왜 나를 노려보고 있는 거야?

Culture Plus

Natural Phenomena 자연현상

+ breeze 산들바람
+ frost 서리
+ hail 우박
+ icicle 고드름
+ mist 안개
+ vapor 증기
+ earthquake 지진
+ volcano 화산
+ flood 홍수

VOCA EDGE_BLUE
INDEX

VOCA EDGE_BLUE

Answer Key

Chapter 1_ Unit 1

Check Again!

A

1. 행사, 경사
2. 축하하다
3. 상징물, 상징
4. 예언하다
5. 영광
6. 연회장
7. 교환하다
8. 영원한
9. 소유하다
10. 건배하다

B

1. ceremony
2. engagement
3. choose
4. intelligent
5. wealthy

C

1. birthday
2. announced
3. exchange
4. challenge
5. glory

Chapter 1_ Unit 2

Check Again!

A

1. 프로그램
2. 사춘기
3. 신체의
4. 정신적으로
5. 경험하다, 경험
6. 익살스러운, 유머스러운
7. 의식하고 있는
8. 어색한
9. 주이하다, 주목하다
10. 퇴짜 맞은

B

1. emotion
2. helpful
3. single
4. beat
5. concerned

C

1. refer
2. reminds
3. fashion
4. pleased
5. treats

Chapter 1_ Unit 3

Check Again!

A

1. 형제, 자매
2. 반짝이다, 빛나다
3. 전쟁터
4. 평범한
5. 졸업(식)
6. 대조, 현저한 차이
7. 취급, 치료
8. 줄무늬의
9. 분명히
10. 불편한

B

1. princess
2. argument
3. costume
4. serious
5. bald

C

1. temper
2. superpowers
3. select
4. thin
5. breath

Chapter 2_ Unit 4

Check Again!

A

1. 설비, 시설
2. 오락
3. 청정기, 정화기
4. 넓은, 훤히 트인
5. ~와는 달리
6. 교육적인
7. 호신, 자기방어
8. 복합 영화 상영관
9. 자주
10. 접근, 이용

B

1. satisfy
2. miss
3. rate
4. violent
5. similar

C

1. taste
2. up-to-date
3. hanging
4. perfect
5. screen

Chapter 2_ Unit 5

Check Again!

A

1. ~을 받을 만하다
2. 행실이 단정한
3. 전형적인
4. 두려워하는
5. 지하의, 지하에서
6. 설득하다
7. 사방에
8. 용변을 가릴 줄 아는
9. 나아지다, 개선하다
10. 보물

B

1. happen
2. remote control
3. pride
4. forget
5. bark

C

1. complaining
2. reward
3. homeless
4. decide
5. trick

Chapter 2_ Unit 6

Check Again!

A

1. 떼어내다
2. 수도 꼭지
3. 연결을 끊다
4. ~인 채로 남아 있다
5. 예보, 예보하다
6. 허가(증)
7. 깨지기 쉬운
8. 주의, 조심
9. 걱정, 걱정하다
10. 위치를 알아내다

B

1. pack
2. trash
3. parking lot
4. pour
5. unload

C

1. empty
2. behaved
3. plug
4. separated
5. certainly

Chapter 3_ Unit 7

Check Again!

A

1. 행정
2. 연극
3. 알려주다
4. 신청서
5. 요구, 필요
6. 적성
7. 연기, 공연
8. 교수
9. 자신만만한
10. 한 학기

B

1. member
2. dynasty
3. record
4. interview
5. peer

C

1. ad
2. submit
3. proves
4. lines
5. greedy

Chapter 3_ Unit 8

Check Again!

A

1. 숙제, 과제
2. 전기
3. 실험, 실험하다
4. 발생시키다
5. 원리
6. 산
7. 화학적인
8. 전환
9. 협력하다
10. 의도적으로

B

1. coin
2. mctal
3. attitude
4. complete
5. share

C

1. discussion
2. success
3. selfish
4. summary
5. thought

Chapter 3_ Unit 9

A

1. 극복하다
2. 대신하다
3. 살아 있는
4. 제거하다
5. 대답하다
6. 묘사하다
7. 장기
8. 공포
9. 강사
10. 기간, 회기

B

1. microscope
2. solution
3. complex
4. magnify
5. stain

C

1. Since
2. operation
3. observe
4. passage
5. structure

Chapter 4_ Unit 10

Check Again!

A

1. 입장료
2. 아마추어(의)
3. 공동체
4. 관객, 청중
5. 참가자
6. 문학
7. 드러내다
8. 열광적인
9. 기회
10. 해마다의

B

1. particularly
2. profit
3. talent
4. poem
5. magic

C

1. admit
2. transforms
3. festival
4. participant
5. enthusiastic

Chapter 4_ Unit 11

Check Again!

A

1. 요금
2. 거대한
3. 목적지
4. 좁은
5. 공격적인
6. 들판
7. 기능을 하다, 기능
8. 열대의
9. 날 것의, 가공하지 않은
10. 무리, 떼

B

1. aisle
2. rural
3. tourist
4. flock
5. tame

C

1. depart
2. barely
3. attack
4. fare
5. rural

Chapter 4_ Unit 12

Check Again!

A

1. 알아차리다
2. 동정, 연민
3. 쓰레기
4. 다큐멘터리
5. 후원자, 응원자
6. 지역
7. 비참한
8. 부끄러운
9. 의심하다, 의심
10. 쓰레기 매립지

B

1. save
2. medicine
3. lack
4. postpone
5. incredible

C

1. polluted
2. sympathy
3. press
4. supporters
5. lack

Chapter 5_ Unit 13

Check Again!

A

1. 부착하다
2. 잡아채다, 낚아채다
3. 기구, 가정용품
4. 운동의
5. 실패하다
6. 연습하다, 연습
7. 분석하다
8. 포기하다, 양도하다
9. 전문가
10. 훈련하다

B

1. stamp
2. tempt
3. paw
4. prepare
5. encourage

C

1. expert
2. competition
3. encouraged
4. attempted
5. exhausted

Chapter 5_ Unit 14

Check Again!

A

1. 학문의
2. 졸업생, 졸업하다
3. 관계
4. 헌신적인
5. 그만두다, 포기하다
6. 중간고사의
7. 통계
8. 고용하다
9. 어려움
10. 마찬가지로

B

1. maintain
2. element
3. retire
4. field
5. colleague

C

1. resume
2. elements
3. supervisor
4. promotion
5. passion

Chapter 5_ Unit 15

Check Again!

A

1. 오디션, 오디션을 하다
2. 적절한
3. 자산
4. 잠재력, 잠재적인
5. 뛰어난, 눈에 띄는
6. ~에도 불구하고
7. 지옥
8. 긍정적인
9. 자기소개서
10. 재판하다, 심사위원, 재판관

B

1. candidate
2. restless
3. inappropriate
4. fierce
5. logical

C

1. final
2. fancy
3. detail
4. potentials
5. positive

Chapter 6_ Unit 16

Check Again!

A

1. 감염
2. 훌륭한, 뛰어난
3. 결국
4. 출석한, 현재의, 현재
5. 귓속말을 하다, 귓속말
6. 세균
7. 약속하다, 약속, 전망
8. 경고하다
9. 추산하다, 추정하다
10. 속도, 비율

B

1. majority
2. bcneficiary
3. victim
4. rumor
5. determine

C

1. Otherwise
2. present
3. whisper
4. estimates
5. boat

Chapter 6_ Unit 17

Check Again!

A

1. 영향을 미치다
2. 소박한, 겸손한
3. 피할 수 없는
4. 결론
5. 유전자
6. 다양한
7. 의학의
8. 도달하다, 미치는 범위
9. 영양
10. 요인, 요소

B

1. advantage
2. result
3. growth
4. alternative
5. injection

C

1. regular
2. genes
3. growth
4. treatment
5. suggest

Chapter 6_ Unit 18

Check Again!

A

1. 순간
2. 제조업자
3. 재료
4. 간식
5. 믿을 만한
6. 위험한
7. 소화불량
8. 용납되지 않는
9. 보장하다
10. 만족감

B

1. severe
2. cruel
3. main
4. dumb
5. depressing

C

1. situation
2. moments
3. mud
4. digest
5. protect

Chapter 7_ Unit 19

Check Again!

A

1. 정확하게
2. 요리사
3. 조수
4. 조리법
5. 재료
6. 저울, 계량기
7. 재다, 측정하다
8. 반죽
9. 급하게
10. 약간

B

1. healthy
2. salty
3. beat
4. heat
5. smoke

C

1. homemade
2. add
3. hopeless
4. undercooked
5. mistook

Chapter 7_ Unit 20

Check Again!

A

1. 속이 빈, 속이 비게 하다
2. 우울한
3. 더군다나
4. 속이다
5. 달성하다
6. 엄격한
7. 공동묘지
8. 불명예, 망신
9. 모욕을 받은
10. 압도하다

B

1. horror
2. demonstrate
3. unlikely
4. superior
5. offend

C

1. injured
2. tends
3. bet
4. layer
5. crucial

Chapter 7_ Unit 21

Check Again!

A
1. 고장
2. 피해, 파손, 피해를 주다
3. 이슬비가 내리다, 이슬비
4. 교차로
5. 고함치다, 고함
6. 수분, 수액, 유동성의
7. 메스꺼움, 구토
8. 술 취한, 술주정뱅이
9. 면허
10. 자동차 수리공장, 차고

B
1. incidentally
2. minor
3. dizziness
4. mislead
5. trivial

C
1. prescribe
2. trial
3. crash
4. fluid
5. remedies

Chapter 8_ Unit 22

Check Again!

A
1. 기념물, 기념관
2. 야심 있는
3. 난파된
4. 무섭게 하다, 겁을 주다
5. 기념품
6. 선박, 배
7. 전시(품), 전시하다
8. 신화
9. 익사하다, 익사시키다
10. 다양한

B
1. conqueror
2. rear
3. foresee
4. retreat
5. supplement

C
1. institute
2. weakened
3. command
4. drowned
5. wounded

Chapter 8_ Unit 23

Check Again!

A
1. 마주침, 마주치다
2. 충분히
3. 증상
4. 행동주의자
5. 털
6. 지속적으로
7. 소중한, 가장 사랑하는
8. 바느질하다
9. 확대하다
10. 갈망하다, 간절히 원하다

B
1. compose
2. revise
3. randomly
4. sensitive
5. work out

C
1. recognize
2. pregnancy
3. steep
4. combination
5. moody

Chapter 8_ Unit 24

Check Again!

A
1. 표어, 모토
2. 가장 중요한 부분, 강조하다
3. 집회
4. 근육
5. 우연히 듣다
6. 근육
7. 유쾌한, 즐거운
8. 설교
9. 규정
10. 역동적인

B
1. independence
2. previous
3. liberal
4. pedestrian
5. condemn

C
1. undertake
2. anxious
3. pierced
4. Unfortunately
5. terrific

Chapter 9_ Unit 25

Check Again!

A

1. 급진적인, 획기적인
2. 미끄러지다
3. 규정
4. 장애가 있는, 불구가 된
5. 특유의, 특색 있는
6. 물질, 재료
7. 바람직한
8. 회상하다
9. 여성의, 여성
10. 미묘한, 미세한

B

1. manuscript
2. run
3. ramp
4. specific
5. install

C

1. Compared
2. improvement
3. sake
4. conform
5. relevant

Chapter 9_ Unit 26

Check Again!

A

1. 끌어내다, 유래하다
2. 실시하다, 행하다
3. 방법
4. 강인한
5. 고뇌, 번민
6. 위원회
7. 심리적인
8. 목표, 목표로 삼다
9. 시도하다, 시도
10. 놀라게 하다

B

1. debate
2. suppress
3. perish
4. tragic
5. prevent

C

1. connection
2. commit
3. consult
4. opposite
5. elegant

Chapter 9_ Unit 27

Check Again!

A

1. 인공적인, 인공물
2. 즉시, 손쉽게
3. 공식적인
4. 맹세하다
5. 부패하다, 부패
6. 대표
7. 미라로 만들다
8. 터무니없는
9. 성인, 어른
10. 풍미, 향미

B

1. resentful
2. scandal
3. deadly
4. wicked
5. uproot

C

1. purpose
2. charge
3. used
4. rid
5. focused

Chapter 10_ Unit 28

Check Again!

A

1. 통용되는 화폐
2. 평가하다
3. 양, 액수
4. 현재의
5. 가치, 값어치
6. 항목, 아이템
7. 새다
8. 짜증이 난
9. 잡동사니, 쓰레기
10. 초안, 초안을 그리다

B

1. investment
2. optimistic
3. retirement
4. autograph
5. carve

C

1. antique
2. doubtful
3. pension
4. gambling
5. budget

Chapter 10_ Unit 29

Check Again!

A

1. 자외선, 자외선의
2. 오존
3. 소비자
4. 상한
5. 격감시키다, 고갈시키다
6. 정리
7. 화장용의
8. 공급, 공급하다
9. 소매업자
10. 처벌하다

B

1. receipt
2. fundamental
3. demand
4. apply
5. wholesale

C

1. bargain
2. swollen
3. impulse
4. overreacts
5. refund

Chapter 10_ Unit 30

Check Again!

A

1. 양
2. 널리 퍼진
3. 예전에
4. 예의 바른, 공손한
5. 관리
6. 직원
7. 식료품
8. 꾸러미
9. 잠시 멈추다, 정지
10. 놀라게 하다

B

1. financial
2. considerate
3. delivery
4. uncover
5. household appliance

C

1. errand
2. suspended
3. robbed
4. Lately
5. part-time

Chapter 11_ Unit 31

Check Again!

A

1. 동창회, 재결합
2. 능률
3. 박람회
4. 향상시키다
5. 더욱이
6. 긴급한
7. 부족
8. ~의 외부에, 외부의
9. 경제적인
10. 지문

B

1. automatically
2. lock
3. eco-friendly
4. detect
5. solar

C

1. hastily
2. contribute
3 furnished
4. forgetful
5. reduce

Chapter 11_ Unit 32

Check Again!

A

1. 독실한, 진지한
2. 세포
3. 증오
4. 왕국, 영역
5. 주장하다, 다투다
6. 치명적인
7. 끔찍한
8. 상업적으로
9. 셀 수 없는, 무수한
10. ~을 기다리다

B

1. divine
2. cloning
3. reproduce
4. eradicate
5. alert

C

1. contrary
2. replace
3. inherit
4. mischief
5. advantage

Chapter 11_ Unit 33

Check Again!

A
1. 프레젠테이션, 발표
2. 적절한
3. 조상
4. 공장
5. 단서, 실마리
6. 섬유질
7. 강의, 강의하다
8. 민감한, 예민한
9. 보통, 대개
10. 이산화탄소

B
1. damp
2. convict
3. sow
4. stroke
5. vital

C
1. daydreaming
2. subjective
3. dissolved
4. mankind
5. progress

Chapter 12_ Unit 34

Check Again!

A
1. 기간
2. 도망치다, 도피
3. 재앙, 재난, 난리
4. 상처, 상처를 남기다
5. 홍수, 범람하다
6. 직업, 천직
7. 저주하다, 욕하다
8. 높이
9. 3배가 되다, 3배의
10. 적시다, 젖다

B
1. grant
2. drought
3. quote
4. framework
5. reservoir

C
1. yearning
2. extinguish
3. sweeping
4. restore
5. odd

Chapter 12_ Unit 35

Check Again!

A
1. 발사하다, 발사
2. 짐, 부담, 짐을 지우다
3. 인구 과잉
4. 빛나는
5. 굉장한, 거대한
6. 산소
7. 다수, 수많은
8. 권태로움, 지루함
9. 애쓰다, 노력하다
10. 훈련, 훈련시키다

B
1. journey
2. zeal
3. survive
4. mining
5. diameter

C
1. Frontiers
2. sacrifices
3. simplify
4. capacity
5. monument

Chapter 12_ Unit 36

Check Again!

A
1. 표류하다
2. 피조물
3. 포유류
4. 우물쭈물하다, 늦추다
5. 금지하다
6. 불법의
7. 줄이다, 감소하다
8. 전달하다
9. 하수
10. 해안으로

B
1. grief
2. excessive
3. marine
4. military
5. stink

C
1. rescue
2. limitations
3. author
4. declining
5. viewpoint

Note

Note